ECOLOGY OF THE BODY

ECOLOGY OF THE BODY

STYLES OF BEHAVIOR IN HUMAN LIFE

Joseph Lyons

Duke University Press   Durham

1987

© 1987 Duke University Press
All rights reserved
Printed in the United States of America
on acid-free paper ∞
Library of Congress Cataloging-in-Publication Data
appear on the last printed page of the book

To Dorothy with love

Contents

Some time ago I gave a seminar on the work of William Sheldon, as part of my long-term project of exploring the possibility of a somatic or biologically grounded psychology. As is well known, Sheldon based his work on what he called the somatotyping of the human figure, in which three major components of the constitution are identified and scaled: the endomorphic component, related to the roundness of the body; the mesomorphic, related to observable squareness and muscularity; and the ectomorphic, related to leanness and the appearance of being stretched out.

In the course of this seminar I was led to consider at some length the modes of behavior that might reasonably be supposed to be associated with Sheldon's three components of constitution. I should at the very outset couple this question with a warning: my mention of the question is not to be construed as raising the issue of "cause," in the sense of whether various behaviors are "caused" by the way one is physically constructed. In the preceding sentence I have enclosed both usages of the key word in quotation marks to indicate that problems concerning causality are not to be taken lightly, are not to be accepted as legitimate simply because they contain some familiar terms, and are certainly not to be taken as already settled. They are problems that deserve extended consideration, which I attempt in chapter 1 and chapter 6 of this book.

In posing a question concerning various modes of behavior, then, I was not reviving the ghost of somatotyping but rather pursuing quite another direction of thought, triggered in this case by my recognition of an unnoticed insight to be gleaned from Sheldon's work. Since the insight became the basis of this book, I will discuss its background.

Sheldon had argued that just as there were three components of one's physical constitution that could be reliably identified and rated, so there were three components of one's personality that could be reliably assessed by means of rating scales.[1] To this relatively harmless proposition he added two others which have since occasioned critique and rebuttal, charge and countercharge, through the years, to the detriment of Sheldon's professional reputation. The first addition was that on the basis of such observation and rating one could classify individuals into "types," either body types—for which he used the unfortunate term *somatotype*—or personality types. His second addition was that positive and high correlations could be shown to hold between the two sets of types, thereby implying a relationship that was other than random. A long series of empirical tests of the latter proposition, as well as a large number of discussions of the former, culminated in a paper by Lloyd Humphreys, which set the tone for professional attitudes toward Sheldon's work for the next two decades.[2]

In his paper Humphreys reviewed and analyzed Sheldon's use of types and his work on personality, concluding that "type concepts [are] unsuited for most research purposes" and that specifically "the use of Sheldon's types in further research should be discouraged."[3] Although many of Humphrey's arguments have been adequately answered since they were first presented,[4] the attitudes engendered by this and similar criticisms have remained. Typology is still in rather bad repute; Sheldon's work is assumed to have a very weak conceptual and experimental basis; and therefore any work acknowledging unabashedly a debt to him begins with a number of strikes against it. I make these points as early and as frankly as I can in order to clear the way for the hypothesis that I present and explore in this book. Its source is in Sheldon's work, or at least in an insight that I think I have detected there, but I must take full responsibility for it since Sheldon did not make it explicit. I also accept responsibility for the typology of behavior that is examined in these pages, at the same time that I disclaim any theoretical tie with the concept of mind-body relations that is implied in Sheldon's writings.

A full discussion of these points will have to be reserved for chapters 1 and 6; but here I may present the insight-argument-hypothesis sequence as it developed in my own thinking. I begin with this insight: no matter what one may say about the specific behavioral traits or types that Sheldon studied as personality, to accept these or any others as reasonably accurate descriptions leads to recognizing that individuals differ in their normal, ongoing behavior. That is to say, if each individual presents some typical mix of personality traits and if the mix is unique to each person, it must follow that—if the traits have any connection with behavior—each person behaves in a way that is different from any other person's unique way.

Here is what may be a truism, and therefore to be dismissed without further serious consideration, or perhaps what may be a fact of fundamental importance that has been unaccountably ignored. It is, in any case, a way of announcing the reentry of the thesis of individual differences into psychological theory. Once we begin to take seriously the possibility that individuals are different, and then try to find ways to make use of such a novel disposition, we are led toward wholly new ways of viewing long-familiar data. Consider, for example, the immediate results if we make explicit the individual differences that are clearly suggested in psychoanalytic developmental theory. Freud's well-known trichotomy of (male) emphases in development indicates that person A might be described as predominantly oral in behavior yet with a slight admixture of the anal but perhaps almost nothing observable of the phallic; whereas person B would be best described as rather markedly anal and phallic, with oral as a very minor element. The theory as stated allows such descriptions, yet curiously, the invitation has rarely been accepted and psychoanalytic clinical descriptions are not couched in these terms.

One reason for this failure to make use of these possibilities of the theory may be that a simple inference immediately presents itself—an inference that our theories are not equipped to handle—that since each individual can and does carry out the same repertoire of behaviors, which is to say that every person at some time thinks, remembers, perceives, learns, or whatever, it is possible that no two persons do these things in the same way. If there are four billion-odd persons alive on earth, there may be that many different ways to think, to remember, to perceive, to learn, and so on.

I do not think we can avoid facing this inference, whatever its cost to our theoretical positions. It is a natural consequence of taking seriously the notion of individual differences. Stated as a hypothesis, it is the thesis of the present book, in which I make a preliminary attempt to examine the consequences for various subspecialties of one usable form of the hypothesis. It is necessary to include a requirement that the form of the hypothesis be usable, for elementary considerations indicate that in its "raw" form the hypothesis cannot be tested. The problem is this, that we begin with as many different patternings of behavior as our measurement scheme allows. In Sheldon's method, for example, each of three identifiable components can be rated on a scale of 1 to 7, with half-steps permitted, as in 1.5 and 4.5. With 13 points on each of three scales, there are theoretically 13-cubed, or 2,197, possible mixes of personality; that is, in Sheldon's theory 2,197 identifiably different kinds of persons. Recall the argument above—that we must assume that these personality traits bear some nontrivial relation to the kinds of behaviors that psychologists study; for the alternative here would be that we eliminate our field of study. If the assessed personality mixes, then, do bear some relation to the significant behaviors of human beings, we are led to the inference that there are at least 2,197 identifiably different ways of remembering, of learning, and so on. And this leaves us with nothing more than interesting, but self-defeating hypothesis. We have in hand an attractive notion, faithful to a thesis of individual differences, but quite useless for most purposes.

We should therefore cut back on the number of different mixes we will deal with. Admitting the full number of possible individuals—in this instance a total of 2,197—puts us very nearly in the position of dealing with one individual at a time; whereas going to the other extreme by assuming no more than two different kinds of behaviors states the case so generally that individual differences disappear. For reasons of parsimony, however, we should certainly cut back as far as we can—and as it turns out, even cutting down to three categories out of the original 2,197 accomplishes much of what I set out to do in this argument. Even if we state my hypothesis in the form, "Every instance of normal behavior can in principle be carried out in at least three distinctively different ways," we will have posed a serious threat to the universalist position. This is the position that general laws, applicable indistinguishably to all persons, suffice to explain all kinds of behavior.

There is one more important reason for stating the hypothesis in terms of at least three categories. Many theorists have based their propositions on an assumption concerning two categories, organizing their data and even their understanding of their data on a model of two parts. Their claim is that the two categories effectively exhaust all the possibilities of significant differences among individuals. Thus, we have left brain–right brain; field dependent–field independent; introverted-extraverted; and so on. This procedure has some heuristic value, but it covers a serious weakness. The two-way division is really no more than an elaborate way of referring to one category. There is no difference between introverted-extraverted and introverted-nonintroverted; each side of the division is defined exhaustively in terms of the other. This demonstration, that a two-category system is no more than a one-category system disguised by a new label, has been pointed out by many writers. Its elegant mathematical demonstration was given by Ekman,[5] in which he concluded that any system of n categories is the equivalent of a system of $n - 1$ dimensions. For this reason alone we are forced to state my hypothesis in terms of at least three categories.

It is of some interest that sets of three categories seem to conform to "natural" tendencies in human cultures as well as in human development. Observational data from children at the age of three or four, when they are still learning the number names, indicates that they easily learn to refer to a grouping of three rather than either two or four. They will count, "one, two, three," but the next succeeding number is for them "imprecise and unreliable."[6] In regard to natural categories in human culture, I turn to the evidence offered by Allen Dundes in his remarkable essay on the predominance of trichotomies, particularly in modern culture.[7] He notes that threeness is very widely used to indicate a limit, as in three cheers or as in referring to an alphabet as ABC's rather than, say, AB's or ABCD's. Folktales and jokes abound with references to groups of three, as in three brothers, three wishes, or the blonde, the brunette, and the redhead. Songs are typically organized in sets of three, as in "Row, row, row your boat." Superstitions rest on groups of three, for example, three on a match. In games and sports the number three is ever-present, from tic-tac-toe to the patterns of scores, players, and acts in baseball—its nine players, nine innings, three outs, three strikes, three bases and fielders, and expressions such as ERA or Runs, hits, and errors. Organizations are almost always named with three words, as in AMA, GOP, KKK, DAR, PTA, MGM, and of course U.S.A.; and their mottoes also tend to be three-worded, as in Liberté, Égalité, Fraternité.

Further, most common expressions have the tripartite form: beg, borrow, and steal; hook, line, and sinker; tall, dark, and handsome; stop, look, and listen; Tom, Dick, and Harry; and so on. Traffic lights use three colors, and settings on switches are likely to be in a pattern of three, as in high, medium, and low. Dundes presents in great detail the evidence for the widespread use of trichotomies in our culture, in the areas of politics, government, religion, language, grammar, science, and everyday behavior. He then raises the question that is pertinent to our discussion, whether this widespread use of patterns of three derives from the data itself or from the observers or users of the data. He asks whether apparently objective schemas may in fact not arise from "cultural pressures" on the scientist. In Caesar's day, he notes, all Gaul was divided into three parts—but according to our present view of the matter, this is no longer "true." Is the land mass on the side of the Atlantic on which I live "really" composed of North, Central, and South America? Is matter "really" to be found in three main forms, solid, liquid, and gas? Is the human psyche composed of id, ego, and super ego? Of these and many other familiar trichotomies, some are still in good repute, some have turned out to be less than useful and so have been abandoned, and all have come under attack at one time or another.

My preference in this matter is to lean toward the idea of a "natural" tendency in humans of all ages to trichotomize the data presented to them. I have already referred to the evidence from young children, and to this may be added a logical argument. Having three anchoring points for our data enables us to use two points as end positions of a dimension and the third as an independent reference point. This amounts to switching from a linear array in one dimension to a surface array in two dimensions, thereby making possible an infinite number of combinations. We then have at hand as many positions as we could possibly want, while still retaining the smallest possible number of categories.

This brings me to the start of the investigation presented in this book. Once I had come this far, however, I became aware of a number of special problems needing to be addressed—some of them already apparent in these opening pages. In chapter 1 I discuss these problems and offer my preliminary solutions to them; afterward, I proceed with a full description of what I will call three behavioral styles (chapter 2) and then apply my hypothesis, in chapters 3, 4, and 5, to a number of substantive areas of psychology—learning, memory, language acquisition, and childhood development—which I feel most competent to explore. The material presented in chapters 3, 4, and 5 will bring me back, in a kind of spiral of reasoning, to a reconsideration of my aims in this book, and so in chapter 6 I will go back over the special problems that were raised and temporarily settled in chapter 1, examining them in what I hope will be greater depth. Finally, in two concluding chapters, 7 and 8, I venture to apply my hypothesis to certain aspects of culture and history, in this way reaching beyond the issues of individual behavior that are discussed in earlier chapters.

The insight that I found hidden in Sheldon's work, that there may be more than one way to carry out any of the processes or activities that are of interest to psychologists, is not meant as a dogmatic pronouncement from the depths of an armchair, and certainly not as a conclusion based on empirically determined evidence. It is a working hypothesis, no more. What I have to say in the ensuing chapters, particularly in chapters 2 to 5, is my set of speculations, guesses, and reasoning on the basis of available evidence, all in reference to the one question: supposing that an activity within the normal human range can be done in more than one observably different way, what would be the consequences for psychological theory and understanding?

In pursuing the answer to this kind of question, I need to establish first of all, in reference to the three or more—2,197 (more or less)—different "ways" possible, some basis for these "ways" in particular. This will involve me in a discussion of typologizing, a methodology that was always suggested, even encouraged, in Sheldon's work. In this respect as in most others, I will tread what appears to be a fine line. On the one hand I will disavow any paternal influence of Sheldon's thought, but on the other hand I will take up a position close to what I think Sheldon's thought might have been if it had been properly interpreted. Throughout, my stance will be, in the broadest sense, phenomenological, not because I pretend to sufficient expertise to rewrite contemporary phenomenology, but because the issues raised by my hypothesis can, in my view, be properly addressed only within a stance as phenomenologist.

PART ONE
Behavioral Styles: A Hypothesis

On History and Method

"The body forms itself in anticipation of the aim it serves, it assumes a shape . . . a shape for doing work, for fighting, for feeling, as well as a shape for loving."—v. e. von gebsattel

If we were to try to divide up all possible behavior so that it fits under a small number of rubrics, how would we do it? The most familiar such division gives us three categories—conation, referring to will, feeling, impulse, and motive; cognition, including the "neutral" thought processes; and the various forms of action or motor behavior. My hypothesis concerning ways of behaving does not attempt such a division. It does not attempt to distinguish one kind of behavior from another but rather to distinguish a limited number of *styles* in which any behavior, in any category, can be carried out. The hypothesis makes horizontal, not vertical, cuts through the corpus of observable behavior. This requires that I begin with some most general statements concerning behavior.

BEHAVIOR AND THE BODY

A foundational generalization is that all normal behavior consists of a biological organism acting in a setting that is meaningful to that organism. The field of study concerned with such behavior is ecology; hence the title, *Ecology of the Body*, immediately suggests itself. The reality that is lived by each of us is lived through the body. There is no other way.

This opening generalization serves not only to entitle this book but also to summarize the critique that it develops of modern psychology. If there is one scandalous lapse in contemporary psychological theory, it may be the omission of any reference to the lived, living, working, behaving body. The word will not be found in the index to any of the hundred introductory texts published each year. In place of a legitimate concern with the whole, functioning body as it is lived by each individual, in place even of a concern with the body's important processes— digestion, breathing, moving—students are given mountains of elegantly organized data on subprocesses such as nervous system activity or hormonal and metabolic action. Indeed, if one were to suppose in fantasy a visit to this planet by a Martian whose only source of information about the creatures resident here was a psychology textbook, in the absence of illustrations the visitor could not help but picture humans as creatures resembling the living brain of a science fiction story. No visitor could guess, from the material presented, that we are also possessed of muscles that move our limbs, of skeletons and stomachs, of skin that itches, and of lungs that respire.

The lapse to which I refer here has been discussed by many writers and attributed to various historical trends. In his introduction to a wide-ranging survey of experimental work on perception of one's own body, Fisher remarks: "For a century there has been a rolling campaign against the body realm. Man has been made to feel that his body is not only dirty and bad but also powerless and useless. . . . The culture tells each individual as he is growing up that he has to master the irrationality of his body . . . [and] parallel with this badness theme . . . there has been a trend toward substituting machines for muscles and by so doing downgrading the worth of the body. The number of human activities in which moving muscles can produce a profit or gain a man honor is steadily diminishing."[1]

From another direction, the view of the critic of contemporary philosophy, the tendency to bypass or degrade the body is attributed to the enduring influence of Cartesian metaphysics. Cartesian thought "conceptually estranges thought about our minds from thought about our bodies,"[2] resulting in a vision of the person, as described by William Poteat, as "an inquirer divested of all previous beliefs, speaking and writing no language—hence without a culture—and armed before the fact with explicit rules of procedure (!), therefore disentangled from his own being in the world in his inquiring activity."[3] If behavior is necessarily grounded in bodies acting in the world, this Martian image of a living person could never act, and to build a discipline of psychology on its presumed behavior leads directly to a conceptual morass in which the proper questions can never be asked. Minds are aspects of bodies, no more and no less. As such, minds are sets of processes taking place in living bodies, and acceptance of this foundational generalization keeps us from the trap of claiming that minds are either things positioned within the skull or metaphors rather than realities.

The Sheldon Array

In this book I will discuss a number of major styles of behavior. I base them on the three "components" of physique around which William Sheldon built his system of somatotyping. I should emphasize immediately that my source is in Sheldon's typology of constitution, not in his typology of personality, my logic in this regard being very straightforward. Given the foundational generalization mentioned earlier, I would search in a constitutional psychology for some hints as to my categories of style. Sheldon's "system" is quite adequate for these purposes—simple, parsimonious, and reasonably based in what we know of anatomy and its development. Sheldon's typology of personality, on the other hand, is poorly grounded in the evidence and is in any case a personality theory, with all the conceptual difficulties that such a theory entails. The typology of constitution furnishes the three categories that, as I have indicated in the preface, would seem to be the optimal number for a first exploration of my hypothesis, and it suggests as well a basis in the living body.

Although I reserve for chapter 2 an extended discussion of the three styles of behavior, I need to indicate here at least their general characteristics and the labels I will be using to refer to them. The terms describing the three styles are taken directly from Sheldon: the endomorphic, the mesomorphic, and the ectomorphic—although for ease of exposition I will usually use the abbreviated forms endo, meso, and ecto. The brief definitions that follow, as well as the extended discussion in later chapters, are my own:

The *endo* style emphasizes passions, values, and deep-seated commitment, with resistance to change; its prototypic activity is absorption.

The *meso* style emphasizes short-term, goal-directed activity, particularly in the arena of social interchange and competition; at its core is the way one uses one's energy.

The *ecto* style emphasizes processes of symbolizing, resting on the mode of activity that I call "distancing."

From these brief descriptions it is evident that my guiding hypothesis goes beyond the simple statement that human activity may be divided into three categories. It proposes, in addition, that each instance of such activity, no matter what category it may be assigned to, can be (and usually is) carried out in some mix of three different styles. From this it follows that if the activity is carried out in some mix of styles with which we are not familiar, we may fail to recognize it as such and may even mislabel it. In this way an appreciation of the three styles, especially as they apply to common kinds of behavior, may allow us to look at familiar kinds of activities in a fresh light.

In stressing at the outset that we must look for continuities between biological and behavioral characteristics, I seem to have taken a position very close to that of Sheldon—in particular, since I also have adopted his terminology and the meanings of his key terms. I should therefore also state at this point how my approach differs from Sheldon's, in order that I do not appear to be proposing a revival of his work on physique and temperament.[4] There are three important ways in which the present work differs from his:

(1) Sheldon compared a person's observed somatotype with scores on a personality inventory of observed traits. In the present work, by contrast, my interest is not in what is usually called temperament or personality but in broader questions of the style of one's total behavior. My hypothesis, it will be recalled, does not refer to relations between body and behavior but only to possible variations in behavior. Once the ramifications of the hypothesis are spelled out—which is the task of this book—an additional task, quite independent of the hypothesis, would be to trace out relations between such variations in behavior and other, independently assessed variations in somatotype.

(2) As I argue in a number of places in the following pages, a

search for causal links, even when it is successful, is not the only way in which an inquiry such as this can be pursued. Indeed, I advance the argument that causal thinking represents only one of the three styles that I will discuss and that at least two other modes of thinking are available to us and may well contribute to our understanding of phenomena. The quarrel over whether causal relations can be found between one's physical structure and one's behavior (or personality or character) is, then, phrased in too restricted a way, closing off too many possibilities. A full discussion of all three styles may serve to reopen the question that Sheldon stumbled over.

(3) In chapter 6 I return to Sheldon's work in order to reevaluate it, and there I suggest that much of it may have been misunderstood, or at least judged too quickly. I argue that a closer reading of the pertinent material indicates a struggle, line by line; within the confines of a nineteenth-century framework of natural science, he may have been struggling to come to a new understanding of that most mysterious of all living phenomena, the body. If we now reassess what he accomplished, basing our review on current thought that has been influenced by advances in phenomenological psychology, we may be able to see where he stumbled and how his failed efforts may be reconstituted. This too is one of the tasks of the present work.

Just as causal thinking, often assumed to be the only way in which logical linkages can be shown, may not be the only approach on which to build an argument, so the terms that we use throughout may have more than one variant. If my hypothesis refers generally to all three styles of behavior, I will need to explore it in terms that are neutral in regard to the styles. For example, if I use the term "accomplish" in a discussion of behavior, have I not already slanted my discussion toward the meso style? The term "achieve" describes a way of doing or acting that is closest to the meso style, this being a style of goal-oriented achievement. Language is our most sensitive behavioral instrument and will inevitably reveal the moment-to-moment leanings of the behavior shown by the writer of these pages. It is a problem that will recur throughout the chapters that follow, and this in itself will indicate that I have no completely satisfactory way of coping with it. As counterbalance I suggest that the continuing presence of the problem may itself indicate that together the three styles come close to exhausting the range of possible human behavior; thus we have no neutral ground left over. I am also comforted to note that others before me have come up against the same problem. In his fundamental discussion of the "structures" of behavior, Merleau-Ponty[5] remarks that he has chosen to use the Hegelian term *work* rather than such terms as "action" to refer to behavior in the most general sense: as "the ensemble of activities by which man transforms physical and living nature."

Sheldon's Contributions

Some background of history will help to fill out the meaning of the terms I have chosen for styles of behavior. During the nineteenth century biological and medical scientists were feverishly engaged in a search for a universal theory of normal and abnormal functioning. Freud was only the best known and perhaps the most gifted of this group of dedicated researchers. One of these, the psychiatrist Ernst Kretschmer, collected observations on thousands of mental patients, which he then organized into gross categories. His interest was in comparing two kinds of observations, those referring to accepted diagnoses of mental illness and those referring to the patient's physique. In his major work, *Physique and Character*,[6] he claimed to demonstrate that these two sets of observations, the physical and the diagnostic, were systematically related.

The relationship that Kretschmer claimed was, however, far from robust and in any case was asymmetrical. He identified three major categories of physique—the asthenic, with what he called a "deficiency in thickness"; the athletic, with a "strong development" of muscles and skeleton; and the pyknic, with a "pronounced peripheral development of the body cavities," which is to say, with a prominent gut. His patient population, on the other hand, fell into two major groups, schizophrenics and manic-depressives. Kretschmer concluded that schizophrenics were mostly of the asthenic type but with some admixture of the athletic, whereas manic-depressives were of the pyknic type. Aside from the fact that quantitative relations between a set of two and a set of three are difficult to show, Kretschmer ran afoul of an error in statistical reasoning that is today familiar to undergraduate students. The mere fact of a demonstrated correlation—which he did find in many sets of observations—is not evidence of a causal relation, since an unknown third variable may be influencing the first two. And this was just what was found on closer examination, that manic-depressives, being usually older than schizophrenics in mental hospitals, also tend to be heavier, thus exhibiting what appears to be a more endomorphic or pyknic structure. The hidden third factor producing his correlations was the patient's age.

Methodological errors of this sort, as well as the weak or negative results of a long series of empirical tests, have helped to discredit the field of constitutional psychology. Yet the conception of a significant continuity between biology and behavior seems to persist, the "gut feeling" (to use an appropriate phrase) that body is not unrelated to behavior and perhaps even to character. As a character in one of Saul Bellow's novels puts it, "The spirit of the person in a sense is the author of his body,"[7] thereby neatly reversing the direction of the causal relation with which we are familiar. Similarly, Cervantes's two major characters, in his *Don Quixote*, demonstrate a close tie between physique and forms of behavior. Both are comic characters, both perhaps less than heroic, yet in quite different ways. The knight is long and lean and doleful, a dreamer and imaginer who is barely in touch with the real world, a comic victim of his overworked ideals and fantasies. The peasant Sancho Panza, on the other hand, is short and stocky, cheerful in the face of troubles and disappointments, with both feet sturdily planted in everyday, concrete reality. Their remarkable correspondence to two of the styles I discuss in these pages should soon be evident. The "types" we see in Cervantes's masterful creations may also be found throughout the long history of the commedia dell'arte and, more recently, in the film characters of Laurel and Hardy.

Since Kretschmer's day the leading figure in constitutional psychology has been William Sheldon. In the terminology that he introduced, there are three major somatotypes or modes of physical constitution.

The *endomorphic* refers to the component of roundedness in the physique, produced most often by an excess of fat over muscle. Under the influence of the endomorphic component, the structure of the body shows externally an emphasis on the stomach and the gut, and internally on the viscera, with a corresponding de-emphasis on the externally oriented organs of contact, such as hands and feet, or sensory organs.

The *mesomorphic* refers to the squareness or muscularity of the physique, resulting from an excess of muscle over the other components. Structurally, the mesomorphic body emphasizes the muscular-skeletal system; it is centered externally in the chest, the shoulders, and the hands and feet as organs for executing action.

The *ectomorphic* refers to the component of length in the physique, expressed as a maximum of exposure of the skin. The structure of the predominantly ectomorphic body shows an external emphasis on the skin and the sensory organs and an internal emphasis on the brain and central nervous system.

In Sheldon's system at least a minimum of each component must enter into the individual's physical makeup, because the three components have their origins in structures formed during embryological development. As a result no one can lack completely any of the components, although in extreme instances one of the components may appear to be virtually absent. The particular and unique mix of components in each case determines that individual's observable physique and therefore judged somatotype.

All typologies before Sheldon, whether offered by theorists or based on research investigation, had referred to the whole body, the physique as a unit, rather than to parts or aspects of persons. In the event that some interesting relations seemed to be discovered, as Kretschmer claimed, the explanation had to be that there was a source within the patients' bodies that was active so as to result in the observed correlations. Usually such sources were called "force" or "principle" and conceptualized as a form of energy. But it was hardly a satisfactory way of explaining one's observations, if only because the resulting theoretical formulations very soon became too abstract to be useful.

Sheldon changed all this by shifting the investigator's focus. In place of the whole body as a target of observation, Sheldon looked for "components" that functioned together and made up the living body that one observed. When he began his work he did not know how many such major components he might find, but it soon became clear to him and his associates that their observations could safely be categorized on the basis of three assumed components. They were looking at photographs of male college students; the test of whether three components were sufficient was simply whether with them they could assign some score to all the photographs. To assign a score an observer would rate a photograph three times, once for each of the components, scoring the component from 1 (for the near absence of the component) to 7 (for its maximum possible value). A person who was, for example, at the observed median in regard to all three components might receive a score close to 3–4–3.

By shifting from observation of the whole person to the search for components, and then by rating the presence of each component separately on a scale of 1 to 7, Sheldon was able to substitute a kind of quantitative scoring for the earlier practice of gross somatotyping. In addition to this he proposed what amounted to a theoretical advance: that the components making up all the varieties of the human physique were an outgrowth of differentiation that begins in early stages of embryological development. During fetal growth the developing organism forms itself first into a cylindrical tube, then into a second tube surrounding the first, and finally into a third tube surrounding the first two—a process first described in chick embryos by Christian Pander in 1817 and later developed by the great comparative anatomist Karl von Baer. Sheldon stated: "The digestive viscera (dominant in endomorphy) are derived principally from the endodermal embryonic layer. The somatic tissues (dominant in mesomorphy) are derived from the mesodermal layer, while the skin and nervous system, which are relatively prominent in ectomorphy, come from the ectodermal embryonic layer."[8]

In greater detail, and beginning with the innermost layer, the endoderm eventually develops into glands and glandular organs such as the thymus, the thyroid and parathyroid, and the liver; the larynx, trachea, pharynx, and tonsils; the esophagus, digestive tube, stomach, and intestines; and the lungs and most of the respiratory system—in short, all that we call the bowel or gut, the digestive and excretory systems, and the respiratory organs. The intermediate, mesodermal layer forms the skeleton with its associated bone and cartilage; the heart and related hollow organs, such as arteries, veins, and lymph vessels; the kidneys and the urinary system; the genital organs; those membranes, such as the peritoneal, which form internal cavities—in short, all the supportive and active structures of the body and their connective tissue. Finally, the ectoderm, or outermost layer, forms the skin (and in mammals the hair and nails as well), the mouth and anus, the brain, spinal cord, and the rest of the central nervous system, the spinal and cranial nerves, the autonomic nervous system, and major parts of the external sensory organs for smell, taste, vision, and hearing—in short, all the systems and structures for contact, communication, and the organization of one's action.

Sheldon's work was clearly an advance on the rather weak conceptualizations of his predecessors. However, we should recognize that his was not a theory in the usual sense of the word. A pair of his most sympathetic critics have summed it up very well: "The theory consists largely of one general assumption (the continuity between structure and behavior) and a set of descriptive concepts for scaling physique and behavior . . . (But) in fairness to Sheldon we must remember that he has occasionally indicated that his position is not to be considered an attempt at a general theory but rather it is intended to account for a limited range of variables and perhaps to offset certain biases that are generally operative among individuals studying human behavior."[9]

It was in the test of his "general assumption" concerning continuity between physique and behavior that Sheldon ran into difficulties. In his major study of this question,[10] he obtained measurements of individuals' somatotypes as well as their performance on a wide range of observations relating to personality. The resulting correlations between his trichotomy of components of physique and his newfound trichotomy of "temperament" were very high—so high, in fact, that they were immediately suspect. One source of error was immediately evident, that Sheldon had himself made most of the behavioral observations on which his temperament measures were based, and if he was also either the author of the somatotype ratings on these subjects or the acknowledged expert on "reading" bodies for their somatotypic characteristics, an error of unknown value had been introduced that could not be eliminated in this research design.

With few exceptions,[11] the matter has rested here since Sheldon's major research a generation ago. In reviewing his work at this point, and in relating the investigation in this book to his studies, I do not mean to stir up an old quarrel or try to make a case against a preponderance of evidence. Rather, I hope to skirt the issue of temperament and physique by dealing with behavioral activities and processes rather than with personality and by leaving open the question of continuity between behavior and constitution. I hope that the results of the investigation I report here may in the end be of some help toward resolving the latter question.

THE LIVED BODY

In proposing that three styles of behavior mix and mutually influence each other in everything a person does, I try not to argue for or against a specific style. It is a temptation difficult to resist, since I am claiming that the three styles are both pervasive and exhaustive of human behavior. Hence in my own behavior as author or in the behavior of other writers as theorists, claimants, or defendants, the behavior that is shown will be some mix of the styles. At the same time the content of their or my reference will, of course, also be some mix of the styles. A writer or theorist may use a predominantly meso style to reason toward the conclusion that an ecto style is the one that should be used in reasoning. It is on these grounds that I take the opportunity very early in my discussion to distinguish among such apparently similar terms as true, useful, and appropriate. To emphasize that a style brings us closer to what is true is, I think, to claim a priority for the ecto style, for truth is a significant possibility and a central notion in an ecto-dominated mode of thinking. Equally, in the meso style it is utility that counts, as appropriateness does in the endo style. Therefore to use one of these terms is itself evidence that one is committed to one or another style of thinking and reasoning, independently of what one is referring to or arguing for.

The Body As Causal Agent

Certain phenomena do perhaps receive more adequate treatment within one style than another. As an example (for which I will argue later), expressive phenomena as a subcategory of observable behavior seem to find their home within an endo style of knowing; and on the other hand, issues in theoretical physics appear to be best treated within an ecto style. Still other phenomena may require, or at least may make possible, a tripartite understanding involving all three styles. I will suggest here that the latter is true of the problem of body-behavior relations, and that to pose the issue in terms of whether causal relations subsist between body and behavior is inadequate. It does not cover the full range of equally valuable answers.

We constitute relations in our observations of nature. Different styles, then, will lead us to constituting different sorts of relations. Two different observers, or even the same observer at two different times, may thus find that the "fundamental" relation subsisting between two observable entities or phenomena is a causal one; or that it is seemingly noncausal even though it evidences a nontrivial co-existence; or that the two "belong" together in the way that, for example, a part belongs to a whole. The central terms here (fundamental, causal, belong) are each part of the vocabulary of a distinct style.

There is, of course, nothing novel in a claim that fundamental relations may be noncausal, but there may be some novelty in looking at body-behavior relations in this light. Much of the historically important discussion of this problem has been restricted to two (implicit) possibilities: that the body in some sense causes behavior, or that it does not. In one of the early classics of experimental medicine, a report published by an American surgeon, William Beaumont, in 1833, there were reported observations he had made on the stomach lining of a trapper named Alexis St. Martin. As a consequence of a fistula, or permanent opening from the outside into his stomach, the aftermath of a healed gunshot wound, St. Martin was in effect a walking display of the stomach lining under conditions of hunger, emotion, and activity. Here was the first evidence that the lining of the stomach directly and immediately reflects changes in other parts of the body, in the "mind," and even in many aspects of behavior. The observations also raised the question of cause, but it is interesting that the assumption made in 1833, and hardly contradicted since, was that the *only* important question raised by the observations was one of cause; that is, in terms of this evidence, what causes what? No other "active" sort of relation was ever assumed.

As a consequence of the particular mode of scientific thinking that dominates contemporary life, it is taken for granted that the most significant relation, the one that counts when we try to understand how body and behavior are related, is the causal one. Once we understand whether and how one of these entities causes the other, we then know in the most fundamental sense how they are related. To the degree that science penetrates our thinking, the causal relation is intuitively accepted as the one that is basic to physical occurrences—and this in spite of the fact that even when the effects of this relation are shown we can never know how it works. The behavioral style that is evidenced in this kind of thinking is the one that I am calling ecto. It is the style that dominates the contemporary physical sciences, as I discuss in detail in ensuing pages, and it has at its core the notion of cause, in particular causation at a distance. When a scientist, thinking in this style, undertakes to explore how body and behavior might be related, the first question that seems proper and indeed self-evident is whether and how the one causes the other. The causation may be multiplex rather than a matter of simple linear effects, but at bottom the causal relation is the only one that is seriously examined.

Yet, as I argue throughout this book, other styles of thinking and reasoning may be possible. Suppose one's thinking, even thinking about causal relations, happens to be dominated by the meso style. In this case quite a different picture of nature may be constituted. One might then unthinkingly, just as though it is the "natural" way to look at things, observe that two entities appear to coexist and seemingly to bear upon each other in some nontrivial way. Then on further examination it appears that the two seemingly related entities constitute mutually reinforcing aspects of a joint or multiple effort.

Such a mode of relationship is, in fact, what most of us, regardless of our usual style of thinking, are likely to observe when we watch a soccer team in action. We will see, for example, that when one member of the team begins a specific offensive move, the other members engage in "related" offensive behavior. This is the way soccer teams operate and therefore how the actions of the members are related to each other. Similarly, this is the way in which the movement of my elbow is related to the movement of my wrist: together, they effect a joint and mutually reinforcing behavior. It would not be appropriate to say that one soccer player's behavior causes the behavior of another, or that what happens in my elbow causes what happens in my wrist, for we accept that in these modes of relating the notion of cause is out of place. On the other hand, when we observe a mother call to her child and the child then run toward her, we accept that in this instance of relatedness the mother's behavior was the cause of the child's.

Our problem, however, arises when we observe relations that might appropriately be viewed as occurring in any one of the three styles, in contrast with the more restricted examples that I have just given. The relation of body and behavior is one such, although as I have said it has not customarily been viewed as other than an ecto-style relationship of cause. I suggest that, depending on one's typical mode of reasoning, observation of the body and the person's behavior can indicate either the presence or absence of causal relations, an ecto phenomenon; or a meso phenomenon in the form of joint and mutually reinforcing action; or an endo phenomenon. Since the latter is by far the least known of the three styles, I will take some space to discuss it here.

In general, when observation and one's thinking are dominated by the endo style, the various aspects of a phenomenon are observed to "belong" together. A familiar model for viewing in this mode is the relatedness that we usually see when we look first at someone's facial expression and then at their stance or posture—for example, seeing first a broad smile and then the arms spread wide and opened in a gesture of welcome. The two aspects of this phenomenon, the facial expression and the stance, seem to us to belong equally to one another and to a "bigger" unit, in this case the stance of friendly greeting. By virtue of the phenomenon itself, we constitute the two aspects as belonging, to the degree that usually we could not imagine it any other way. Try, for instance, to imagine the conjunction of a wide open posture with a frowning and angry facial expression.[12] It is not, as it is in observations conducted in the ecto or meso styles, that alternatives are possible on the grounds of utility or truth, but that this is the way it is, all together, irrevocably. Observation and reasoning in the dominantly endo style result in "conclusions" of this sort, often in instances in which other persons break the phenomenon down according to dictates of the other styles. In the extreme endo case, the smallest detail is viewed as an aspect of an all-embracing cosmic vision; and closer to home, the body and its behavior are seen as, let us say, two of the many ways in which the life process may appear, frozen, for observation.

On Object and Process

In an influential work on this topic by Gabriel Marcel, a meditation that he called *Being and Having*,[13] the distinction is made between two modes of possession. I may own something in the sense of having it as a possession, as I do my home, my automobile, and in one sense my arm. I may also own (and be owned by) something in the sense of being that thing, as I do my name, my personality, and in quite a different sense my arm. The difference is that I might sell my house without effecting a central change in all that I am, whereas if I changed my personality I would simply be a different person. Any possession might occupy one or the other categories—for example, I might be so attached to my house and it might mean so much to me that only if I were a different person would I sell it—but the meaning of the two categories, and the difference between them, is clear. We use the verb *have* in both senses, often unfortunately, saying that "I have a certain type of personality" as well as "I have two sets of keys to my office." The body is remarkable, perhaps unique, in this respect, that we cannot help "owning" it simultaneously, in everything we do, in both senses. I have my body and any part of it, and at the same time I am my body, living it. It is both this object that I have and this set of processes that I am, or in Sartre's terms, both my property and my being; it brings together two "levels of being," being-for-itself, which is pure interiority, and being-for-others, which is the body in the eyes of an outside viewer.[14]

All our acculturation having predisposed us, we understand very well how the body can be an object, a kind of property, something that is had as I have my typewriter. It is the other category that causes us trouble—so much so that our cultural tendency has been to ignore it. What do we mean when we say that a definable and knowable entity is not had but lived, not known from the outside but lived from the inside? Let us attempt a science fiction image. Imagine that somehow we could build a living thing and that having finished it we want to insert in it somehow a knowing, a mode of self-reflective consciousness such that when we look into it, as we might if making love to it, we would be sure that we would see a person looking out. If our project fails we will be left holding in our arms a perfectly formed being whose eyes are lifeless, but if it succeeds we will have built, somehow, a person. The distinction, I submit, is simple enough to be appreciated by the most philosophically unsophisticated person.

Now imagine that phenomenon of the living person as it might be experienced from the inside, from the point of view of the person who has just been created in this manner. We are, each of us, "inside" a body, looking out—but now in spite of all my effort I cannot find words that fit what I am trying to describe. To speak of a person as inside a body, as somehow positioned so as to look out through a shell called the skin, immediately misses the point, for once the notion of person and the correlative notion of living has been introduced, these terms descriptive of mere objects located in space are revealed as inadequate. We cannot describe what it means to *be* a body, although we usually have no difficulty in referring to what it means to *have* a body. Marcel puts it thus: "What we have obviously presents an appearance of externality to ourselves . . . I can only have, in the strict sense of the word, something whose existence is, up to a certain point, independent of me."[15] "The statement 'I have' can only be made over against another which is felt to be other."[16] This is to say that the object, as such, is bounded and so its boundaries can be known; we experience it as constrained by observable limits, or, as we quite properly say, we can apprehend it, which means that we can take it in our grasp.

By contrast—which is perhaps the only way we can come to an adequate description of the body as known and lived rather than had—the body as process rather than object can be known only from within; hence it is not experienced as bounded but simply is, as it is. Its boundaries are then experienced not as limits but as potential. The difference is well stated by Umberto Eco in the following, which was made in quite a different context but is strikingly applicable here: "Thus God knows the world, because He conceived it in His mind, as if from the outside, before it was created, and we do not know its rule, because we live inside it, having found it already made."[17] The rule we live is the one that we do not know, nor know that we do not know, and do not obey or disobey but simply live. In the terms of the science fiction image that I offered above, if the person were already "in" the body before it is built, it would then be known but only as an object and then could be apprehended, perhaps even ordered, but not lived.

Understood in this way, the body as lived is both determined by its givens and capable as well of directing itself toward new givens that may exceed the old. The latter alternative, in which the body is lived as process, occurs each time our behavior eventuates in growth; whereas when the body is apprehended and utilized as object, one uses what is already there and either wears it out or engages it so as to wear out the environment. In a later section I discuss this adversary relation that subsists between an object and its surround, as compared with the way in which a lived body grows into and with the situation of which it is a part. My reference to, and contrasting, these two modes of relation between the body and its world provides another justification for referring to my topic as an ecology of the body.

The three styles of behavior that I will discuss and compare have each their own mode of knowing; although it should be kept in mind that any style of thinking or knowing can be directed toward any target. The distinctions arise in regard to what is then constituted, in that target, by the particular style of knowing. In general, as I show later, in the ecto style it is objects that are constituted—discrete, bounded, at a distance, grasped as other, able to be broken down or else combined in an infinity of ways. When we know our own bodies as objects, we are behaving primarily in the ecto style. The other way of knowing our bodies, as process, is in some combination of the meso and endo styles—and this may help to explain why we have no vocabulary for talking about knowing the body as process, why we find it so difficult to present a systematic and reasonable argument in its support.

Merleau-Ponty: The Body-Subject

In his early work, *The Structure of Behavior*,[18] Merleau-Ponty took a major step toward a phenomenological psychology in his analysis of the key term *behavior*. It is, he said, "not a thing, but neither is it an idea. It is not the envelope of a pure consciousness and, as the witness of behavior, I am not a pure consciousness. . . . Behavior is a form."[19] It is grounded in the biology of the organism, such that "the efficacious relations at each level define an *a priori* of this species, a manner of elaborating the stimuli which is proper to it."[20] In this view, organism, behavior, style, and learning all mesh in a new set of significations, in "a kinetic melody gifted with a meaning. . . . Situation and reaction are linked internally by their common participation in a structure in which the mode of activity proper to the organism is expressed."[21]

This conception of behavior, biologically grounded and identifiable as what I term a style, may be taken as the starting point of the present book. However, Merleau-Ponty's later conception, the *body-subject*, which was presented in a second work, *The Phenomenology of Perception*,[22] plays no part in the argument that I present here. By his term "subject" he means something like "person," in the sense that it is a meaning-giving existence. In the words of one commentator, "our body itself is already a subject, an existence, an intercourse with the world, [such] that the world's structure depends on the structure of our body."[23] Merleau-Ponty shows in careful detail the ways in which the body constitutes the meaning we find in space, in movement, in sexuality, in the realm of the senses—but all at a preconscious and prepersonal level. The body forms the "original intentionality" of ourselves as subjects so that it is appropriate to refer to consciousness, not as an "I think that" but as an "I am able to," that is, as bodily rather than "psychic."[24]

This powerful argument is welcome as a preparation for a systematic phenomenological psychology. To the traditionally accepted conception of a meaning-world constituted by a "psychical" consciousness, he has added a second but prior meaning-world of the body, showing, for example, that certain experimental results can best be understood as a demonstration of the body actively organizing itself to establish a ground of meaning. But as a philosopher Merleau-Ponty is not content with proposing a new groundwork for understanding past and future evidence gathered in psychological experiments. His field of inquiry extends to an ontological analysis. Thus he distinguishes two realms of existence, that which is free and called consciousness and that which is bound and called concrete existence or corporeity. He will permit to the latter a world of constituted meaning far beyond what one can find in the work of earlier phenomenologists, a contribution as significant as that of Freud, who also argued for a realm of the unconscious with its own meaning-giving powers. At the same time, Merleau-Ponty would insist that we retain a privileged realm of conscious knowledge, looking down, as it were, on a busy and prior and indeed necessary realm of concrete corporeal existence.

It will be clear in subsequent pages that in this book I am taking another tack entirely. I approach the issues from another angle—not steeped in consciousness, as we surely must be as self-reflective persons, but poised on the middle ground of behavior that Merleau-Ponty explored in his earlier work. On this ground, I will claim, all behavior is a mix of the three styles of bodily existence. I then need go no further toward ontological distinctions, for all the phenomena that I will discuss are at hand. I will be involved, then, in an extended set of exercises in phenomenological description, rather than a phenomenological analysis.

The Question of the Author's Style

If, as I have claimed, the three styles are exhaustive of the range of normal behavior, what justification can I offer for using predominantly one of the styles—as I surely must—to discuss the use of styles in general? To answer this question in regard to myself as author, I need to discuss, if I can, how my own writing and presentation in this book are related to the three styles of thinking and writing.

A useful distinction is sometimes made in regard to the place of mathematics in the human sciences. On the one hand, mathematics may be adopted as a method, an aid, a tool; and on the other hand mathematics may serve as a determining approach, a kind of language with which the scientist chooses to operate. Most researchers, including many who are not mathematically inclined, will perforce use mathematical methods as part of their armamentarium of tools. Only those who are, in a sense, themselves mathematicians, however, will normally think in mathematical terms or treat questions as though they were problems in mathematics.

I remind the reader of this distinction because it helps us to understand a related distinction that may be made in regard to one's predominant behavioral style. One can, on the one hand, behave primarily in reference to material that belongs mostly in one of the styles—as, for example, when I occupy myself with the interrelated propositions and the logical structure of theory in psychology. Or on the other hand one can think or reason in a specifically styled way, whether or not the content belongs in that style. Merleau-Ponty, who both wrote about phenomenology and wrote as a phenomenologist, was aware of the difference, as when he reminds us that phenomenology can be both practiced and identified as a manner or style of thinking.[25] The distinction has also been discussed in a recent perceptive critique of Polanyi's thought by William Poteat. He describes Polanyi as being in his "explicit" arguments less radical, less "broad in its general philosophical import," than in his "often quite unwitting innovative use of [these] concepts."[26] In the terms I am using here, he may be said to have used one style of thinking, perhaps one close to his "natural" way of behaving, in order to pursue an argument explicitly couched in a different style—the former being noticeably more powerful. To this Poteat adds that these are somatic modes, that they are expressed by way of language, and that by virtue of the character of language one may at the same time both comment upon a phenomenon and "instantiate a particular case of it."[27] Thus, in the most general terms, some of Polanyi's implicit "assumptions . . . are embodied in therefore implied by what he does and are therefore grounded in his mindbody; . . . [others reveal] the very actuality of his mindbodily being as such."[28]

Although it is difficult for a writer to clearly identify the stylistic nature of the content of his or her thought, it is for evident reasons even more difficult to recognize, much less to write about, the stylistic "language" of what is produced. In my own case an honest attempt at both tasks indicates that the content of my writing, the target or topics with which I am concerned, is predominantly ecto in style. I will be discussing mostly those kinds of issues that naturally arise within an ecto style of thinking about issues. However, my personal "language" of thought and expression, including how I approach and then deal with the issues and finally how I express myself about them, does not seem to be primarily in an ecto style. Quite evidently, I do not naturally express myself in the style of reasoning or writing that one finds in the experimental articles of scientific journals, and to the degree that my style of presentation reflects the thinking that led up to it, we may assume that my thinking, too, is not primarily in the ecto style.

The reader of this work should therefore expect to encounter fairly traditional topics, as well as questions about them, which are handled in a nontraditional way. The writing in the pages that follow will not present a hierarchically ordered set of propositions nor will it follow in linear fashion a chain of causal links. In place of links that are connected in an if-then sequence, my presentation of points to which the reader is led will usually be sensed as "followable" (to use Ricoeur's apt term), in a manner that has been well described by Paul Tillich: "The test of [this] description is that the picture given by it is convincing, that it can be seen by anyone who is willing to look in the same direction, that the description illuminates other related ideas, and that it makes the reality which these ideas are supposed to reflect understandable."[29]

The physical model most appropriate to my style of reasoning and presentation would be a spiral, its successive plateaus stated as intuitions grasped rather than as facts adduced, its connections in the form of networks of associations rather than chains of evidence. I will lean heavily on examples, with their burden of allusion and suggestion, rather than on ordered linkages of proof and disproof. Finally, my style of thought will affect what I write, so that the reader should not expect to find here either a set of explanations or a rigorously established proto-theory. Beyond these caveats I am not able to penetrate— not because, as so often happens in the case of talking about one's own character, the talker may be the last to know, but because it is only when one's style is primarily ecto that one has access to a means for talking about it. That is one of the great glories of the ecto style, that it is automatically and intrinsically self-referential, and in it one can talk about oneself and then talk about oneself talking about oneself, endlessly. If, as happens in my case, the style is closer to the meso or endo, a self-referential quality is not readily available and one is then left with, at best, the demonstration of the style and some of its results. One might with effort talk about what the style is not but not be able to talk meaningfully about what it is.

I may also emphasize at this point that the approach I use in the present work intends no bias either for or against any of the styles, or their mixes, that I discuss. My purpose is not to evaluate the styles but to compare them, and in particular to explore some traditional areas and problems from the point of view of three different styles, rather than, as is customary in the scientific community, in terms of one style at the expense of the others. My reliance throughout on an endo-meso mix of styles of thinking and writing is, then, only a reflection of the way that I most comfortably behave. This book, or one very like it, might just as well have been written by someone else in an ecto style.

RELATED WORK BY OTHERS

The work I present here has its sources in important work by others, some of them already mentioned in passing. In the capsule discussions that follow, it will appear that I can make no claim to originality, that much of what I say is adumbrated in more thorough treatments by earlier writers. While recognizing my intellectual debts, the only kind that one cannot easily repay, I want at the same time to disclaim any reading of these writers as supporting the arguments I advance in these pages. As far as I know, what I present here is the first explicit statement of its central hypothesis and the first attempt to explore the hypothesis across a range of familiar areas in psychology. What is original here, then, is the application of some insights which have been more or less explicitly offered by a number of others before me.

Sigmund Freud

It is an unsettled question whether Freud's conceptual system, as he worked it and reworked it over a span of four decades, is as biological as he and some of his followers have claimed. On first view it would appear that from the start it was a pronouncedly biological theory. Freud's work began with his case studies of what was then called hysteria, in particular the condition known as hysterical paralysis or the question of a nonorganic disability masquerading as organic and thereby determining the patient's psychological functioning. He went on to postulate as the origin of psychic life a biological entity, the reservoir of biological impulse that he called the id. To this he coupled the notion of instinct, which he described as on the boundary between the biological and the psychological. A second basic conception, the ego, fed by perception as the id is fed by instinct and representing reason and commonsense,[30] "is first and foremost a bodily ego; it is not merely a surface entity, but is itself the projection of a surface."[31] (In this Freud was faithfully followed by some psychoanalytic theorists, for example, Otto Fenichel with his conception of an ego-like entity at the core of the Self which he envisioned as one's body image.)[32] Freud also outlined a scheme of biologically determined stages of childhood psychosexual development which he identified with the locus and functioning of specific areas of the body. And, of course, beneath the entire scheme, like a single foundation stone, was the unshakable proposition: anatomy is destiny.

Surely this adds up to a system that is basically biological. To all this may be added that the idea of individualized styles is often at least implied in Freud's theorizing. Aggressive impulses, for example, may be expressed in a circuitous way, as in the case of the hard-driving entrepreneur, this style of behavior then coloring the person's entire behavior. The psychoanalytic treatment of character comes close to making these ideas explicit. However, they are never fully developed, and they are not applied so as to furnish an explanation of an individual's behavior. As a result, Freud never came close to exploring the kinds of problems that are the concern of the present book.

It appears that in spite of some tendencies toward a biological, individualized psychology, the case for psychoanalytic theory is by no means clear-cut, the evidence by no means definitive. The psychoanalysis that we see today, the result of nearly a century of work by its practitioners, fails to show evidence of its biological origins. And when we take a fresh look at the history of Freudian theory, as I attempt in chapter 5, we find that from the very beginning Freud seemed to be trying to find some way out of a biologically based scheme. Although there have been from time to time some suggestions that the conceptual pillar known as the unconscious might profitably be defined as unnoticed or denied aspects of the lived body, these suggestions have come from those, such as Alexander Lowen, who have been strongly influenced by theoreticians outside the Freudian fold. Indeed, it may be argued that a biologically based theory of personality and clinical practice is more likely to be found in the writings of Reich than of Freud.

For these reasons it would be difficult to claim that Freudian psychoanalysis, either as theory or as practice, is strongly biological. What I present in this book, then, might at best be considered as not incompatible with Freudian thought but to only a minimal degree derivative of it. Freud was not greatly concerned with placing the lived body at the center of his psychological scheme, and probably for this reason he did not seriously concern himself with such basic issues as mind-body relations. He did, however, make use of a kind of typology of character, linking the types to specific stages of psychosexual development. The well-known trichotomy of oral, anal, and phallic characters may even seem to be the basis for the endo-meso-ecto triad I discuss in these pages. I should therefore clarify the similarities and differences at once.

The similarities between the two trichotomies are evident, and they may be mapped to each other about as follows: what I call the endo style corresponds approximately to a combination of oral and anal characteristics; meso to a mix of anal and phallic characteristics; but ecto to post-oedipal characteristics rather than to important elements of the pre-oedipal triad. Counterbalancing these rather weak similarities is an important difference. Psychoanalytic characterology was forged in the heat of clinical sessions and is therefore meant to refer to one's character or personality and to sources of one's psychopathology. The trichotomy that I offer here has a more modest origin and a smaller aim. It refers to narrower and more local modes of functioning such as remembering and perception, as well as to the range of everyday behaviors that sustain "normal" but probably not pathological functioning. It is precisely because of this restriction to normal, everyday, basic behavioral functions that I feel justified in attempting to map my trichotomy to larger groupings such as societies and even historical eras, as I do in chapter 8, an effort that would be out of place with the familiar Freudian characterological triad.

Part of Freud's genius lies in the multilayered complexity of his system as it finally developed. The result is that its depths permit almost any other view of human behavior to find some appropriate reflection. I would not want this circumstance to make it appear that I am presenting a reworded or transliterated psychoanalytic scheme. What I offer here is not completely independent of the Freudian scheme, not orthogonal to it, but related and somewhat tangential, a useful addition and perhaps enrichment rather than a substitute.

The Post-Freudians

Among the many thinkers who were originally inspired by Freud but who later went off in their own directions, to a greater or less degree independent of the thinking of the master, mention should be made first of all of Alfred Adler. As early as 1926 he started using such terms as "plan of life," and in 1929 he adopted the expression "style of life" from the sociologist Max Weber. My usage in this book is so close to his that it may legitimately be said that I have borrowed from him. For Adler, the term style of life refers to "an individuality . . . expressing itself and molding itself in an environment."[33] One's style of life is a "unity" derived from a lifetime of striving against life's difficulties and organized around the goal attainment that comes from this striving. One's style of life is therefore one's "consistent movement" toward one's major life goal.

The notion of style in Adler's thinking is to be distinguished from the related notion of type. The latter are no more than "convenient abstractions" based on an "intellectual device" to help us understand

people's similarities.[34] Style of life, on the other hand, refers throughout to the individual, in the sense that every person has a unique and
personalized style of life. This central point, that types refer to group
classification and style of life to individuals, is perhaps uniquely Adler's contribution. The childhood precursor of the adult life-style, its
developmental core, is what Adler calls the *prototype;* the shift from
early prototype to adult and lifetime style is made about the age of
five, and thereafter "for the most part" never changes, although of
course it can be altered through treatment.[35] A very closely related
line of thought may be found more recently in Sartre: to attain to
consciousness in childhood is to embark on one's own (free) project
by which the self is then constituted and so expresses itself completely
in each self-defining act.[36]

A system much closer to a true typology may be found in the work
of Carl Jung, developed most completely in his volume on psychological types.[37] In this view one's character is compounded out of the interplay of two major "attitudes" and four "functions." The two attitudes, extraversion and introversion, are determined for the person by
the primary established direction of libidinal flow, outward or inward.
The four functions include two referring to distance, the thinking and
the feeling forms of judgment, as well as two referring to the immediate, the given, the nonrational, sensation and intuition. (The overlap
with the styles to which I refer, ecto on the one hand and meso/endo
on the other, will be apparent.) Multiplication of two attitudes and
four functions makes possible eight primary types, with other possibilities available in the various shadings. Jung's interest was clearly in
developing a system that was sensitive to individual differences, as
opposed to a psychology of general laws or principles, and to this degree the exploration in this book moves in the same direction. The
psychiatrist Hermann Rorschach,[38] an early Swiss contributor to psychoanalysis whose untimely death cut short a career of great promise,
built the interpretation of his inkblot test on some distinctions similar
to those made by Jung. The dichotomy of "turning inward" *versus*
"turning outward" is scored on the test as M *versus* C, referring to
perceived movement and perceived color. M scores are interpreted as
indicating the subject's tendency to give up graceful "outer" move-

ments in favor of introversion, withdrawal, and awkwardness, resembling the style that I describe as ecto; and C scores are interpreted as a tendency to turn outward and participate in active, colorful, lively interchange with the world, in a combination of my meso and endo styles. In his test scoring Rorschach seemed to have transformed the Jungian "mentalistic" distinctions into terms that are more clearly somatic.

More closely within the psychoanalytic movement itself, modern ego psychology and its ego analytic school have resulted in a number of attempts to deal systematically with observable behavior across the span of the normal. Thus, in a psychoanalytically inspired longitudinal study of children's development, Escalona and Heider refer to "the inherent continuity of behavioral style and of the child's pattern of adaptation,"[39] and some years ago George Klein and his associates created a flurry of interest in the useful concept of the individual's "cognitive style."[40] More recently we have had David Shapiro's valuable contribution to characterology, *Neurotic Styles.*[41] By the central term style he means "a form or mode of functioning—the way or manner of a given area of behavior—that is identifiable, in an individual, through a range of his specific acts;[42] . . . one's generalized, stable, and characteristic modes of functioning."[43] His discussion is, however, restricted to psychologically inner states and activities such as perception, emotion, and "modes of subjective experience in general."[44] He deals with behavior only in regard to "various pathologies." As in the argument that I present, there is no claim that the notion of style becomes a determiner of everything one does, a foundation for theory: "I do not mean to say that any single mode or style can describe all areas of an individual's functioning, but only that styles or modes may be found that are capable of describing general aspects of function (such as cognition, emotional experience, and the like), modes that themselves will then be related and organized."[45] One of his major sources is Wilhelm Reich and his concept of character,[46] although he ignores Reich's emphasis on the body musculature and stresses rather the role of the ego. The specific styles that he discusses are taken from psychoanalytic characterology and include the obsessive-compulsive, the paranoid, the hysterical, and various "impulsive" styles.

Georg Groddeck

The figure within the psychoanalytic movement whose work comes closest to the present book is surely Georg Groddeck. A German physician whose professional career was limited to operating a clinic at a well-known German health spa, Baden Baden, he became interested in Freud's work in its early years and trained himself (as was possible before formal schools of training) to become a psychoanalyst. Although throughout his career Groddeck was admittedly a "wild analyst" whose thinking was far from conventional, Freud always thought highly of his original approach to treatment, in particular the treatment of psychosomatic disorders. Groddeck's best known contribution was what he called the It (das Es), from which Freud derived the related concept he called the id. By the term It, Groddeck meant "the deepest nature and force" of the individual, embracing "all the powers which govern the formation and further development of the individual man."[47] It is a force "unknown and forever unknowable,"[48] comprising both the conscious and the Freudian unconscious, "the sum total of an individual human being, physical, mental, and spiritual."[49] One of Groddeck's students has suggested that "Lao Tse's Tao is perhaps nearest to the It in its workings as a guiding function."[50]

Whatever the theoretical value of this conception within some total picture of the personality, it is clear that it refers to a mode of intelligence that is closer to a biological imperative than to the cognitive capacity which usually serves as a definition of intelligence. Groddeck insisted that the It is the power in our lives, determining what we do and what we are, from our hunger for air to how we see and sleep and move. "What we think we do is really only what is left unrepressed from the whole of life, what the It allows to our vain, arrogant consciousness."[51] If one accepts some such conception—which Freud, for all his sympathy for Groddeck's work, was unable to do, without, as he said, "civilizing the It"—the first step has been taken toward undercutting a simple view of monolithic activities of the personality. If you believe that there may be modes of intelligence, of reasoning, of perception that refer to activities of the It and therefore are not restricted to the cognitive realm, you have started to undercut the assumption that there is only one kind of intelligence, reasoning, or perception.

Groddeck did, in fact, take one more step toward making explicit what is implied in the concept of the It. He proposed that we think of three "minds" rather than one. "Countless incidents of ordinary life give evidence that in certain circumstances the belly-mind is felt to be in opposition and dangerous to the head-mind and the breast-mind."[52] Although he pursued his conceptions into the realm of obscure and farfetched sexual symbolism, thereby antagonizing even his fellow psychoanalysts, he always insisted on our recognizing an active, intelligent biological process with its own vocabulary and its particular modes of "expression." "We belittle mathematics," he remarked, "when we limit it to the domain of rational thought. See how accurately a dog can gauge the speed of a motor-car before he crosses the street"[53] or, one might add in a more modern analogy, see how accurately the dog can aim to catch a Frisbee in the air. "I believe the human hand has its I, that it knows what it does, and knows that it knows";[54] this is a statement to be made only by someone whose logical starting point is a proposition very similar to the hypothesis of this book. It was, in fact, largely because Groddeck recognized the various ways that the individual, as a living organism, carried out all its acts that he was able to accomplish some of his remarkable cures in the field of psychosomatic medicine. For example, in speaking of "the self-protectiveness of the head-mind and breast-mind in face of unwanted impulses from below,"[55] he referred to the behavior of the throat and then noted: "We all know how hard it is to swallow our pride, to eat humble-pie, to stomach an insult,"[56] the first use of such metaphoric data in modern medicine.

There is one more aspect of Groddeck's work to be mentioned here, since it has to do with a topic treated earlier that will come up in later chapters. It should be clear that if we accept the hypothesis of this book and then attempt to explore some of its consequences, we are faced with dual consequences in the case of someone who, like Groddeck, writes about psychological processes such as thinking and reasoning. He can, as Groddeck seems to do, write about the processes as though he had accepted the hypothesis; in which case he will, as Groddeck in fact did, postulate more than one mode of carrying out the processes. But he can also, in the style of his own work as a thinker and writer, demonstrate a mode of expression that suggests what the hypothesis proposes. This Groddeck does as well. Not only does he describe, for example, modes of thinking that are different than what we usually call thinking, but in his own writing he seems to demonstrate such different modes of thinking. In one of his letters to Freud he described at some length how he and Freud differed as thinkers, and his words are worth quoting here because they exemplify one of the styles that I will be examining in this book. Groddeck writes, "In this comparison, I appear to myself as a plow, and you the farmer who will use this or perhaps any other plow for his means. . . . Because the plow has no eyes but fears the rocks, it balks at times to make the farmer who guides it more cognizant of his pushing. . . . For the plow, it is a matter of life. For the farmer, in the last analysis, it is a matter of money."[57]

Although I will reserve for chapter 2 a discussion of the characteristics that Groddeck here attributes to himself, it should be noted that in his analogy he aptly sums up a true stylistic difference between himself and Freud. Groddeck is the "blind" yet intelligent instrument, guided yet guiding, engaged in a life-and-death activity, while Freud is the intelligent user, the traditional perceiver and thinker whom we all have assumed is in control of what is happening. To the farmer, the plow is only one possible instrument among many, whereas to the plow, the farmer who may often be out of touch with what is happening needs to be prodded and even directed from below. Two intelligences, expressive of two styles of action, which may work in unison but just as often may be in conflict.

Paul Schilder: The Body Image

I turn now to a topic that has been claimed by many as central to the development of a somatic psychology: the topic of one's *experience* of one's body. This refers to what one knows of the body that is one's own, what one thinks of it, feels about it, and senses in it, consciously and unconsciously. It is clearly a large and important topic, in the eyes of some writers, the heart of a viable psychological theory.

The phenomenological conception of the lived body would appear to be related as well. Not only is the idea of the experience of one's body a way of talking about how the body is lived, but equally important from the point of view of tactics, the concept of body experience appears to be the route by which thought about the lived body has been permitted to enter contemporary psychology.

The hypothesis directing my discussion is, as I have noted above, about behavior, not about the rather fuzzy psychological concept of experience; and indeed, I have introduced the conception of lived body only as a way of talking about the biological grounding of behavior. Thus, although I have said that one's behavior is grounded in the lived body, I have not said that one's behavior is caused, markedly or weakly, by the lived body. Writers who stress the importance of body experience, on the other hand, do so in order to be able to argue that one's attitude toward or experience of the body causes, or at least mediates the causation of, one's behavior. It is for these reasons that it would be inappropriate for me to say that this is a work about body experience or about any of the terms related to that topic.

However, it is important for me to include in my survey of sources some mention of the term *body image* and the pioneering work of Paul Schilder.[58] His outlook as a psychoanalyst was much closer to the psychiatric school of Adolph Meyer, which he called psychobiology, than to the thinking of the European analysts around Freud. "I have always believed that there is no gap between the organic and the functional. Mind and personality are efficient entities as well as the organism."[59] Here Schilder stated clearly what has come to be called a holistic position, or as he labeled his own thinking, "a biologic, organismic philosophy and psychology."[60] He saw the organism not as a mere "theoretical entity with merely perceptive qualities,"[61] but as an active organizer of one's world, in this way foreshadowing much of the thinking of contemporary phenomenological psychology. The conception that he developed as a way of organizing his observations along these lines was the body image: "the picture of our own body which we form in our mind, that is to say the way in which the body appears to ourselves, . . . the tri-dimensional image everybody has about himself."[62] It is important to note that the "picture" or "image" he refers to here is not just a psychic process with "merely perceptive qualities," but a way in which the organism lives its somatic ground; in this way Schilder's concept is appreciably broader and philosophically richer than its more recent derivatives in psychology.

It may be because of this weakening of the concept that the notion of body image in recent psychological writings is so vague. Seymour Fisher, in his very thorough summary and discussion of empirical research in this area,[63] equates the terms experienced body, postural model, body concept, body schema, and body image, referring at times to "the act of beholding one's body"[64] as well as to the attitudes, feelings, and ongoing experiences one may have in references to one's own body. The conception of body image—to give it the most neutral label—is not seriously discussed in relation to an understanding of consciousness. Missing as well in this attempt at ordering the data is any appreciation of the central problem involved in advancing a conception of body image: that is, how can one's body as lived be both the source and the target of these kinds of experiences?

A somewhat narrower but perhaps more useful conception of body image is found in the suggestion that you generally act in terms of how you think someone of your structure should act. Behavior, in this view, can be understood as mediated by your body image and by your response to perceived social pressures. Some recent work by investigators in Australia[65] moves in this direction, as does the notion of "optative identity" advanced by Burton and Whiting,[66] that is, the body image status a person would like to have and which therefore helps to determine the person's behavior. Schilder[67] had offered some suggestions along these lines, especially in his discussion of the social relations of body images, but the problems remain largely unexplored.

Edmund Husserl and Phenomenology

It might be argued that what I present in the following pages is in large part a phenomenological critique of what Giorgi[68] and others have termed "natural science psychology," or academic psychology in the tradition of the natural sciences. I hesitate to make such a broad claim, although I am not unsympathetic to the results of such a critique. Rather, I would prefer to view this work as phenomenologically influenced, perhaps as establishing some of the basis for a thoroughgoing phenomenological critique. In addition, I hope that what I offer here may help us to understand the place of phenomenology in the contemporary human sciences—which is a statement that deserves some explication.

Phenomenology, at least in its exposition in the writings of Edmund Husserl, is not usually considered a biologically grounded school of thought. Indeed, philosophy as a discipline has the reputation of being, in Erwin Straus's apt term, rather completely ex-carnated. But in fact in Husserl's thought every cognitive act, every movement of consciousness, is conceived as, so to speak, wrapped around an act of perception; or, in other terms, perception is presupposed in every cognitive act. Implied in Husserl's thought and explicit in phenomenology since the work of Merleau-Ponty is the further proposition that perception is necessarily bodily—and contemporary phenomenological psychology, as seen in recent studies by Kenneth Shapiro and others, has in effect placed the lived body at the center of the system. To this degree, then, the direction that I pursue in the present work fits comfortably within the implicit aims of modern phenomenology.

But I mean as well to say something more, and it constitutes a kind of critique of phenomenology itself. Since my hypothesis is meant to apply to reasoning in general as it is practiced by any thinking person, I mean it to apply to philosophers and how they go about their own work of casting a light on the work of other thinkers. On these grounds I offer that phenomenological philosophy, insofar as it is basic and introductory to all the sciences (as Husserl boldly claimed in 1910), is an attempt by way of the meso style to undercut the dominance of ecto-style thinking in science.[69] I would argue this as follows.

The central conception of a phenomenological philosophy is intentionality, which is the claim that every psychic act has its object, that to perceive is necessarily to perceive something, to remember is to remember something, and so on. By means of this conception the Cartesian impossibility is resolved: the puzzle contained in the circumstance that with every cognitive or psychic act an abstract and unreal entity (such as a thought or perception) gets connected with a real object in the world. For Descartes the world of mind is irretrievably lost to the world of matter, but for Husserl, who based his view on intentionality, these two worlds find each other again in every psychic act.

But in terms of my hypothesis in this book, I would say that Descartes and Husserl were referring by way of two different styles to two different modes of cognition. Consider the world of psychic activity as it functions within an ecto style. Its basis is in the central nervous system, whose very structure is a network of connected-yet-disconnected fibers; its great evolutionary significance being that its parts are not solidly connected with one another but linked while separated, gapped at the synapses yet joined in function at these junctions. In this way the central nervous system grounds in a physical structure the basic characteristic of an ecto-style system: a connection to its objects while at the same time setting up a gap, or distance, between cognitive element and cognitive object. In a real sense what the central nervous system handles is never the thing itself but, just as Descartes claimed, some representative of or reference to the thing itself—and this describes in its every other respect the ecto style. It is a style in which everything is handled as symbol, as reference, as about-the-object rather than as the object itself. Descartes's world of two "substances" was in fact a crude but accurate picture of the ecto style in operation.

But as my hypothesis leads to claiming in this work, there is always more than one way to carry out any act—including acts of thinking. We are not restricted to the Cartesian picture, even though if we follow it we produce finally all the marvels of modern science. We might, for example, offer a picture of thinking carried out in a meso style. In this mode, whose model is the physical act, the doer and the doer's object are joined, irrevocably; and in fact only because of this joining is it possible for the doer to effect a change in the world. If the blow that I aim misses its mark, it is as though I had never aimed it. Hence we have no memory of "missed" acts in the muscles, only in memories that are carried out as ecto acts which are in turn *about* our physical acts.

The concept of intentionality is a way of substituting for the Cartesian picture a model of psychic acts as though they were kinds of physical movements, their origins in doing always tied to their objects in the real world. Subject and object poles are no longer separated by one or more gaps, no longer in two different worlds, but linked as soon as the one aims for the other. And in Husserl's founding his analysis on this concept we can see, I suggest, his attempt to reconstitute human consciousness by way of a meso model, thus enabling him to undercut the "ownership" of rational thought (and science) by an ecto style.

I hope it is clear just what the foregoing argument does and does not do. On the one hand, it purports to show Husserl's work as exemplifying predominantly a particular style, in the sense in which I use that term. But on the other hand, it does not mount a critique of phenomenology. It does not, for example, prove in any sense that styles are ontologically prior to structures of experience. This is consistent with what I try to do in this book, and so should stand as an example of what I try to do. To speak through a rather coarse example, my argument that phenomenology operates in terms of one style rather than another is equivalent to my demonstrating that Husserl's exposition in one of his essays is, let us say, long-winded rather than concise or dogmatic rather than suggestive.

Howard Gardner: Multiple Intelligences

A recent work on the nature of intelligence, by Howard Gardner, argues a position very close to mine, with some important differences.[70] Gardner quotes with approval a "pregnant idea" advanced by the eighteenth-century anatomist and phrenologist Franz Joseph Gall, that "there exist different forms of perception, memory, and the like for each of the several intellectual faculties, such as language, music, or vision."[71] In addition, he mentions without disagreement Jerry Fodor's proposal, based on recent research on information processing, that "mental processes are best thought of as independent or 'encapsulated' modules, with each operating according to its own rules and exhibiting its own processes."[72]

By the term *intelligence*, Gardner means a set of problem-solving and problem-finding skills, with the proviso that the problems involved must be valued by the culture.[73] On this basis he argues for "the existence of several relatively autonomous human intellectual competences . . . (or) intelligences."[74] How many? This is not yet known.

What is their nature? This is not established. But to identify such multiple intelligences he reviews bodies of evidence that appear unrelated and looks for convergent evidence in regard to either, (a) special intelligences that appear in "relative isolation" in special populations but not in the normal population, or (b) psychometric evidence in regard to relevant "core abilities that, in effect, define the intelligence."[75] He lists eight signs or criteria, most of which have to be satisfied, for defining an intelligence: most important, it can be either spared or destroyed in isolation by brain damage; special individuals, such as prodigies or idiots savants, demonstrate it; it is associated with one or more "core operations" for "basic information processing; it shows a distinct developmental history as well as identifiable final levels of performance; we can locate what seem to be plausible "evolutionary antecedents"; we can adduce psychological research evidence; psychometric evidence in the form of test results is available; and it can be encoded in a symbol system.[76]

By these means Gardner discovers six intelligences—linguistic, musical, logical, spatial, bodily, interpersonal—which comprise autonomous modes of "know-how" or "procedures for doing things."[77] They are clearly, as he claims, types of abilities other than those usually tested by IQ tests, and to this degree he has taken a major step toward reconstituting the field of intelligence testing as a subspecialty within the domain of individual differences.

Gardner's work, however, has much less of a biological emphasis than does mine, although he does mention in passing the "biological and evolutionary roots of cognition."[78] In large part this difference resides in the fact that for Gardner biology refers to the activities of the brain and central nervous system, not to the muscular and visceral processes as well, and certainly not to the lived body. In his view the various operations observable as modes of intelligence—language, music, mathematics, and so forth—probably involve different "symbol systems"; the theoretical problem then becoming one of how the different symbol systems "might be represented in the human nervous system."[79] His chapter 3 is entitled "Biological Foundations of Intelligence" but refers entirely to the properties and processes of the central nervous system.

Embedded deep within the cultural foundations of the contemporary human sciences is the assumption, never examined and therefore never questioned, that what we call cognitive processes are the exclusive province of the brain and central nervous system. Within such a restrictive view, which rules out the possibility of significantly different styles of cognition, Gardner has made the very best effort to date toward an extended definition and analysis of intelligence. "Findings from the brain," he notes, "serve as the court of last resort, the ultimate arbiter among competing accounts of cognition."[80] We may hope that his findings, coupled with the hypothesis put forth in the present book, will serve to keep the options open for further progress.

Erwin W. Straus

Of the important figures in modern phenomenological psychology—among them Merleau-Ponty and F. J. J. Buytendijk[81] in particular—the one whose ideas come closest to what I argue in this book, and for this reason has been a significant influence in its writing, is Erwin Straus. His early career was spent in Germany during the first three decades of this century, where he gained a reputation in both neurology and psychiatry. His seminal work *Vom Sinn der Sinne*[82] appeared, unfortunately, just at the time of the collapse of German intellectual life with the advent of the Hitler regime.

In this book Straus distinguishes between sensing and cognitive knowing. The latter is very similar to our traditional conception of psychological processes, but the former, with the new weight of attributes given it in Straus's thought, is something new in modern psychiatry, even in modern phenomenology. Sensing does not occur in a kind of pre-experiencing limbo, as so many other formulations would have it; it is not pre-world, for one's experience of a world takes place in sensing as well as in more familiar modes of experiencing. Sensing is not a playground for mere stimuli, for objects as such already exist in a world of sensory experience, and it is for this reason that Straus chose as the subtitle of his work in English the claim, "A vindication of sensory experience."

If organized objects already exist in our world of sensory experience, they must have been organized by some form of intelligence—and here the door is opened to the explicit statement of the hypothesis of this book. Straus is not always clear as to the exact nature of this mode or style of intelligence, although he occasionally comes close to likening it to a form of motor skill. Thus, "Only a being whose structure affords it the possibility of movement can be a sensing being,"[83] by which he always means a movement that is in the service of the organism's values and is responsive to the organism's felt situation. The bulk of Straus's book, for reasons that were pertinent in the 1930s, consists of a sustained attack on Pavlovian learning theory; what is significant for our purposes here is that his attack on Pavlov rests throughout on his insistence that the Pavlovian laboratory dog is not simply making cortical connections in the course of its learning. It is also, and perhaps more importantly, acting in other modes which will remain unrecognized as long as we define the animal's behavior solely in terms of one style, the ecto. Although Straus nowhere defines these alternate modes more precisely, the direction of his thinking and the implications of his argument surely fit the claims I am advancing here. This will become apparent in the following pages.

Michael Polanyi

A number of modern philosophers of science need to be mentioned here, one briefly and one at greater length—not as a way of profiting from the positions they took but in order to indicate the links that connect my hypothesis with some other directions of recent thought. The first of these, to be noted briefly, is Alfred North Whitehead. In his *Process and Reality*[84] there appears, within a philosophy of process and change, the notion of the body as a living and lived "turmoil of activity" (in Anthony Quinton's phrase). Here perception is not modeled on vision, as in almost all other contemporary writing on the topic, but on touch, thereby opening his treatment of cognitive processes to other than ecto styles. Whitehead never aimed to compose a psychology; but it is to be regretted that his contributions toward this end have never been fully realized.

The second figure, who merits a great deal more discussion than I can give him here, is Michael Polanyi. One of the most influential of modern philosophers of science, he is perhaps best known for his conception of "tacit knowing." It is best defined in his well-known statement, "We can know more than we can tell,"[85] implying succinctly that the form of knowing in which we talk about what we know does not include all the knowing that is possible. The examples that he presents include: recognizing a familiar face, making sense of the moods of another's face, and "descriptive sciences" in general.[86] Polanyi sees such organizing of our experience, of which our understanding of the human physiognomy is perhaps the prototype, as occurring by virtue of a certain "tacit power by which all knowledge is discovered and, once discovered, is held to be true."[87] It is clear that his reference here is to something other than the neutral cognitive activity customarily identified with thought. It is closer to understanding than to explanation, in the tradition of that school of continental psychology called *Verstehende*.[88]

The structure of all knowing, Polanyi says, consists of two terms, the proximal and the distal. Since we attend from the proximal in the course of attending to the distal, we know the former only insofar as we are aware of attending to the latter. For example, we customarily rely on our awareness of the features of someone's face (a proximal knowing) for attending to the "characteristic appearance" of that face (our distal knowing). We know the face in and through its features; yet it cannot be said either that we know the features or that we know the face because we know the features. The meaning resides in the features, yet it is the face which "has" or carries the meaning, and we deal with this seeming paradox by displacing the meaning from proximal to distal, as in the common example of learning to use a cane to feel one's way. If asked how the cane is being used, the person would have to say that the characteristics of the sidewalk are truly experienced at the tip of the cane—that is, whatever meaning exists in this experience is at a distal locus—yet the person would also have to recognize that the elements of this meaning exist as such in a proximal locus, back where the hand feels the cane's movements.

Certainly the commonest instance of such a structure is the case of visual perception, which, in addition, has always posed what seemed an insoluble problem for theories of perception. The fact is simply that, in spite of the fact that it is retinal stimulation and nothing else that constitutes the physical basis of our seeing, we never see the world at our retina but rather "out there" in space. The question then is how we get it from our retina to "out there." Polanyi's formulation takes care of the problem: what we are aware of, so to speak, consist of "efforts" in our bodies, but what we are attending to is the perceptual object with all its recognizable characteristics. It is like the way we use a cane, feeling the cane at our hand but attending to the world at the cane's tip. This is not to say that in the usual sense we are consciously aware of what happens at the retina or at the hand. Rather, we are aware of the proximal only in our perception of the distal. In this connection he quotes experimental studies in which subjects who were not in the usual sense aware of electrical activity in certain muscles could still be trained to turn the electrical activity on or off in order to stop an unpleasant noise. Their "awareness" of the muscle activity, as the proximal aspect of normal distal experiencing, is what Polanyi has called the mode of tacit knowing.

His general statement is, "wherever some process in our body gives rise to consciousness in us, our tacit knowing of the process will make sense of it in terms of an experience to which we are attending."[89] This would seem to be a reference to at least two organized and functioning modes or styles of knowing (including whatever processes might go into one's knowing), although Polanyi is not any more explicit concerning the alternative characteristics of the tacit form. However, he does add to the above statement the crucial point that the prototype or exemplar of proximal knowing is our experience of our own body. "Our own body is the only thing in the world which we normally never experience as an object, but experience always in terms of the world to which we are attending from our body. It is by making this intelligent use of our body that we feel it to be our body, and not a thing outside."[90] Finally, it is in fact when we are aware of something as proximal in this sense, tacitly, that "we incorporate it in our body—or extend our body to include it—so that we come to dwell in it."[91] The concepts to which he refers in this connection, thereby furnishing a conceptual basis for understanding them, include Lipps's notion of empathy, Dilthey's concept of indwelling, and the notion of interiorization. In Polanyi's view, whenever one "dwells in" something in this sense, the process of tacit knowing is begun. What is implied here, although without spelling out its characteristics, is a general mode of experiencing that differs in every respect from what we usually refer to as conscious experiencing. It is for this reason that I feel justified in considering it as compatible with the inferences we might base on the hypothesis of this book.

2

Three Styles of Behavior

On mottoes: The endo motto might be: "I'll take whatever I can get." The meso motto is: "Go for it." The ecto motto is: "Let me think about it."

Any kind of behavior can be carried out or expressed in any combination or mix of the three styles; this is the hypothesis I will be examining in the remaining chapters of this book. In its "pure" form, which admittedly occurs very rarely, the style appears as a describable type, and since for purposes of exposition I will be referring most often to the "pure" form of a style, it may appear that I have nothing to describe but types. It should be kept in mind, therefore, that most of our behavior, and most of what we see in others, is a mix of the three styles and that my examples and descriptions are couched in a language of types for heuristic purposes.

Consider, as an initial example, the matter of emotions. The familiar state of anger is most familiar to us in the meso style: quick to rise, ready to strike out, sharply directed, a first stage of aggressive action. Once expressed, it is usually gone, as though a goal had been reached and overcome. Ecto-style anger, by contrast, is usually satisfied through substitute behaviors such as insult and verbal attack or by related states such as sarcasm, and so it may continue for years in the form of vengefulness, closer to a memory than to an action. Finally, anger in the endo style is slow to rise and slow to die away, suffusing the person like a blush. It is more like a mood than an emotion, calling for descriptive terms such as sullen, brooding, sulking. Endo anger fills the person and so creates an atmosphere, fulfilling but not active.

These three descriptions of the emotional state of anger are meant to be helpful as signposts describing the "pure" form, although in fact most instances of anger will appear as a mix of the separate characteristics described. To repeat what I have said in earlier pages about the most general characteristics of the three styles: endo functions have to do with absorption, with cyclical changes, with the way the gut might respond to self and world; meso functions center on energy, action, goal-direction, with movement and interaction in the social arena, in short, with the ways of behavior that fit the activity of the muscular-skeletal system; and ecto functions have to do with sensation, information processing, and symbolizing, all at a distance, as befits the structures of the skin and central nervous system.

In this chapter I will begin with an extended example of two pre-historic cultures whose way of life and chief artifacts strongly suggest two of the behavioral styles in almost pure form. After a discussion of some problems associated with typing and typologies, I will describe the three types at some length, and then conclude the chapter with a discussion of the experiential structure that most characteristically defines the ecto style.

VENUSES AND WARRIORS

The major determining influence on prehistoric human cultures was probably temperature, in particular the extreme swings of temperature that produced a sequential advance and retreat of four glacial masses over most of Europe and Asia. In the warmer interval between the third and fourth of these glacial eras, lasting from about 175,000 B.C. to about 110,000 B.C., Neanderthal humans appeared and established the genetic and cultural line that led to present-day humans. Somewhat later, most probably between 40,000 B.C. and 30,000 B.C., the Neanderthal type was replaced by the Cro-Magnon type, the latter physically indistinguishable from contemporary humans. They differed from their predecessors by having a lighter skin, smaller and often absent browridges, a more bulbous forehead, and a slightly smaller brain size—and most importantly, by the fact of their having introduced representational art on a culture-wide scale.

The Neanderthal had already invented the needle and learned to sew garments to protect them against the prevailing harsh climate. They wore bracelets and necklaces, utilized collective strategies to kill large animals, buried their dead in ceremonial fashion, and had even produced isolated examples of decorated weapons and small carvings or engravings of animals. But it remained for their successors, the nomadic Cro-Magnon hunters of the Upper Paleolithic era, to found what may be called a "school" of art. Beginning just before 30,000 B.C. and continuing for perhaps another ten thousand years, they produced an identifiable type of statuette that was evidently done by different persons, in widely scattered locations, over the course of many generations.

A vigorous and far-ranging people who occupied their tents, rock shelters, and open-air campsites over an arc extending some seven thousand miles from France to Siberia, they tracked a corridor along which migrated huge herds of bison, mammoth, deer, and horses. The term *art mobilier*, or portable art, has been given to the small sculptures in stone, ivory, or bone that they produced in sizable quantities and, apparently, carried with them as valued possessions. Many of the sculptures are of animals, as might be expected in a culture of hunters, but these are almost never the equal in quality of their statuettes or figurines, chiefly of women, which have come to be known, with scholarly irony, as Venuses. The figures are all small enough to be carried in the hand or in a pouch, the range in some sixty known examples being between two and eight inches in length, and they are remarkably similar in design. The well-known Venus of Willendorf (figure 1) is perhaps typical. Discovered in the debris of a Paleolithic campsite in Austria in 1908, it is a five-inch figure of an obese woman with the hips and breasts portrayed in exaggerated but naturalistic fashion. The figure seems to be all belly and hips and breasts, with the small and thin arms laid over the chest almost as an afterthought. The head is round and featureless, set on a short, thick neck, and the hair is carefully detailed in curls and ringlets. Hands and feet are almost completely absent.

Yet this is not simply a grossly fat body lacking in some important features, for it has evidently been carefully, indeed almost exquisitely, carved in limestone by a master of the flint. Close inspection reveals, for example, that the shoulders and upper back are not merely rounded masses of flesh but are remarkably expressive of a kind of sturdy strength. Significantly, and like all the other Venuses within this tra-

Venus of Willendorf

dition, the figure has been carved in such a way as to emphasize certain features that we associate with female sexuality and to de-emphasize or even eliminate other features such as the hands and the feet. Similarly, other statuettes consist of a body that is rounded at the middle to show breasts, stomach, hips, and vulva, and then tapers off almost to a point at top and bottom (figure 2). For example, in the Venus of Dolní Věstonice, from a campsite in Czechoslovakia (figure 3), the sculptor has achieved within a space of five inches a remarkable combination of the realistic and the abstract. The lines of the figure flow down over heavy breasts and then into a protruding middle section that is bisected by what looks like a girdle string; from there the lines fall along the full hips and down the sharply tapering thighs. Even in terms of technique the work is outstanding; it was modeled in a yellow clay that had been mixed with ash from burnt mammoth bones and then baked to produce an enamel-like surface. And in still another Venus, this one from Lespugue in France (figure 4), a riot of curved

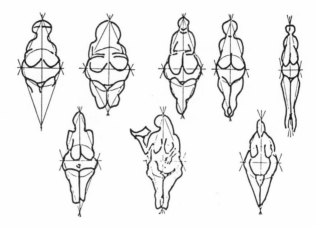

Body shapes of typical Venuses. Illustration from page 203 of *The Creative Explosion: An Inquiry into the Origins of Art and Religion,* by John E. Pfeiffer (New York: Harper & Row, 1982). Copyright © 1982 by John E. Pfeiffer. Reprinted by permission of Harper & Row, Publishers, Inc.

Venus of Dolni Vestonice   Venus of Lespugue

 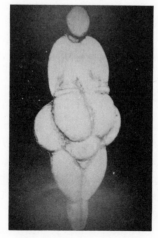

volumes manages to represent the same physical characteristics but this time in a treatment that is totally abstract.

In the stylistic tradition I have just described, the art appears to be a kind of celebration of the female generative impulse, this determining just about every feature of the works that were produced. By contrast, consider now another school of art produced some 20,000 years later—the precise dates are not known and probably not knowable—by a distinctively different culture along the northern portion of the Mediterranean coast of Spain. Known as Levantine art, it was done entirely in open-air rock shelters and consisted of paintings rather than carvings or engravings. They are in monochrome black or red, done in swift and lively strokes, and restricted entirely to groups of humans and animals engaged in vivid scenes of hunting or battle. In a typical drawing, this from a rock shelter at Valltorta (figure 5), we see what must be a battle scene in which dozens of figures, most of them male, are shown in swift, almost violent action; they are all armed with bows, all in movement, and all have exactly the same physique.

This is what is most striking about Levantine art, that just as in the tradition of the Venuses, the bodies all look alike. The bodies of the Venuses are female and heavy, with pronounced emphasis on the structures associated with the gut and pelvis. The bodies in Levantine art, by contrast, are all male, quite tall, with almost abnormally long, thin waists, quite muscular shoulders and chests, and with wiry legs dressed in what appear to be pantaloons. Indeed, in the Levantine males the waists are so attenuated as to have almost disappeared, by contrast with the very evident stomachs but disappearing hands and feet of the Venus figures; whereas in the Venuses the energy seems concentrated at the middle, in the Levantine figures all the strength and energy is concentrated in the puffed-up chests, muscular shoulders, and active arms and hands.

Both types of figures are almost, but not quite, caricatures—but equally important, what is being celebrated in the two traditions is quite different. It is evident as well that the artists who worked within these differing traditions restricted themselves to specific stylistic features, the most obvious of which were the structural characteristics of the bodies they portrayed. Perhaps all women of these Paleolithic cultures were in fact short, heavy, and round, with a strong emphasis on

Typical Levantine drawing and detail of figure.

the anatomical features associated with female sexuality, while all Levantine men were tall, lean, and wiry, with thin waists and muscular upper chests and shoulders. On the other hand, the artists who produced the Venuses or the Levantine wall art may have purposefully selected and even exaggerated certain bodily features in order to make a celebratory point.

We need not try to settle such questions one way or another. What may be more important is to recognize two wholly different styles and traditions in art, expressed through two different styles of the physical body. A question that follows naturally from the recognition, then, is this: can we discover, in association with these differences in artistic style, equally evident stylistic differences between the two cultures in which the art was produced? And if so, are the cultural differences reasonably associated with the differences in their art? These are the questions to which we now turn.

Two Styles of Hunting

Enough is now known about the habits and culture of these two groups to make sound speculation possible. Both cultures, the Paleolithic and the Levantine, organized their lives around the ways of the hunt. Their customs and their movements, their weapons and clothing and other possessions, even their social organization, and quite possibly their ways of dealing with one another as individuals or in subgroups were probably derived from or strongly colored by the ways they found to solve problems of the hunt.

Consider first the style of the Paleolithic hunt. These people lived and traveled very close to the slow-moving herds on which they lived. Theirs was a kind of face-to-face existence, always within reaching distance of the herd animals they knew so well, animals whose pace and organization became determiners of how life was to be lived, who were killed and used but only when necessary, and who entered into the very being of their human followers by supplying just about all the material needs of everyday life. What is strongly suggested here is, of course, the phenomenon of the totem animal, that creature with whom the hunter feels a tie of blood brotherhood, who becomes an inspiration for every important act and the very source of one's life. The tie that links hunter and animal at the source of their lives is the blood they share, not only when the hunter kills and eats the animal but in every act that they share in a mutually determining pact. Given the nature of the animals held as totems by Paleolithic hunters, we can imagine that life for both human and animal was lived in a sequence of slow tidal waves; time was endless and seasonal, and space too was either closed-in or endless, the space of the blind. And when the kill occurred it was always close at hand, as the animals were trapped in dead-end ravines, chased and then pushed over cliffs, or mobbed at close quarters, always by groups of warriors rather than by single hunters.

Our knowledge of these techniques of the kill among the Paleolithic hunters is based on the observation that their weapons were without exception made for fighting close at hand and not in groups. They made knives and hatchets, and they certainly used stones and sticks, but their chief weapon was the spear or javelin. Even after the introduction of their major innovations, the barbed spear or harpoon and the notched spear holder for increasing their accuracy, their game still had to be killed at not much greater distance than the unaided hand and arm could reach. Nor could such weapons outrun another adult or most animals. Thus, in both time and space these hunters were limited in their successes to no more than minimal extensions of the human reach and the hand-to-hand encounter.

As the centuries passed without change, marked only by the long waves of cyclic migration in which human and animal were held together, variations in forage as well as in temperature finally led some of the herds to settle more or less permanently in river valleys. Here the hunters also settled, moving into caves or rock shelters on the north banks of east-west rivers so as to face the warmer south. These hunters now began to develop an art of painting and engraving, done on cave walls, of an astonishingly high order. But for all its magnificence this art was not changed in its inspiration from the way of life of earlier centuries; as we can see in the cave of Altamira in northern Spain or at Lascaux or Font de Gaume in the valley of the Dordogne in France (figure 6), it was still a celebration of the monumental. It aimed to present in heroic stance the still, grand figure of a totem animal sharing a timeless space of immediate contact with its hunters or

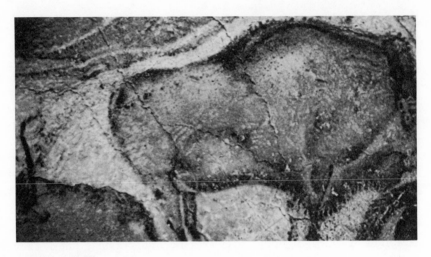

A Lascaux bull

viewers. We preserve at least some of this image in the rituals associated with the modern bullfight.

Siegfried Giedion has described it very well. He points out that the
portable art of the Upper Paleolithic era and the wall art of the cultures
that followed share one feature: what is depicted is not aligned with
the perceived horizontal or vertical of the viewer. The latter is gravity-
determined, whereas this art, whether carried in the hand or embla-
zoned on a cave wall, is always in a space that is "unconfined or universal," a space like that of the heavens. In its time as well as in its
space, too, it is unconfined and universal; it exists in what Giedion
terms an "eternal present, the perpetual interflow of today, yesterday,
and tomorrow."[1]

These generalizations are meant to be no more than suggestive, for
I do not intend to explain all the protohistory of human culture in
terms of only one of its aspects. Yet certain differences in the style of
hunting, that most central of activities in these cultures, do distinguish
between Paleolithic and Levantine cultures, and they appear to be related to other aspects of the cultures as well. The single most important distinction may have been that the Levantine hunters quite
possibly invented and most certainly used the bow and arrow.[2] Here

is a weapon that makes possible a completely new mode of control over both time and space. With a bow and arrow even the lone hunter can kill fairly large game at three or four times the distance at which a spear can be accurately thrown, and he can do this so swiftly that neither human nor animal can outrun the arrow's flight. As a result, hunting now comes to take place within an arena many times multiplied in space and appreciably foreshortened in time. One conquers whatever one can see, once the necessary motor skills have been perfected. The target is now no longer one's totem, a part of one's very being that is held, touched, felt, but anything or anyone, at any distance or moving at almost any speed. Both space and time are at last under the warrior's control. Now it is possible to kill the stranger.

It is therefore not surprising to find that in Levantine art the stable, grave, and weighted image of the foraging animal or of the generative human female has disappeared, to be replaced by sharp and vivid images of action, conflict, control over the movement of groups. Space is no longer a setting but an arena for acting. Nor should we be surprised to find that in Levantine art a quite different kind of bodily structure is celebrated; it is a type that naturally engages in all the varieties of movement. Where Paleolithic art, from its origins in the Venuses to its culmination in cave paintings, depicted its subjects as totems, emphasizing the living, vibrant volumes of a body ceremonially at rest and accomplishing this by careful sculpting and shading to show a space-occupying body, Levantine paintings were done in swift, bold strokes, each one as quickly finished as a bit of active movement. In a perceptive discussion from which I have greatly benefited, one critic has noted that in Levantine paintings the very limbs of the figures suggest "the slenderness and direction of well-aimed arrows . . . [and] the tension of taut animal sinew is transferred to an idealized human body drawn out from the hips as the bow is bent for stringing"—in direct contrast with the "ponderous, earth-bound solidity of Upper Paleolithic sculpture."[3]

From this perspective it is understandable that in the extensive corpus of Paleolithic painting, sculpture, and engraving, there does not exist a scene—that is, the presentation of a space of action that is peopled with figures moving in relation to one another. On the other hand, it is just this sort of presentation that uniquely identifies Levantine art: the celebration of encounters, even of violent action, between humans or between animals and humans. But in addition to these differences between their respective kinds of art, Levantine and Paleolithic cultures may also have differed in regard to the everyday behavior of the group members themselves, or in regard to what I am here calling their behavioral styles. The style of hunting, for example, differs in ways that go beyond the matter of which weapon was used. We need have no doubt that a Paleolithic hunter might with some brief instruction have been capable of using a bow and arrow to bring down an animal at a distance. It is not such details as kind of weapon or size of waist that makes the difference I suggest here but rather the way in which these and a thousand other details were lived. The term I suggest to sum up this kind of distinction—because no other term is available—is "style," and I suggest further that Levantine and Paleolithic hunters differed in their behavioral styles. This would include the very way they walked, their mode of perceiving other persons and most animals, their attitudes and accompanying motives and feelings, how they learned or failed to learn, and how they apprehended time and space—or in short, what today we might sum up as their respective psychologies.

TYPES AND TYPOLOGIES

Most persons seem to carry around with them certain central, guiding images onto which they can map their significant experiences. For the person who is predominantly meso the central image is something like "the light at the end of the tunnel." It came naturally to the lips of military men during the Vietnam war, perhaps coupled with other images related to intensive, goal-directed action, a straight-ahead direction, and a single, clear-cut, "well-lighted" outcome. For the meso thinker it is the outcome that explains the total meaning of the struggle after the fact and so resolves all doubts and questions left behind in the action. "Thinking my way through" is one such related meso image; it suggests that thought too is a form of action against opposition.

In the field of politics one says that electorates contain two major types of voters: those who customarily lean toward candidates and policies of the right, and those who are more sympathetic to candidates and policies on the left. But it is clear that the distinction made here is a product of their observers' mentality, not of the data in and of itself. Other observers, pursuing other aims, might add a third major grouping, the independents who occupy a middle position; and still other observers might not be satisfied unless the distinctions were made much finer at one or another end of the political spectrum. Indeed, as experimental evidence has shown,[4] judges or observers who themselves occupy extreme positions on such a scale tend to insist on, even perceive, fine distinctions at their own end of the scale while being satisfied with very gross distinctions at the opposite end of the scale. This leads to the familiar phenomenon of extreme left-wingers perceiving everyone to the right of them as "reactionary" or "fascist" while arguing fiercely over fine sectarian distinctions among splinter groups of the left or, equally, extremists of the right wing judging everyone to their left as communists while sharply distinguishing among groups on the right.

The problem is that in creating a typology, an infinite number of possibilities arise, most of them justifiable only on the basis of the typologist's personal preferences. If a proposition—such as my hypothesis—that rests on the making of such distinctions is to be of some use, it will have to begin with some built-in restrictions. Some scientists who would like to make the best possible use of clinical data—Hans Eysenck is a leading example[5]—have proposed that in place of fixed types one adopt a functional approach, for example, by assigning each individual a position on one or more scalar dimensions such as introversion-extraversion or degree of neuroticism. This procedure might be extended in the direction of a typology by labeling all persons whose positions on two orthogonal axes fall in a certain quartile area as, let us say, Northeast types. If the scalar dimensions or axes in question have been derived by a statistical procedure such as factor analysis, it would then be argued that the preferences of the observer or investigator have been minimized.

In support of this approach Eysenck argues that "there is much evidence to show that individual differences are systematic in their effects, and that they are subject to theoretical formulation in terms of general laws."[6] One such formulation that he has proposed identifies two statistically independent "dimensions of personality," the one labeled emotionality or neuroticism, and the other extraversion *versus* introversion. Recognizing that individuals may differ along these two dimensions enables one to uncover the "true facts" that may be hidden in conventionally stated group data. For example, to the question of whether children are better motivated by praise or by blame, a question that does not usually yield unequivocal results, the evidence when assessed in terms of such individual differences reveals that the introverts need praise but that the extraverts are better motivated by blame. He therefore argues for a "suitable typology,"[7] particularly as a counter to the universalism that we owe to the legacy of Edward L. Thorndike[8]—the notion that members of each species, perhaps even of each phylum, are "formally" identical in their intelligence and their character. Eysenck's procedure involves two stages that are relevant to my inquiry here: an initial "descriptive approach" in order to isolate the main dimensions of, say, the personality, followed by a set of experimental procedures to develop measures of the described dimensions and then to validate them.

Unfortunately, Eysenck's complete procedure is not open to me in the present work, given the absence of quantitative data in regard to my hypothesis. I can at most go as far as his first stage. I should therefore offer some additional justification for what may appear to be a less than adequate typology.

In his discussion of the rationale for his approach, Sheldon refers to his somatotypes as "biological identification tags in a field where no comprehensive taxonomic system [has] yet been applied."[9] The somatotype therefore simply "identifies a person as belonging to a biological group or family."[10] The distinction that is implied here, between a typology and a taxonomy, is a useful one. In his own words Sheldon's work was not a typology but a taxonomy, a form of classifying, an attempt to bring a preliminary order to a set of observations that were too large. A taxonomy divides up the given instances in whatever way seems immediately appropriate.

A type, on the other hand, would seem to imply something more—at the very least, the suggestion of an ideal, unflawed representative of some process or function, perhaps an individual member of the set who approximates this ideal picture. Thus, there may exist no pure Apollonian or Dionysian types, but the type itself can still be described, for the type comes into being as soon as one has a theory or rationale in regard to the function involved. The distinction, then, is between a taxonomy that is simply the product of reliable differentiation and a typology that rests on some theoretical foundation. This is why we often have at hand a complete description of a type in the absence of any existing representative of it. Typologizing is a form of proto-theorizing, its results telling us how closely an existing specimen comes to representing what the type stands for, whereas taxonomic division is not concerned with such division but serves rather lesser purposes of classification.

Since typologizing arises out of theorizing, we can understand how theory may sometimes begin with a statement of types but then lead us in quite a different direction. For example, Freud's early theory concerning the vicissitudes of the sexual instinct led him first to postulate levels or stages of psychosexual development in infancy and childhood. He might then have postulated that some rare individuals developed personalities that represented in pure form a specific fate of instinctual energy, that they were representatives of the oral or the anal type. But the theory led him in a different though related direction, toward an exposition of the course of libidinal development, rather than toward the identification of kinds of individuals. What he devised was a theory of personality development, not a typology of psychoanalytically understood persons. The latter course was, however, still open, as David Shapiro showed some years later in a work (briefly discussed in chapter 1) that he called, most appropriately, *Neurotic Styles*.[11]

In addition to its foundation in proto-theory, typologizing would also seem to call for conceiving of the person as an unbroken unit. To assign an individual to the niche known as a type is in effect to state that everything about that individual "belongs" in the niche. What might have started out as taxonomy, a neutral classificatory procedure, now turns into a kind of restrictive categorizing. The danger that tempts one at this point (which I deal with at greater length in chapter 8) is that the theoretical turn we call typologizing may become the attitudinal stance we call prejudice. I have deliberately avoided this turn in the present work, primarily by keeping my discussion throughout at the level of pretypology or taxonomy—as I think that Sheldon did as well. My use of a phrasing such as "the ecto [person] typically does this" is always meant as a shorthand way of saying, "It is typical of the ecto style of behavior that in it the person. . . ." I hope in this way always to stop short of turning from taxonomy to typology, from description to theory.

THE ECTO STYLE

One important difference between the ecto and meso styles is well caught in the distinction between anxiety and impatience.

There are a number of reasons for beginning with a discussion of the ecto component and the style related to it. The first reason is that the ecto is the style, and perhaps the structural component, that of the three is by far the most familiar to us. It is, as we are taught, the way that people are known as individuals and the source of whatever makes individuals do and be what they are. In addition, and for related reasons, it is the style that we usually consider the most typically human, the style that we feel is basic to our highest forms of functioning, perhaps even the style that enables us to know how things really are in the world. For example, we would consider it absurd for an adult human to rely on the functioning of the body's interior in order to gauge how to get along in the world. For this reason many persons are sure that the ecto mode is, in a sense, all there is to human functioning; that the other modes are there only to carry out whatever directives come down from ecto-style centers. In this view it is then incorrect to speak of equivalent components or styles, since human experience and behavior consist simply of a range of ecto activities to which various secondary phenomena are attached from time to time for reasons of practical utility. We will see this view expressed very clearly in some approaches to teaching and learning that I discuss in chapter 3.

A second major reason for beginning our discussion with the ecto style is that, uniquely among the three, it is almost defined by its accessibility to analysis. Related to this characteristic of the ecto style is the fact that since its activities are always about, or in reference to, something else, the style itself is self-advertising, as it were. You behave in the ecto style in such a way that you automatically behave in reference to your own behavior as well, a special feature that is called self-consciousness. Finally, because the ecto style is usually considered the very prototype of any act of talking-about, serious discussions are usually couched in its terms. This in turn then helps to determine what can legitimately be talked about and even how such an activity is to proceed. As a result it is inconceivable to most persons that a serious discussion might proceed out of either a meso or an endo style.

Yet in spite of its importance as the very basis of our life of thought and reason, the ecto style is not easy to describe. Sheldon always had a great deal of trouble in pinning down the essential characteristics of the style, which he considered a closely related set and which he called "cerebrotonia." In the end he opted for defining the style negatively, in terms of an absence rather than a presence of any major characteristic; it consisted, he said, of an inhibition or "hushing" of the body's activities.

This definition, as we shall see, is quite understandable, but I think it fails to capture all that is implied in the ecto style. Like the other two, the ecto style when it is dominant tends to inhibit the operation of other styles. One cannot, for example, be primarily occupied with endo absorption at the same time that one's total behavior is defined by surges of meso action. In addition, as Sheldon sensed correctly enough, the activities of the ecto style are often marked by the characteristic of inhibition—as distinct, say, from the energetic outgoingness that marks activities in the meso style. But the ecto style is by no means to be defined entirely in terms of how or what it inhibits. It does not consist exclusively of hushing activities, for it has its own mode of activity and of active influence. To see this we need only broaden our conception of the term active to refer to more than physical action. The game of chess, for example, is a nearly pure ecto activity—as are most such board-and-table games—and, as is well known, it is so demanding of the player's energy and vitality that, like more physical sports, it is primarily an activity for the young.

In Sheldon's view the basis of the inhibition typically seen in the ecto style is the phenomenon that he terms "conscious attention." As a consequence, he then notes, cerebration tends to be substituted for direct action. Further, in the ecto style one prepares for significant acts of cerebration by means of a conscious concentration on "exteroception," or outwardly directed processes of sensation and perception. Finally all this is usually accompanied by such activities as thinking about, recalling, or working over the cerebral activity just completed. In all, Sheldon presents a rather extreme portrait of someone who seems to be obsessed with thinking, first in advance of it, then as a major activity, and later in retrospect—and since one can always think about what one is or has been thinking about, in an endless retrospect as well. One might speculate that Sheldon was not talking about ecto-style activity from the point of view of an insider personally familiar with it but rather as a person predominantly non-ecto in style who had devoted a great deal of (non-ecto) thought to ecto behavior.

He does, however, take note of other aspects of the ecto style, all of them related to the central features of restraint and inhibition. The person who is primarily ecto is often uncomfortably aware of his or her internal tension, for it goes on as a continuing sidelight of the person's general awareness. As a consequence, sleep may be light or poor, even broken, often punctuated with brief dreams. Difficulty in recovering from such nonrestful sleep may lead to an inability to relax during the morning hours and hence to a preference for working late into the evening. Eating is usually done in short and quick sessions, with one's hunger felt sharply at first but then easily satisfied. To these observations of Sheldon's I would add that as a logical consequence we would expect that persons who go on hunger strikes—for example, idealistic and self-sacrificing martyrs for a political cause—are of an ecto rather than a meso or endo temperament. Indeed, it is the ecto group in general who are ideologues, willing to die for their abstract principles; for it is, as Sheldon puts it, a Promethean style. It often takes the form of a dream, to act out ideals in terms of some overarching vision that, being generated in one's imagination, is free of the demands of muscle or gut. The ecto vision, which is the equivalent of a meso goal or an endo passion, may, unfortunately, often become simply disengaged from the demands of a practical or passionate reality.

Like the other styles, the ecto is expressed not only through those structures to which it is most closely related—for example, being expressed in cognition because that is primarily brain-related—but in many other kinds of functions and behaviors as well. As a result, when the ecto component is predominant in a person it results in an observably distinct kind of individual. We may describe the person as one who is unusually exposed to the world yet cannot act freely in it and is therefore both skittery and inhibited; who may be preoccupied with recall and then with recalling the recall and thinking about it; whose normal experience is to be engaged with an interior that is, somehow, not quite the interior *of* anything. Such a person's behavior will typically be carried on without dogma, apparently always in response to what is reasonable, logical, effective; for conviction, especially when it is passionate, is only an embarrassment to the ecto-style person. The attributes of the reasoner dominate this person's personal style—dogma becoming preconception and conviction becoming opinion whose sources can often be explicitly stated. Thought and its expression have the qualities of the reasonable, the probable, the arguable, and the more organized such thought is, the more aesthetically pleasing it is to the ecto person.

Such individuals take an almost unique pride in being good citizens, for ordered social awareness of this sort is in fact the way that the ecto style is expressed in the arena of social relations, in a personification of the Enlightenment. Of course, one does not have to behave in the ecto style in order to be a good citizen, for that quality or most others can be well expressed through one style as much as through another, but the self-conscious pride in the exercise of good citizenship is uniquely the mark of an ecto style. In this style order and reason in the service of abstract and nonpersonal ideals are elevated to a high principle and allowed the freedom to be expressed, while passion and direct action are either ruled out or else tightly reined in by means of an edgy control. As Sheldon clearly saw, the net effect is an overworked holding-in, accompanied by a pervasive irritability of the exposed skin: "He may be kind and affectionate, according to the strength and quality of his first (endo) component, and he may be fond of action, according to the strength of the second (meso) component, but he is not in the final analysis dependent upon affection or action. In the face of trouble the cerebrotonic must always fall back upon the system and organization which is in his own head, even though the resulting delay may be fatal."[12]

In his valuable work on the strengths and weaknesses of computers—which I would read also as a discussion of the strengths and weaknesses of a pure ecto style—Dreyfus defines the world as a "field" organized, for the purposes of our activity, in terms of regions of value, that is, as an arena of (meso) action colored by (endo) values.[13] He then credits Heidegger with having been the first to point to an overriding aim of contemporary science: to define the world in abstract terms that reduce a world of concerned actions to a world of impersonal control over neutrally defined objects. To this Dreyfus adds that "insofar as we turn our most personal concerns into objects . . . they no longer organize a field of significant possibilities in terms of which we act but become just one more possibility we can choose or reject."[14] Or, in the terms of our present discussion, once the thinker gives up behaving in terms of some mix of all three styles and resorts exclusively to the ecto style—as an extreme scientism would propose—the world is then reduced to the defining characteristics of ecto behavior, choosing on preplanned grounds among an array of more or less equivalent and nonpersonal entities. As we consider at greater length in the concluding chapter, this is the result if the ecto style of thought is pushed to its extreme.

THE MESO STYLE

Silicon Valley managers, executives, even scientists, have a lot to teach us about the meso style, for here we find one of its more obvious manifestations. This is a high-energy, high-protein culture, a setting in which the skills of these modern scientific warriors will flourish dramatically and then decline rapidly with age.

A Meso Caricature

In American culture the pure meso style is familiar enough that it can be introduced through an example that is almost a caricature. Not long ago there appeared in the comic pages of some Sunday newspapers an advertisement for a forthcoming film. That these pages should be used as a medium for reaching potential customers is itself a fairly clear indication of both the nature of the film and of the kinds of persons who would be expected to be interested in it. The advertisement in question was for a film called *Megaforce,* a title that is revealing of its style and content. The main element of the advertisement, a large drawing, shows a muscular man, lightly bearded and with a sweatband around his appropriately coiffed hair, dressed in an aviator's jumpsuit and holding at shoulder height, ready for quick use, an elaborately engineered pistol. Across his chest there is strapped a panel of push buttons, as though he himself is wired as an instrument of destruction. At his belt, into which his left thumb is hooked in imitation of a style affected by some cowboys, there depend a number of grenade-like objects in their leather cases. On all sides of him, even coming from behind him—almost as though his body is their source—one sees small-scale instruments of warfare erupting into explosive action—a tank, two racerlike cars mounting cannon, an armored motorcycle whose blazing tail pipe indicates its roaring speed, helicopters, and hordes of fighter planes. In the background explosive flashes light the sky, small against the figure of this martial god who fixes the reader with a fearless and penetrating gaze. It is a look that is meant not to communicate or to reciprocate but to make a unilateral declaration, expressed in the caption above his head: "Batman, back to your cave! Spider-man, bug off! Aquaman, throw in the towel! The ultimate hero is here! Ace Hunter!" And above his words, enshrined in the space just behind his head, a motto sums up both the style that is conveyed by the advertisement and the response that it means to call forth: Deeds Not Words.

This is all so exaggerated, so nearly a caricature of the meso style, that it comes close to being silly, and I do not mean that it should be taken too seriously. Yet it does provide us with a convenient summary of the more obvious meso features. The motto might be restated as: Actions, not Thoughts—although it is interesting to note that the word chosen for the film, deeds, is a stronger and more "virile" term than the one I have used. Note, too, some of the other words that are used. None of them are soft in sound, none indecisive in import; all are strong, direct, hard in both feel and tone. As expressions these words resemble the blow by a fist that is so often the epitomized expression of the meso style. To add to the overall effect, exclamation marks punctuate everything that is said, again with the effect of a sudden and decisive blow.

It is, in short, all masculine, even excessively masculine, and as such it represents one kind of extreme of the meso style. But in other respects as well it is heavily meso in style, not simply that it is "male" in the crudest sense. To take one example, the movie's story line is completely indicated in advance, even in this preliminary public announcement, and this is a significant characteristic of the meso style. It is not a style that, like the ecto, considers itself reflectively in advance or in retrospect. Rather, in the meso style one finds a straightforward declaration of what is going on, followed by an immediate and simple expression of the thing itself. And so we are told without further qualification that a single heroic figure, aptly named Ace Hunter, will dominate the film as hero and protagonist. A loner, he is not dependent on nor associated with others, even when they are his equals, and, indeed, one of the commonest plot complications in such movie tales consists of the quarrels and conflicts between associates who are both on the same side of the battle and are equals. His relations with others will be in the form of relatively brief clashes, or tests of power, or if need be of brief contacts to satisfy passing urges, much in the manner of birds that mate in flight. His true profession is that of hunter, who is blood brother to the warrior, and his only goal is to destroy his enemies utterly by means of his command of superior weaponry.

Like all other heroes in the meso mold, Ace Hunter will do all this with never a thought about why he does it. It is an attitude that was perfectly expressed by William F. Buckley in an autobiographical account that he called, with marvelous precision, *Overdrive: A Personal Documentary:* "It is easier to stay up late working for hours than to take one tenth the time to inquire into the question whether the work is worth performing."[15] In the same vein, Ace Hunter could probably never imagine asking advice before plunging into the clash of battle, much less question himself about what was and what was not worth doing. Rather, he sees the scene before him as though it is a battlefield and then moves toward his only goal, to wipe out the forces that gave rise to the goal in the first place. For it is in the nature of meso goals that they are never reached; they are annihilated. This is why the meso style permits striving repeatedly for the same goal, and this too is why the person fully committed to the meso style can say, "What counts is not reaching the goal but playing the game."

The meso person will not talk to others, and certainly not to himself, about what he is doing. He will prefer to be involved in action, trusting wholly to the intelligence of his muscles and to that buried spirit that is sometimes called the hunter's instinct. His purposes remain simple, pointing as directly as an arrow toward their desired end. The film in which he appears may well have loose ends but it will not have grey areas. Only in the more unusual westerns, for example, films such as *High Noon*, do we find the Ace Hunters pausing to say, "Why am I doing this, anyway?" They are driven, as we can see, but never in the sense of being impelled by deep-rooted value systems or high principle. Rather, it is a matter of being pulled ahead, like the reader of a mystery novel or the hero of a search (for example, Indiana Jones in *Raiders of the Lost Ark*), never stopping until one runs out of energy. Consider, for example, this interior monologue by a fictional character who, although a sedate college professor, acts out her fantasies by being a successful amateur detective: "Odd, Kate thought, the years it took to learn one simple fact: that the prize just ahead, the next job, publication, love affair, marriage, always seemed to hold the key to satisfaction but never, in the longer run, sufficed. However one tried to savor one's gifts—leisure, health, money, a room of one's own—one always ended peering ahead, to the next chance. . . . And so one asked: What next, what new purpose to life, what new community or service?"[16] In the ecto style no such question would arise, even in moments of dissatisfaction, because there would be felt a constant sense of some overarching principle that made one's constant striving seem meaningful. One might argue with oneself over the principle, but one would not be in the position of searching for a principle. Nor could such a monologue arise in the case of the person who acts entirely in the endo style, for this would give rise either to a slow savoring of one's gifts and blessings or else to some passionate need to accomplish, regardless of one's gifts or goals.

But we should also note here that although in the meso style there is the constant shadow of action, meso-style behavior is not always objectively physical. Not long ago *Time* magazine described, in its heavily personalized style, the life pattern of a Wall Street consultant, identified as the "chief portfolio strategist" for a major investment banking firm. Described, interestingly enough, as a "ruddy-faced Yankee," this man was said to keep in shape for the "intense" action of Wall Street by pumping a bicycle in a gym for "up to forty-five minutes at a time." Yet we can guess that his work was probably not actively physical but consisted rather in talking persuasively on the phone and attending with care to appropriate source documents. Thus, it is not in his objectively observable actions that his meso style would be apparent as in the way that he experiences and then organizes his life situations. The same act, in a physical sense, can be carried out quite differently in each of the three styles.

One other consequence of the meso style being heavily action-oriented is that it soon runs out of words. It is then reduced to the repetitive use of words that repeat the same action: the *wow* and *bam* school of expression. In general, repetition is at the core of the meso style; habit is one of its commonest signs, and habits tend to go on, repetitively, until they are brought to a stop by extrinsic causes. That type of TV viewer, usually male, whose greatest pleasure is to watch football games, will often do it almost endlessly if that is possible. On New Year's Day, when a true surfeit of college football is presented on American television, the dedicated fan will finally stop watching out of a kind of physical exhaustion rather than because his viewing has reached a logical stopping point or because he is now satiated. He can, finally, be bored but he can only rarely be fulfilled. In one of its more bizarre manifestations, this is the mentality of the jet-setter.

Although the meso style may seem at first glance to be very much goal-oriented, particularly in regard to achieving them quickly, the goals are most often immediate or short-term. This may be one reason that organized games are so appealing to the person whose preference is for the meso style. Such games are made up of a string of short-term, easily visualized goals that are either gained or not gained rather quickly. They are not goals that—as in the case of the ecto style— lead to one reaching them and then contemplating how things have changed as a result. In the meso style reaching the goal is experienced, rather, as the end point of some limited effort rather than as a change point in one's life. Thus, persons who are predominantly meso seem to be able to learn endlessly yet without undergoing personal change. This may be one reason why the field of learning in psychology, which is largely restricted to manipulating meso-style episodes of behavior, has never developed an adequate theory of change or managed to forge links to its sister specialty, developmental psychology.

Watson the Engineer

Not too long ago it was quite unusual to find expressions of the meso style in the public statements or actions of prominent figures. In order to find relatively pure examples of the meso style one had to turn to lower class activities or else to places where athletes performed with "deeds not words." The image that leaders of public opinion tried to present was that important personages were thinkers, dealing with words rather than with actions—and this held true even though in fact many public leaders were heavily meso in their style. Members of the better classes might perhaps enjoy their (endo) pleasures and the (ecto) nuances thereof, but they tried to avoid involvement with the (meso) activities of workers, animals, and other mindless doers of labor.

During this century, however, this picture has changed profoundly, particularly in the United States. Theodore Roosevelt—who was the first president since the very meso-styled Andrew Jackson to be called by his nickname, which is a small sign of the meso style—may have been the person most influential in bringing this about. He was a much admired public figure, yet quite exceptionally for his day, he was also an athlete, an outdoorsman, a soldier who both looked and acted like one (as Grant, for example, certainly did not), and a persistent spokesman for the values of healthful outdoor living. As he summed up in his motto, "Speak softly but carry a big stick," his style was that of the well-armed but cautious warrior who is ready for battle in a warlike world.

An even more interesting figure, who may indeed have introduced the meso style into the public life of academics, was the psychologist John B. Watson, well known as the founder of the school of behaviorism. Photographs of him show the square and somewhat prominent jaw, the stocky physique, and the bold and penetrating gaze of the structural mesomorph, and his activity as well displayed a similar style. He expressed nothing but disdain for what he described as "what goes on inside the head," by which he referred to all the abstractions and symbols inhabiting the domain of the mind, a realm that William James had once called "this tumbling ground for whimseys." This is the realm of the ecto style, and Watson saw it as his enemy; as for the endo style, in common with almost every other scientist and thinker of our day, he never took it seriously enough to criticize it. As far as he was concerned, all that counted was the concrete, tangible, observable, physically present datum, the hard fact—that is, the basic elements of a world experienced in the meso style. He approached his material in exactly the same fashion as a later mesomorphic hero was to do: Sergeant Friday, whose famous dictum, "Just the facts, ma'am," expressed a sturdy and simpleminded inability to sense the multiple mysteries hidden in every observation.

In his public posture Watson presented himself as quite the opposite of the stereotypic intellectual, even though he was himself clearly a person of appreciable intellectual gifts. He approached his audiences as a straightforward and plainspoken man of action rather than a thinker or theorist. He claimed to be above all a practical person, and even when he was obviously engaged in theoretical speculations of the wildest sort, he made his pronouncements as statements of fact rather than of theory. Nothing in psychology so aroused his righteous anger—and nothing was later to get him into such theoretical hot water—as his insistence that the brain was literally empty of everything that (ecto) thinkers had ever associated with "mind." In this he was being simply self-consistent, for in the meso view, preoccupied with deeds rather than words and with actions rather than thoughts, the mind is nothing but a trap set by philosophers.

In one of his more controversial public statements, which he presented to a group of his fellow professionals at a symposium on the unconscious,[17] Watson showed that unlike most of his colleagues in psychology he was well aware of a possible somatic basis for behavioral styles. He distinguished between what he called manual and verbal "dominance" in action (paralleling the distinction in this chapter between ecto and meso predominance), and he laid out a plan of education and training in "mental hygiene," meaning by this term a practical, working knowledge of how one's own body functions. Even today such a suggestion would probably be startling to educators. His vocabulary in elaborating on this suggestion was surprisingly like that of the artisan or the workman, as in his frequent references to training, working, and functioning—or perhaps it might be more appropriate to say that he spoke like an engineer in an area that had heretofore been preempted by theoreticians. In one instance he raised the question, "Then can't we teach them [the children] enough physiology for them to grasp what the function of each main part is and how the various parts function together?"[18] From the terminology alone, one might imagine that his reference here is to a piece of machinery. His aim is totally practical, and his method is to break it down into a series of subgoals or working parts whose separate but interlocking elements perform just like a complicated (but not complex) clock or engine. One feels that Watson would also have made a superb teacher of auto mechanics.

One of the lessons we can learn from studying the careers of persons like Watson is that the engineer as much as the athlete exemplifies the meso style. Since it is so largely action-oriented, the life of the athlete might at first seem closer to the meso style, but in fact each of the styles is action-oriented in its own way and each expresses its continuing embeddedness in the ongoing life of the body. This is to say that all three styles may be somatically grounded, and that differences arising when one or another style is dominant do not refer to whether the person lives in and through the body but rather to how that living is expressed.

Typically, the engineering approach will be to attack every situation as though it were an opponent; if the situation is a problem, it will be experienced as a challenge and dealt with by reducing it, usually by trying to break it down into smaller parts. It is one of the axioms of the meso style that all wholes have true parts to which the wholes can be reduced; and an important corollary that follows is that all such parts are accessible in themselves. Hence the terminology we find in documents expressing the meso style: construct, reconstruct, strategy, tool, expertise, system, resources, steps, stages, blueprints, and so on.

All these words have been taken from one page of a recent brochure that advertises an approach to self-improvement called "Neuro-linguistic Programming." As its terminology indicates, this program is in the style of the engineer and the planner, at times to such an extreme degree that it begins to sound like that perfect example of the meso style, militarese.

Other characteristics of the meso style as Sheldon describes them fit the examples I have been discussing. He refers to the solid and compact meso body, often marked by a ruddy complexion, to eating habits that are often based on wolfing one's food rather than savoring it—and to this I would add, the high protein diet, the diet of the carnivorous hunter—to a daily schedule marked by early morning rising and vigorous morning activity, and to qualities of stability and dependability rather than deep-rooted teachability. Another common finding, according to Sheldon, is the meso-style person's unique response to sensory stimulation, especially in the auditory realm. The meso style is to tolerate and even welcome a high level of noise in the background, hence the surprising decibel level of the music one hears in the rooms of some students as they study or in their cars as they drive and, of course, the almost painfully high sound level associated with such meso-style activities as rock concerts and motorcycling. The warrior's yell is found in meso-dominated cultures all through history; it is very well described in Mary Renault's historical novel *The Bull from the Sea*, a fine account of both the strengths and the weaknesses of the meso-style hero Theseus.

Sociability, in the sense of sharing sensation, is central to the expression of the meso style, much more so than in either ecto or endo styles. As Stanley Keleman has shown, the muscles are the first and most basic of our social systems. The muscles of the face, as they express interest, attention, happiness, or distress in the very earliest years of infancy, serve as important organizers of the infant's developing social world. Other muscle systems are the basis of its earliest modes of joining, clinging, reaching, or rejecting. The sociability that develops on this muscular basis is uniquely meso. It does not show the neutrality that belongs to the ecto style or the mutual absorption one finds in instances of the predominantly endo style. Rather, the meso style structures a face-to-face confrontation in which independent protagonists meet head-on within a space of physical contact. As the ecto world of contact is a world of distances and the endo a world of touching at the interface we call the skin, so the meso is a world constructed at arm's length, a distance bounded at one end by the embrace and at the other by the blow. The most appropriate word for the mode of contact that occurs within this meso distance is *encounter.* It is a term that may be more appropriate than we think. It is an interesting word, one that has recently exchanged its root meaning for another meaning that is in fact a little false. The root of the word, and of its cognate in other languages as well, is a term that means "against," as in the Latin *contra*—for at its basis an encounter is a kind of mutual countering. In the typical encounter, muscles are fixed and ready to be used, and that is just what the meso style typically expresses in its own form of sociability. Only very recently, under the influence of a shallow romanticism, have we permitted the term encounter to be changed so as to mean a meeting in which partners share their good feelings about one another.

I should not leave this preliminary discussion of the meso style without pointing out that its seat in the body is in the chest, its center the heart. The heart is the very core of emotional life in the hearty meso style, as the gut is the seat for the endo style and the skin for the ecto. It is therefore appropriate that the heart has the rhythm of *bang-bang,* just as the rhythm of the gut is tidal and that of the skin is electric, responsive, and irritable.

THE ENDO STYLE

There is a characteristic of endo thinking that is called serendipity, *or the art of being open to what one might "accidentally" discover. The term comes from an ancient Arabic name for Sri Lanka, Sarendib. One might consider its opposite—which would be, on the geography of the globe, the Andes mountains of South America—for which an apt name would be* andeity. *By the opposite of serendipity I mean the price one pays for being open in serendipitous ways. To avoid paying this price, one would be closed in the manner of andeity, unable to see other than what one directly expects to see. Serendipity and andeity, then, would be the two poles of the endo style of thinking and perceiving.*

It is characteristic of this style that at the very beginning we encounter difficulty in talking about it in an organized manner. The reason is that by the very nature of the endo style it eludes systematization. In this respect at least it appears to resemble the meso style, which also lacks any means to refer to itself. But the endo style is nonreflective in unique ways, which can perhaps best be elucidated by means of examples. In this section, therefore, I will be falling back again and again on examples of varying length, in the hope that they will add up to a coherent whole.

A skilled group leader once tried to explain to me the procedure by which she selected persons to compose the groups she led. It appeared to observers, after the fact, that her choices were always intuitively right; she made her selections in such a way that the group formed a satisfactory working unity, the members fitting together in the most productive possible gestalt. Yet although she was able to do this, as her results repeatedly showed, she was quite unable to give me a systematic explanation of the selection process that she used. Indeed, when she talked about the matter she seemed much less in command of the situation than when she simply went ahead and made her selections. Whatever her knowledge was, however her intelligence functioned, they enabled her to know at the proper moment what was right, even though she then lacked any means for talking or even thinking about what she had done.

It is the gift of the endo style to make form out of chaos in this way, just as though the form emerges out of a formless mix, inexplicable and unexplained. Those whose style it is to behave in this way, being unable to report on their own processes, find themselves the victims of their own style of intelligence. There is a certain analogy here to the case of the brain-damaged person who, whatever accomplishments can still be shown, appears unable to talk about them or even to repeat a successful performance. One consequence is that the endo style offers no assurance in advance that the correct behavior will occur and then no way to know after the fact that the correct behavior did in fact occur. Much of what we term organized memory is thus lost to the person; it is not there to be of use, for there is no framework by which one may judge or explain or even talk about what one has done. The consequences of endo intelligence, then, constitute a gift from the past that, being buried, cannot be brought out to be deliberately used.

When something occurs in the pure endo style, an observer may perhaps learn something from watching it as it occurs but not from asking any questions of the doer as to what went on or how to go about doing it again. The endo style therefore has no teachers, if by this term we refer to a person with the requisite skills who can talk helpfully about some mode of behavior. At best one can hope for models or examples in the endo style. One may learn what the style is not, but that is not the same. In regard to the endo style—just as is already evident in my discussion on this page—there is lacking any system or framework on which to hang an explanation, and even more, there is lacking a working vocabulary to use in the discussion. As we will see in chapter 8, for reasons that are of critical importance to our culture and its intellectual life, the endo style has no vocabulary of its own.

Let me then turn to another example. I am sure that if a hundred reasonably perceptive adults were to be shown samples of the behavior of some persons who are celebrated for their social skills and attractiveness—some stars in the entertainment world, for example— there might ensue a fairly high consensus that the target persons possess the elusive quality we call charm. Suppose, now, we question our hundred judges. We ask them to tell us just what it was they perceived in the target person, how they made their judgments, what they used as a basis for deciding that one person did or did not display the quality of charm, and how they might go about instructing beginners in making judgments that were as accurate as theirs. I am sure the answers we receive would be unsatisfactory. The judges might well show a consensus in their judgments, but it is probable they would not be able to give us usable information *about* how they did it. In this respect they would be like my friend the group leader who can regularly and with confidence accomplish just what she cannot explain to another person. The hundred appear to be able to do well, or correctly—at least by the criterion of consensus—and perhaps even confidently what they do, but they probably could not tell someone else what goes into the doing.

Yet the word charm remains in our vocabulary. We do not drop it from common usage just because we cannot develop a system for explaining it in a systematic way. Rather, we assign it to a special category, to which also belong such terms as beauty, justice, and perhaps even intelligence. We seem to be aware that some kinds of acceptable information and observation have to be accepted in their own right, sui generis, and that we have no right to raise additional questions. Such is the fundamental quality of observations made in the endo style.

Put more directly, in the endo style there is lacking any possibility of developing an independent schema on which we can hang an explanation of endo activities. At best, rather than talking or thinking about the activities carried on, we may participate in their expression or we may at least make some empathic contact with a model or example. To this I would add that perhaps there is a structural basis as well for this essential characteristic of the endo style. It is that the gut, in contradistinction to the muscles and the sensory organs, is lacking in any social probes or means of interpersonal contact. The gut is blind to the world, even though it is called upon in everything we do to "know" the world and to respond to the world. We must conclude that the gut possesses its own ongoing activities of relating to the world, its ways of getting along, even its own interior and exterior to which these ways are directed—even though all this is mediated by way of passion rather than perception. Actions of the gut occur in the long, slow, repeating cycles of the viscera, in a time that is timeless, tidal, and without history. The link here—and this is the central point to be kept in mind—is that the endo style is as though it were located in the viscera.

In our necessary preoccupation with the adult world and our investment in it, involved as we must be in engagements, foreknowings, consequences, and ties to our known pasts, and occupied as we are with the equally busy doing of other persons, we too easily ignore the endo component in all that we do. We tend to forget that the endo component is necessarily a part of all our behavior, even though it may often be expressed only minimally. Because of this continuing neglect, our terms for understanding and explaining ourselves and others are all either ecto or meso, and all our terms for talking about our understanding are ecto. The result is that we end up being unable to take the endo style seriously, although this is the one style that can never be taken in any other way. We find it easy to react to what we perceive as the negative side of the endo style, as when we quickly spot and then dismiss someone as a slob, but when we come across the endo style in its more aesthetically pleasing form, as in the character of the intelligent endo portrayed by the actor Sidney Greenstreet—whose name in the film *The Maltese Falcon*, interestingly, was Mr. Gutman—our immediate response is likely to be to dissociate our response from the person. We may experience admiration but not the identification that occurs in the case of the meso hero James Bond or the ecto hero Dr. Who.

Only recently, in some of the teachings that have come to the West in the form of Zen disciplines, have we been exposed to the first terms of an endo vocabulary. In one such description by the German philosopher Karlfried Dürckheim, the notion of *hara* is introduced.[19] This refers to a mode of tranquility in which one's personal "center" is joined fully with nature. It is a posture something like that we experience in a dream, halfway between waiting passively and reacting actively, as though it were possible to receive life and participate in it without planning or trying. Dürckheim's description is remarkably close to that of Sheldon, who refers to a desire to "embrace the environment and to make its substance one with the substance of the individual's own person . . . to remain close to the earth (in) a dominant mood not far from the mood of the nourishing soil . . . unhurried, deliberate, and predictable."[20] If this comes about, controls and directives become deeply buried, hard to reach and so hard to change. For the person committed to the endo style, somewhat labile but deeply conservative, other persons may be lived with, leaned on, perhaps joined or helped, but never opposed, never encountered, and never experienced as teachers. It is a style that makes for a realistic and traditional world of slow changes and abiding passions.

The Endo Act

Our usual conception of the acts that make up behavior depicts them in some combination of meso and ecto styles. Acts are goal-directed, more or less planned, and serve the purpose of getting something done. When faced with someone's activity that has none of these characteristics, we are at a loss as to how to define it and therefore how to understand it. Here are typical acts in the pure endo style:

In 1974 a man in Amarillo, Texas, bought ten Cadillacs and half-buried them in the ground. In 1984 a woman in San Francisco obtained ten worn out televisions sets and half-buried them in her garden.

Consider the woman's answers when she was interviewed about her "act." She was, she said, a conceptual artist, and she showed the interviewer that she had earlier made some books out of cement and put them on her bookshelf. In each case, she said, she was "making a statement." This was as close as she came to answering the unspoken question: but why did you do this particular thing? It was clear that these acts were not done for a purpose, that they had no goals in the usual sense, that they did not serve to get anything done. Yet the notion of an act without a goal seems like a self-canceling phrase. We ask, how can this kind of behavior, which is not random but organized, occur in the absence of a purpose, a goal, some relation to the ongoing work of the world?

To their credit, these artists appear to have accomplished a revolutionary breakthrough in the world of work. In the face of a universal consensus on what constitutes an act of work, they have produced a redefinition and perhaps a new kind of act as well. It cannot be fitted into conventional notions of what is meant by the common expressions "doing something" or "getting something done." Indeed, one cannot imagine the acts described here as being anything other than the work of artists. In one of his remarkable case studies, this one of a young man whom he calls "the autist artist," Oliver Sacks describes the curious artistic ability of a patient who had been kept hidden at home all through his childhood, diagnosed as autistic, severely epileptic, retarded, and probably aphasic.[21] Under Sacks's encouragement and with the help of a hospital staff, however, he was able to demonstrate a talent for drawing which, in turn, aided appreciably in his recovery.

Sacks's comments are very suggestive in the light of the description I am attempting here of the endo act. In regard to the patient's copies of flowers, "fastidious, botanically exact . . . rather similar to, and not inferior to, the fine vivid flowers one finds in medieval botanies and herbals," he notes that this occurs "even though José has no formal knowledge of botany and could not be taught it or understand it if he tried."[22] This, according to Sacks, is because "his mind is not built for the abstract, the conceptual. . . . But he has a real passion and a real power for the particular—he loves it, he enters into it, he re-creates it."[23]

I suggest that we may learn from what this patient lacks just what it is that the endo style has to offer. In place of the abstract and categorical, there is the concrete, the particular, the singular, as Sacks puts it. Living in a world of "innumerable, exact, and passionately intense particulars," theirs is "a mode of mind at the opposite extreme from the generalizing, the scientific."[24] "He grasps the world as forms—directly and intensely felt forms—and reproduces them, . . . hence the piercing directness, the absolute clarity of his perceptions and drawings."[25] One is reminded, in thinking of this patient's grasp of the world, of the "interpenetrating unity" that is supposed to hold for the mutual relations of yang and yin. He both holds and is held by the world, in a direct and primary and passionate act of embrace.

The Endo World

In order to understand more fully the endo style, we may ask the obvious question: what would the world be like if grasped predominantly in the endo style? It is a question we can answer easily in regard to the other two styles, but in the case of the endo style we are seemingly in the position of trying to describe what is not there in the usual sense. It is like talking about the sounds of silence. Fortunately, we have at hand a set of insights that brings us very close to this elusive goal: the essay by Fritz Heider that is a classic contribution to perceptual theory, *Thing and Medium*.[26] Originally published in German in 1926, it remained relatively hidden until its translation to English in 1959. I hope it is clear that in discussing this essay for the purpose of this chapter I do not mean to take over Heider's contributions as in any way my own or to imply that my usage is what he had in mind. I hope rather to make some use of his insights in order to clarify the terms of my own presentation.

Heider's paper concerns the most general properties of the environmental macrostructures that are perceived by the thinking and acting person. Given any object of perception, that is, a "thing," there is also a medium through which the perceptual object is made evident to us. In the most familiar possible example, the ticking of a watch, as object of auditory perception, is the relevant thing; the vibration of the air between watch and ear is the medium. Heider's contribution consists in systematically elucidating the differences between thing and medium, such that it is possible to construct a portrait of what the world would be like if, say, one had access to only the medium in each case. This is how I mean to make use of his essay.

In table 1 there are listed for convenience the major characteristics of the thing, in column 1, and the medium, in column 2. The listing is not meant to imply that there are two categories of perceptual target to which we can, if we want, direct our attention. Rather, perception is normally directed to the object, and all that can be said of the other category is that "we see the thing through the medium."[27] What Heider has done is conceptualize the "unknown" or "hidden" category, the medium, so that we may understand the total perceptual process rather than just the part of it concerned with the overt target. As an example, when we write we are not normally conscious of making marks—the medium through which the writing takes place—but rather of "what" we are writing. Here everything between the initial act of conscious attention and the subsequent product constitutes the medium, yet out of it all we are aware, or we perceive, only the "objective" form of our thought as it appears on paper.

Personality will serve as an excellent example of the characteristics of thing and medium as they are listed in table 1. The personality that we perceive—and it is what we normally perceive as a totality—is the thing in question; but it is made up of a multitude of independent, single movements that are dependent for their meaning on an "objective unit," a thing, in this case "the person and the sequence of psychological events."[28] The personality "moves" as a whole, so to speak, whereas the parts of it, as medium, are pliable; and the less the move-

Table 1   Characteristics of Thing and Medium

1. The thing	2. The medium
Directly perceived	Not in consciousness, not perceived
What meets the sense organ is co-ordinated to the thing	No coordination between the medium and what appears to the senses
The process is conditioned internally, by the nature of the thing	The process is conditioned externally, by the nature of the impinging process
In the form of a unitary event that is "released by an external influence and then takes its course."[1]	In the form of "composite events in which a continuous influence is exerted from the outside."[2]
Parts of the process are "dependent" on each other and therefore move rigidly as a whole	The parts of the process are independent of each other, therefore the process is pliable
Acts like a "single wave impact", therefore does not indicate which of many different causes could have produced it	Each element, separately produced, acts like a messenger, and together they point "univocally" to the cause
Appears as an object of perception, standing by itself	Appears as a mediator, having no "reality" without its cause
Thing events are important for us	Medium events are irrelevant unless "coupled with something important"[3]

1. Heider, F., Thing and medium, in F. Heider, On perception, event structure, and psychological environment: Selected papers, *Psychological Issues* 1, no. 3 (1959): 5.
2. Ibid.
3. Ibid., p. 13.

ments are internally conditioned (by the rigid movement of the whole), the more expressive the movements are. This formulation applies not only to a process such as the working personality but also to an event such as the curve of a chain or a string. An object such as a stick moves as a whole; it is rigid; and therefore it cannot follow any curve except that of its own shape. A chain, on the other hand, can follow a curve; the smaller its links and therefore the less the parts of the chain are dependent on the totality, or the more independent they are, the better it will conform to any curve. In the extreme case such as a string, the way its parts arrange themselves is entirely conditioned by influences external to the string, not to the nature of the string itself, and therefore it can perfectly follow any curve.[29]

It should be clear from these examples that the concepts of thing and medium, and the qualities ascribed to them, though modeled on the example of an act of sensory perception, are not limited to such an event. I therefore feel free to utilize Heider's insights in a direction of thought that he certainly did not intend. I will suggest that what appears to the person whose perceptual behavior is predominantly in the endo mode is a world made up of the medium rather than, as we are accustomed to know, a world of things. I do not mean that the medium itself appears when one is behaving in terms of the endo style but that the medium, as Heider discusses it, is a prototype of what would appear in such a mode—that is, if the world were, so to speak, entirely endo. It would be a world that is not object-dominated but rather carries some other, more "final" meaning or identity.

Under these circumstances, improbable as they may seem, what appears is entirely externally conditioned. Therefore to apprehend it one cannot either encounter it or resist it or take up a distance from it, in either the ecto or the meso style, but must accept it or absorb it totally, and be absorbed as well. Only then will it appear to be externally conditioned. Further, everything will now appear as parts independent of each other, not "naturally" cohering in wholes; as flowing rather than rigid; as proximal rather than distal; as lacking any final meaning in itself; as a non-object, a no-thing, as absent from the socially relevant action that gets things done. There will be only the flow, seemingly conditioned by what is external to it. This, I suggest, is perhaps as close as we can get to a description of the complete endo-dominated experience.

THE INDEPENDENT SCHEMA

In earlier sections I introduced and discussed some problems that arise when one undertakes to utilize categories, and I hinted that such use may be directed by this or that principle. By the term "principle"

I mean, of course, some general statement that is applicable to a range of individual cases. I now raise the question of whether such general statements are instances of only one of the three styles of thinking or whether they might be said to belong to two or three of the styles. Here I want to argue that it is a unique characteristic of the ecto style that it rests on the use of such very general principles. The term I will use for such principles is *independent schema*, for reasons that will soon be apparent; the term *schema* was adopted because it has a long history of related usages. The neurologist Henry Head introduced it to refer to our individual and objectively conceived postural model of ourselves,[30] and in a major work on memory Bartlett[31] used it to mean one's personal core of past memories and organized attitudes.

Consider what we mean by a principle. We define it as a general statement or truth, meaning that it has been defined in such a way as to be applicable in a wide range of cases, regardless of what those cases are about. A characteristic of principles, then, is that they are, so to speak, independent of what they refer to; their usefulness or their power comes rather from the fact of their wide and neutral applicability. It is as though they had no content but functioned rather by being *about* other things. Principles are not tied to particular situations or instances. In these respects they resemble the mass-produced tool or appliance, as distinct from the tools and weapons of earlier and simpler societies. The warrior in a preindustrial society possesses his spear in so personal a sense that the weapon may almost be said to be a part of him, for he has often made it himself or had it made to his personal specifications and through long use has molded it to his own characteristics as a hunter. Today this is true only for the preeminent performer, the tennis star or the concert violinist, persons who can afford, or deserve, to have their equipment molded to them.

In our day the equipment available to most persons is a mass-produced item like the push-button appliance, whether dishwasher or home computer. It is built anonymously and is meant to be used by anyone who can follow the book of instructions. The "user friendly" computer is built to be friendly to everyone, without distinction. In this sense it is to an important degree independent of the characteristics of the person using it or the situation in which it is used. It functions just like a general principle, independently of what it is working on, whether the family wash (if it is a washer) or the family bank balance (if it is a computer).

These characteristics of the equipment that surrounds us are important enough to our lives to merit extended discussion, and I take up this theme again in chapter 8. At this point I want to discuss at greater length one set of characteristics, for which I have used my general principle as an example. In a discussion of this topic some years ago,[32] I applied the term independent schema to arrangements of this sort that are general, abstract, and logically independent of what they refer to. Examples that I have already mentioned include the general principle and the push-button appliance. An even commoner example is our number system, which is a perfectly abstract and general arrangement of symbols and their rules, all organized for the purpose of carrying out formal operations using the elements of the system. Although the number system needs a set of numbers in order to operate, any set will do; it is therefore logically independent of its content as well as of the content of the problem to which it is applied.

All systems of rules are, in this way, instances of the independent schema. This leads to the point that is relevant here, that the independent schema is therefore a perfect example of the ecto style of thinking and reasoning. In this style activities of this sort are carried out by means of abstract symbols, that is, by means of elements that are both general and independent of specific content.

The distinction between activities carried out in terms of an independent schema and those carried out in some other mode is clearly made in a discussion by Dreyfus of computer programs. He distinguishes between a gestalt, which is a system for defining "what counts" in the elements that it organizes, and a plan or rule, which "simply organizes independently defined elements." Because of this relation to its elements, a plan "can be stated as a rule or program, independently of the elements."[33] Polanyi makes a similar point in reference to the nature of commitment. In discussing whether it is possible to "formalize" the act of commitment, that is, to organize some scheme for planning acts of commitment in general, he concludes that it is not possible. This is because "you cannot express your commitment noncommittally,"[34] that is to say, you cannot handle the notion in any way that is independent of the notion itself; the rule you develop will never be free of the very content to which it is meant to refer.

Because the independent schema is almost the hallmark of an ecto methodology, it will be helpful to consider it at further length, in the form of an extended example. Suppose that you undertake to write a book. Even before you put down the first word of your first draft, you will have to decide what your book will be about. You may make all sorts of changes before you are finally done with the manuscript, but the fact is that you cannot begin it unless, in a certain sense, you already have the whole book in hand. For example, you cannot say to a colleague, "Well, I've decided to write a book," if you are not prepared to furnish some sort of answer to your friend's obvious question, "Oh—what about?" What you have in hand is precisely this answer; it is a statement *about*.

We might then say that a book must begin as an independent schema, or as a known and describable arrangement that is about something— although the ways in which the book can be about that something may be very large and may vary independently of the plan. This is true at least of nonfiction books and of textbooks in particular. It is somewhat less true of novels, for the novelist may often take the risk of letting the novel write itself, especially if it already contains a strong character or a compelling situation. At the other end of the spectrum, however, is the book of poems, as we see in the fact that only rarely can the author provide an answer to the question, "What is your latest book of poems about?" For the book of poems, even though it is bound into one set of covers and then sold as a single item, is not a book in the same sense that a nonfiction work is. Poems appear as books only because of our modern convention, which is not much more than a century old, that poets should not sell their poems individually but put them into a bundle first. Painters or musical composers are still expected to sell their works individually.

As the prospective author of a book, you begin by knowing about it as a whole; your writing is then a form of dissection in which you gradually come to know its parts. Once you have decided on the general statement of the whole, you come to a decision about how to arrange the contents so as to best present what the book is about. You may then provide a table of contents, which is your own statement of how you fit the material of the book to its general plan. All of your actions as author are determined by your reliance on an independent schema, which in this case consists of your conception of the book as a whole.[35] And if your book is now published, it will be packaged exactly like any other neutral, mass-produced product; all its instances will be alike as it is sent out to be sold to readers who are anonymous to you. The process by which in modern Western history the book as an example of the independent schema was developed is very well told in Neil Postman's account of some of the effects of the invention of printing.[36] Like all schemas, like all generally applicable rule systems, the book is experienced as all-knowing, as powerful as a god.

Each of the many anonymous readers of the modern book comes to it by way of some version of the independent schema. Each of them, that is, will know something of what the book is about, perhaps on account of having read a review of it, perhaps by reading the blurb on its jacket or its table of contents, in some instances simply by knowing the title or the name of the author. The reader will then take up the book and start to read it because the independent schema fits in with his or her purposes as a reader at this moment. But if, for example, your book appeared in a college bookstore with the title "Introduction to General Psychology," your reader would be justifiably upset to open it and discover, say, a volume of love poems or the autobiography of a saint.

Still other aspects of the production and use of books are related to their roles as independent schemas—for we should note here that the book is related to the independent schema in two ways. First, the book is organized around such a schema by virtue of it being about something, being organized so as to express that something, and being packaged and sold as an anonymous entity. Second, an independent schema enters into the nature of the book insofar as the book is built around some general plan that is independent of the elements through which the plan is worked out. Lacking such a plan, the book would have to write itself, an activity that might or might not produce a book that could appropriately be considered to be about anything in particular. It would seem that objects that are organized around the independent schema tend to take on an existence like that of the schema itself. Thus, books are written in such a way that they are quite unrelated to how author and reader might meet. The effect is that they do not meet at all but merely trade signs of recognition, make their exchange, and go on their individual ways, the particular time or place or circumstance of the exchange being quite independent of the book itself. The book becomes a marketable item moving silently from the author as anonymous (or perhaps pseudonymous) agent at one end to a large group of equally anonymous and indistinguishable readers at the other. Compare the book in these respects with a letter, a one-of-a-kind message that is usually dated, signed, even handwritten, all because it is meant to function like the reaching of a hand, going from one particular person to another at a time and in a place known to both of them as well as meaningful to them.

In the sense that I have been describing it, the modern book demands that one or more independent schemas come into play and, as I have said, then functions like an independent schema in its own right. Perhaps we can now begin to see that the invention of printing, making possible the modern book, had as one of its most profound effects that it introduced the independent schema into human communication. More than this, as should now be evident, the independent schema is a perfectly apt example of an ecto style of thinking. The invention of printing, then, may be considered as the major step in making possible on a large scale the application of the ecto style to human communication. Built around the independent schema, a book is wrought so as to transcend any situation of immediate or personal sharing. It is meant to be bought, borrowed, stolen, or found by anyone, anywhere, and then to be read as each reader decides, alone or in public, in one sitting or in successive sessions, in whole or in part. The book is an abstract symbol writ large. Perhaps this was what Emily Dickinson referred to in her melancholy line, "Publication is the auction of the mind."

The Independent Schema: Meso and Endo Styles

There are, however, events to which the independent schema cannot be fitted, and they will be found to arise out of either a meso or an endo style. For example, some of us may have had the experience of knowing someone who was usually helpful and occasionally even inspiring as a friend and helper, but whose exact mode of being helpful could not be pinned down and talked about. You might meet with such a person and on leaving say something like, "Now, just what was it my friend said?" The exact words might never be recalled; what remained would have been only a sense of what was conveyed, an experience of helpfulness. You might even ask your friend, "Tell me what system you use. Tell me your rules." I suspect that your friend in all honesty would be no better able than you to spell out such a set of rules. The two of you would then be left with a set of events that occur predictably, not randomly, but that could not be reduced to an independent schema by which some anonymous third person might be instructed.

It might then seem that nothing of this kind of event can be transmitted, taught, or learned, that it must remain forever private. But the history of medicine and of the various arts teaches us that the styles in which such non-ecto events occur, even though they lack the possibility of an independent schema, may have their own means for passing them from one person to another. In terms of our example, you may well find that as your contacts with your friend continue and you permit yourself to be modeled unreflectively on what your friend does, your own contacts with other persons change in ways you would have wanted. You will then have discovered that you have indeed found out just what your friend does, and you have even incorporated it into your own activities but without interposing an independent schema between your friend's work and your own.

It is one mark of meso and endo styles of behaving that what one does is rarely planned in advance or reflected upon while being done. In place of thought or action that is organized in accordance with some independent plan, as in the ecto style, meso action is carried by its ongoing physical meaning and endo action is sustained by one's sense of continuing participation. If the prototype of action in the ecto style is to thoughtfully and self-reflectively solve a problem that is stated in abstract or symbolic terms, then the best model for the meso style is a physical test such as running a competitive race.

In running a race there is surely no problem to be solved by anyone, yet there is certainly an issue of sorts to be resolved by each of the participants, in the sense that all of them as competitors mean to act in such a way as to beat out the others. Thinking about it in advance—

that is, "pure" thinking, in the absence of such other operations as imaging—will be of only limited help, and thinking about the race during the running of it may even be a hindrance; worse, thinking about one's own thinking will probably guarantee the runner's defeat. Yet a certain kind of awareness of self, both before and during the race, must occur in some detailed sense. This suggests that more than one kind of self-reflection may be available to those who are properly prepared for it.

It is true that rules for running races, or for training to do so, can be developed and that some coaches have even worked up elaborate "systems" for training runners. For this reason it might seem that some form of the independent schema is applicable to meso just as much as to ecto activities. But even if some kind of plan seems to be applicable to meso activity, it functions in a way quite different from the ecto-style independent schema. Even when such a structure is available to the athlete, as in a system that a coach has developed and published for improving one's game of golf, it will benefit the learner only when it functions as though it were forgotten. As long as it is kept in awareness, as a plan or a set of rules that can be stated on demand or with which one can remind oneself what to do in order to be correct, it will not only be of little use but will probably get in the way.

This is, in fact, just what happens in the course of learning a motor skill. At the beginning of training most of the rules can be stated by the learner, but as training proceeds the rules appear to be forgotten, although, as we know, they are not but are simply used in a different way. An example that will serve here is the relatively simply motor skill of typing. The independent schema that functions as a set of guiding rules is the organization of the keyboard and the accompanying requirement that only a certain finger can be used for each of the keys. But once the learner has committed the keyboard to memory and then learned which finger goes on each key, what seems to happen is that both keyboard and finger placement are "forgotten," although perhaps in different ways. The finger placement is forgotten in the sense that it can be brought back for display only if the typist literally physically moves the fingers, that is, goes through the correct movements. If shown a picture of a keyboard and asked to say which finger is placed on a specific key, the skilled typist will usually be able to answer correctly only with the help of surreptitious finger movements.

The picture of the keyboard, on the other hand, seems to be forgotten in a different and more usual sense. It can usually not be drawn correctly from memory—even though the skilled typist will at the same time do touch typing without an error. Just as happens to all of us when we learn a telephone dial through hundreds of trials, becoming familiar and then overfamiliar with it—a phenomenon that is appropriately called overlearning—the independent schema that guides our learning is forgotten; if asked, we cannot draw a picture of the telephone dial that is correct. I suggest that it is forgotten in the sense of an ecto-style memory, but that it is not forgotten in the meso sense. It is buried in a new place, in a new motor attitude. I suggest further that only if this happens can motor learning occur in the first place, and that once it does occur we have the odd circumstance that beginning typing students can draw the keyboard better from memory than experienced typists, while none of us who are experienced telephone dialers can draw the dial from memory without error.

Actions carried out in the meso style, in which an early independent schema becomes contained in a motor attitude, are in many ways like handwritten signatures. They are always available but then carried out without thought, as though they were canned and prepared, suggesting the presence of an imprinted pattern of muscle activity producing their occurrence, again and again, in exactly the same way. Yet they can hardly be directly dependent on a specific set of muscles or muscle patterns, since people will make their signatures in recognizably similar ways even when they use quite different sets of muscles, for example, if they write with the pen held between the toes.[37] A schema seems to be operative here, but it is clearly not the independent schema of the ecto style, for it is not a plan that can be talked about, abstractly considered, or taught to another person. The meso activity appears to have its own form of schema, serving as one possible organizing mode for meso intelligence. Although the schema is not in the form of a neutral set of principles that can be abstracted from the doing of an act, it makes motor learning and the existence of motor skills and habits possible. Endo activity, however, appears to be unique in that it goes on without schemas that can be identified. "Pure" endo activity seems to be lived as it proceeds, without preparation, without reflective consideration as it goes along, and without organized reflection once it is done. It must follow, then, that what we call planning or ongoing experiencing, even what we call memory, are all different in the endo style than in the other two styles.

PART TWO

Applying the Hypothesis to Topics
in Psychology

3

Thinking, Learning, and Teaching

The main intellectual accomplishment of the nervous system is the world it-self.—GEORGE MILLER

In Western culture at least, the activities of thinking and learning have traditionally been considered to be functions of the mind—or of its physiological basis in the central nervous system, as in Miller's statement above—and therefore, and necessarily, ecto functions. To entertain the view that these activities may be in part functions of both meso and endo styles may seem at best irrelevant and at worst simply wrong. I hope that what I present in this chapter will help to open up a discussion by suggesting that other than ecto modes of thinking and learning are possible if we but know where and how to look.

THE ECTO STYLE OF THINKING

Thinking and the Brain

In the ecto style, thought is all. It is the natural model for every function and the self-evident peak of any hierarchy of functions. Its essential mark consists of a glorification of the irreal. For evident reasons, Erwin Straus has referred to these characteristics of the ecto style as forms of "excarnation," a freeing of organismic functions from all the biological limitations of the body. When experimental subjects are required to engage in a task that demands a high level of imaginal thinking in the ecto style,[1] they show clear bodily indications of such excarnation. They are positioned facing away from a blackboard and required to write on it, behind their backs and with the nondominant hand, some unusual pattern—for example, to print the letters USA so that an observer facing them would see the letters as though they were being viewed in a mirror. To accomplish this task one must manipulate the letters in imagination while at the same time testing the results of the manipulation against the requirements of the task. The subject is thus required to handle a self-generated, abstract representation of an entity, or what we call a thought, an idea, or an image, and to do this solely by means of "mental" processes. It is, in short, a completely ecto task.

Motion pictures of subjects' performances show that first they position themselves firmly, usually by setting their feet solidly and a little way apart, almost as though they wanted to be sure of a firm "home base" to return to after their anticipated "flight" of thought. Once established on this base, they attend to the task. The head tilts to one side or a little to the back, the mouth loosens and the jaw begins to sag slightly, and invariably the eyes de-focus from the immediate environment. It is in the eyes, those "windows of the soul," or more prosaically, those portals for the ecto processes of attending, surveying, and scanning, that one notes clearly the process of excarnating. For when the eyes have de-focused subjects are no longer in informational contact with the immediate, tangible physical surround. The de-focusing carries the thinking person out of the realm of the practical everyday. Close examination of stills from the motion picture film, as reprinted in the Straus paper, shows that some subjects peer or stare straight ahead, seeming to look right through the camera, or more commonly will drift away, up, or to the side with their gaze. In this way, through their posture and their eye contact they indicate that they are attending to a realm removed from that in which our physical actions take place. The phenomenon is so automatic and so easy to produce that one may have confidence in the excarnation that it implies.

It is our bias as thinkers to refer to these functions as thinking and then to restrict that term to these and only these activities of the head and eyes and brain. For reasons important to the intellectual history of the Western world we have come to believe that the processes involved take place inside the skull, in the brain itself. Yet some two thousand years of study, research, and speculation have failed to teach us just how the irreal domain of ecto thinking is connected with its presumed basis or with the real world that the thinking is supposed to be about.[2] While we have little reason to doubt that neither muscles nor viscera can function in the ecto style, we should at least be open to the possibility that each of these other important loci may have their own modes of thoughtlike processes.

Characteristics of Ecto Thought

Thinking that is directed toward the irreal, as ecto thinking is, has the capacity to play in an infinite variety of ways with its target objects. I can, for example, think of or about anything, then imagine it changed in any way at all, and have it then revert to the way in which it was first thought of, canceling out all that had gone before; and I can keep doing this, on and on, without fatigue until I am brought to a halt by boredom. What I cannot do, however, is not think of something, or deliberately unthink it once having thought of it. My thinking processes seem to work on what is available to them, but the availability itself is much less subject to my control.

As a result of the infinite play associated with thinking, there is always available to the ecto thinker an additional and parallel line of thought. It bears something like a target relation to the first line of thought. Thus, if I think of A, it is almost always possible for me to think of me-thinking-of-A in addition. In both these processes, the initial thinking and then the additional, parallel thinking, very much the same thing happens. A curious relation is set up between a function, thinking, and what the function is directed to, its target. The relation is not one of direct physical contact, for one of the two sides of the relation is, as we know, always irreal. Yet the process and its target are powerfully linked, so much so that while the thought is happening the link cannot be broken. To think is, on principle, to think of or about something, as the phenomenologist's principle of intentionality succinctly states. Further, to think of that something is to not think of some other something, and as we just noted, to think of something means to be unable to not think of it. Because this is the way the process works, we find ourselves unable to unlearn at will, or to deliberately forget. It is a circumstance that the humorist George S. Kaufman once ridiculed when, having first prepared for a trip to France by learning some French words, he had the trip canceled and then reported to his friends that he was now engaged in forgetting one word each day: "Today, for example, I forgot what the noun *gare* means."

In these respects all thinking is the same, no matter what its target, a characteristic that has two consequences. First, if thinking is not defined in any way by what it is about, one can develop general laws that refer to all thinking; and second, thought is essentially neutral toward any of its objects. Like the sun that shines equally on the rich and the poor, ecto thought casts itself toward any possibility and then functions in the same way regardless of what it may contact. The ultimate expression of thinking in the ecto style is the symbol of a mathematical formula, which must of necessity be utterly neutral and free of human value.

Equally, this cipher, which is thought at its purest, is free of time and space as well, and this in turn leads to the noblest characteristic of all, that thought may be self-reflective. Some writers have defined this characteristic as the ultimate end of evolutionary development; perhaps for this reason they locate it in the prefrontal cortex and insist that it uniquely defines the human animal. As a consequence of not being in any place, not limited to the evident bounds of time and space as we normally experience such limits, thoughtlike experience can turn on itself—and then, in an endless regress, can turn on itself turning on itself. The "what" of ecto thought, or that which thinking is "of" at any moment, is not fixed but infinitely variable, endlessly manipulable, truly what William James once called "a tumbling ground for whimseys."

Floating free, such thought can "repeat" endlessly, without consequences. Thus the obsessive neurotic, trapped in a repetitive sequence of thought that requires that the same thought be had, meaninglessly, is in fact an example of the perfect, even if limited, ecto thinker. The thought that keeps recurring to this poor wretch has no history, never tires of being repeated, and has no consequences in its own realm. Modeling on the obsessive, the true thinker can always repeat the thought, can think about the thought, and can finally repeat the thought about the thought as required. Further, the true thinker cannot have a thought without at the same time having a thought about that thought or its expression; the reflection follows as a shadow, impossible to dismiss. Ask a thinker to say it again, that you had missed what was said, and the result will often be a flawless repetition. But try to get any but the most expert and practiced athlete or dancer to repeat on demand a specific movement or reproduce a pose and unless they are highly skilled, they will have to include the movement or pose within a larger movement, and they will have to practice it at different speeds, even though they had done it perfectly once before. There is a sense in which repetition belongs to the ecto style and to that style alone; repeating by talking about, by referring to, by recalling and then replicating.

For the person whose style is predominantly ecto, something is so if it resembles thought. Expressions that carry values are always suspect, and an emotional coloring to thought or word is a sure sign of its limited value in discourse. The rock-bottom reality of the ecto world is a symbol, just as theoretical physicists are fond of telling us. The person in the ecto style, just like the rest of us, sees what is outside in terms of what is inside—and so the world is then conceived as being made up of the symbols of an irreal domain, mirroring the ecto style itself.

Thought and Ecto Reality

This helps us to understand a curious characteristic of the ecto thinker, which can best be explicated by means of an example. Suppose that you awaken from a sound sleep and in the very dim light of your bedroom you make out, at the foot of your bed, a ghostly white shape projecting above where you think your foot is. Since as a good burgher you keep a pistol under your pillow, you immediately aim it at the shape and pull the trigger. The shape disappears—but to your pained dismay so does your big toe, for that was what was producing the projecting shape. But let us assume an alternative ending to this grisly tale and suppose that when you fire away at the shape it does not disappear. In the one case, then, your action directed toward the shape makes it disappear, and in the other case your action does not make it disappear. One of the most important ways we know whether something is real is by testing to see if we can make it disappear by action toward it. If it does, as in the first case, we know that it is real, but if it does not, as in the second case, we know that it is unreal—or, as we say, only a figment of our imagination.

This sort of everyday ontology establishes that in the practical world of ordinary action there does exist a physical world to which we can choose to attend or not, and that whether this world appears to us will depend on whether we attend to it. It is our sensory functions that define for us what is there, and we control the results of these functions by bending toward or turning away, by paying attention or not, that is, by continuing choices regarding what will be present for action. However, if the target to which we try to attend persists in spite of our chosen mode of attention, if it is not demonstrably under the control of our sensory functions, then we are compelled to say that it is not real. The mirage, for example, presents itself whether or not we choose to see it, it persists in its same form no matter how we position ourselves for attending to it, and it may then disappear without consulting us, so to speak. The afterimage whose effects can be so neatly demonstrated to psychology students arrives, persists, then fades away in spite of all our attempts to see it in the ordinary way.

The real things of the world, on the other hand, will appear only if we are properly positioned and attentive; they will change position or shape or appearance as we move in relation to them, as we squint or focus our eyes, as we turn toward or away from them, as we gain or lose information about them, or as we develop or lose sensory skills or acuity in reference to them; and they will finally disappear when we choose that they do. What remains of them after they disappear, in the form of what we term memories, is of course not "real" for just this reason, that it persists in spite of us and will like a mirage then appear and disappear, often unchanged, according to some laws of its own.

That the reality status of things should in this way depend on whether we are able to make them disappear—and so, in our example above, the shape that remains in the face of our violent action must be nothing but a ghost—is rather hard to understand. This is certainly not true of the ordinary world of action and the things in it. Other persons come and go without my control over them, the sun rises or sinks below the horizon, yet I do not for this reason immediately conclude that because I cannot control their presence they must be unreal.

It is in fact only in the purely ecto style, and in regard to the phenomena belonging in this style, that this curious formula holds.

When we exist in a purely meso mode, as for example if we are totally involved in a physical struggle against some tangible resistance, we are of course often unable to control what our opposite number will do. This is in fact the nature of what we encounter in the ordinary world of action: it will present itself as a kind of opposite number, something or someone to be confronted, a resistance to our doing. We take all this for granted when our behavior is dominated for the moment by the meso style. We learn as perhaps our very first lesson in sharing a world with other persons that what we want or do may well conflict with what others do or want. Freud, with his fine sense of the complexities of human development, turned this basic characteristic of the world of action into the very foundation of all thought processes; that is, he accepted this meso necessity as prerequisite for ecto development in the human. Thought, he said, begins in the infant when an act following on a wish is blocked, as typically occurs when the infant's wish or reach for the nipple is frustrated because the mother is not there; the infant then hallucinates the absent breast. As we grow up we come to know that all action is accompanied by effort and that the amount of effort we expend will not necessarily be an indicator in advance of the results of the effort. The meso world is resistive, effortful, conflicting, and hard at work for its own ends, no matter what we do in it or against it—or perhaps just because we are constantly acting in it and against it.

OTHER VIEWS OF THINKING

I want to get my hearers to be able to accept the view that the It guides human science, makes scientific discoveries, and then leaves them to be logically worked out and based on rational grounds by the conscious mind.— GEORG GRODDECK, *Exploring the Unconscious*

In his concluding discussion of the future of artificial intelligence, Hubert Dreyfus[3] distinguishes four types of intelligent activity. The first of these, which he terms "associationistic," operates in the absence of meaning and context and consists of innate or rote behavior, often in response to programmed patterns. In regard to computer operations, one finds here trial-and-error routines or the simple matching of patterns against given templates. In the terminology of this book, such activity would be in meso and endo styles. A second type, in Dreyfus's formulation, would be the "simple-formal" and constitutes the formalized and calculable domain best fitted for artificial intelligence. All meanings are completely explicit, so that games such as tic-tac-toe can be played with great skill and theorems can be proved using fixed and mechanical procedures. In our terms, this is a meso intelligence. A third type would be the "complex-formal" in which the behavior "is in principle formalizable but in fact intractable," primarily because of the very large number of elements involved. The game of chess belongs in this category, and although computer programs for playing chess, and playing it well, continue to be developed, it is generally recognized that even the best such program is no more than an approximation of the skills of a chess master. Some form of intuition that is founded on an internal situation dependency seems to be required, which cannot be furnished through any form of artificial intelligence. This type of activity most closely resembles ecto thinking. Dreyfus's fourth category comprises what he terms "nonformal" intelligence, including "regular but not rule governed" activities. Pattern recognition, guessing riddles, the use of natural languages are examples of typical activities. Because these activities require "a sense of the global situation" in order to avoid knowing the infinity of possible facts that may be relevant to solutions, the requirement here is for intelligence of a radically different order than the intelligence of the other categories.[4] I would suggest that in our terminology what is referred to here is the individual use of all three styles in their mutual interdependence. In any case, in neither our formulation nor Dreyfus's can the possible varieties and the range of intelligent activity be contained within one narrow type. To state the matter more positively, we turn now to a description of meso and endo styles of thinking.

The Meso Style of Thinking

In a recent review of experimental studies of thinking, Paul Aikin[5] concludes that the evidence strongly supports this conclusion: that "neuromuscular activity plays an essential role in emotional, perceptual, and cognitive processes." This is to say that thinking, the major form of our cognitive activity, does not consist entirely of the operations I discussed in the preceding section. That constitutes a style, but only one style, of thinking. The evidence supports the additional claim that muscle activity is importantly involved in most instances of thinking. According to the results of intensive research by McGuigan,[6] this activity includes a number of organ systems, the viscera, the skin, the throat and mouth, the visual system, and the autonomic nervous system. In McGuigan's summary statement, the data overwhelmingly support the claim that we think with our entire bodies. The supporting data for this claim come from hundreds of studies in which electromyographic measurements were made at specific locations on the body surface during periods in which subjects were thinking, dreaming, and fantasizing. The action potentials produced by this technique can be measured in the hand during sessions of mental problem solving, or in the mouth and chin during sessions of silent reading, and even in the appropriate muscle groups when subjects think about such actions as throwing a ball or running. As Jacobson has shown during some decades of research on muscle relaxation,[7] if muscle activity is lessened during deep relaxation, subjects' thought processes also diminish to the point where they fall asleep.

These experimental data support the view that at the very least the process of thinking involves two modes of functioning, the ecto and the meso. Whether the structures associated with the endo style, the organ systems of gut and viscera, are also involved in normal instances of thinking does not seem to have been tested on a systematic basis—although much anecdotal evidence would seem to support this possibility. Joseph Chilton Pearce,[8] arguing for a mode of children's education that contains many of the elements of the endo style, remarks that educational development proceeds best when the learner is involved in an "unbroken continuum with the world," a phrasing that well describes the psychological situation of the endo learner.

Most views that differ from traditional Western psychology, however, seem to be describing a meso style of learning and thinking. Karlfried Dürckheim, in presenting what he calls the "Japanese cult of tranquility,"[9] makes use of terms very close to those that describe a meso style. All situations of stress, he writes, and in particular situations arising out of desire, which is probably the commonest case, begin with a tension between the unfulfilled subject and that subject's target of desire. The tension is released only when the object is attained, but since it may then soon be aroused again, mere attainment of the object after a struggle is not sufficient to provide enduring satisfaction. What the person must learn to do is to attain the object so easily, so perfectly, that tension simply does not occur. And this can only be accomplished by exercise, by the actual, concrete doing of the attainment over and over until it becomes automatic. Only in this way will the person experience the goal of all self-development, a "consciousness of unison . . . a sense of release or deep satisfaction" that is realized "at the harmony of subject and object . . . undisturbed by subject-object tension."[10]

Dürckheim does not mean this prescription to be read simply as a truism, something to the effect that we feel satisfaction when our desires are satisfied. Rather, he seems to be pointing toward a specific mode of resolving tensions, one that is not "mental" in an ecto sense but concretely muscular in a meso sense. Thus, he quotes some advice from a wise old Japanese, "If something is to acquire religious significance, it need only be simple and capable of repetition."[11] To this he adds, "The most natural actions are then made the object of particular exercises—walking, standing, sitting."[12] In short, it is the movements themselves, in the absence of cognitive activity—indeed, apparently in their necessary absence—that will lead to tranquility as the highest of all goals of living. The emphasis here is after all not very different from what we may find in other spiritual disciplines in Japan, China, and India, particularly those in the Buddhist tradition. Archery, flower arranging, swordsmanship, measured walking have all been advocated as activities basic to personal spiritual development—again, just as though the activities themselves, in the absence of any cognitive operations, will bring the person to a higher level of thinking. The Western tradition of defining cognition in ecto terms is here almost completely replaced by a definition in meso terms.

A quite different attack on the traditional Western view of consciousness, this from modern phenomenology, takes a very similar position. Its clearest expression is to be found in the work of Maurice

Merleau-Ponty.[13] In an extended discussion of a brain-injured patient named Schneider whose deficiencies light up, by contrast, the ordinary capabilities of normal persons, abilities that escape our notice simply because they are so evident, Merleau-Ponty notes that "the space in which normal imitation operates is not . . . a 'representative' space based on an act of thought. It is already built into my bodily structure, and is its inseparable correlative."[14] Because "a movement is learned when the body has understood it,"[15] pure motility is able to endow meaning to a space, an object, a situation. Therefore it may be said that "consciousness is in the first place not a matter of 'I think that' but of 'I can.' "[16] These are surely descriptions of the characteristics of a meso style of thinking and learning, one that is founded in action, one in which "the body has its world" in a way that is distinct from how a world and its objects are present to ecto thought. But we should also note that for Merleau-Ponty this alternative, posed against a restricted, ecto view of consciousness, stops at the boundaries of the meso style. He does not even hint that a third mode of intelligence, in the endo mode, is possible, and in this respect his thinking follows that of Husserl, the founder of modern phenomenology.

The Endo Style of Thinking

I shall begin with an example, this one based on an aphoristic statement by Ludwig Wittgenstein. Discussing the problem of "the meaning of life," he remarks that it is not a problem at all but a riddle, and therefore is not to be "solved" as a problem might be. The reason for this, he says, is that we are inescapably inside this question; therefore there is no way for us to pose it as a problem and then solve it.

It might seem that here Wittgenstein has failed to understand the nature of problems. How can he say that we are forever inside the problem of the meaning of life? As we all know, the very nature of a meaningful theoretical question is that we are not inside it but rather outside it, by virtue of having been able to state it properly. If we are still inside it even after the question is asked, then we have not asked a meaningful question but something else—perhaps a . . . well, perhaps a riddle.

At this point it may occur to us that Wittgenstein might not, after all, have failed to grasp the nature of problems, but that instead he has understood them quite well. He has realized that there may be more than one kind of question. There is the familiar kind, which is a product of the ecto style, in which we leap beyond our present, time-bound situation, somehow grasp more than one of the possible answers to our question, and then build the question around the answers we have grasped, working backward from answers to question so that the latter now coherently encompasses the former. Since our two or more possible answers are equivalent as regards the question, we are prepared to accept any one of them as correct. In this sense we are neutral in regard to the outcome of our question, and it becomes simply a kind of test. We are not inside the question but external to it, therefore it is neutral as far as we are concerned.

However, there may be questions, or expressions that appear to be questions, that do not permit us to be outside them in this way. The question-marked expression, "What is the meaning of life?" is, as Wittgenstein saw, one example. Unless the question is asked as a joke, with no personal involvement in any of its possible answers, there is no way this question can be meaningfully asked unless the questioner feels at least some stake in one or more of its possible answers. We are all of us, inescapably, inside this question, or of any others that catch and hold us in the same way. We are like fish, who are forever unable to wonder how big is the ocean; for even to get as far as posing the question, the fish would have to become amphibian. We should note that this is not because we—or the fish—cannot figure out a technique for arriving at a good answer, nor is it because we cannot choose confidently among alternative answers. Rather, it is that we are forever unable to get outside of the question, to pose it in the ecto style. For us it is not a question but, as Wittgenstein saw, a riddle, therefore never to be solved as we might a problem or a neutral question.

Wittgenstein might have taken one more step and suggested, as he did not, that riddle-making, which greatly intrigues children, is just as worthwhile an enterprise as question-framing, one of the favorite games of adults. I will take this step here and offer, somewhat tentatively, that endo thinking typically takes the form of being caught in questions the prototype of which is, "What is the meaning of life?" In endo thought the answer to riddlelike questions is not one among a number of possible answers and never merely a neutral statement. It is, rather, always a matter of there being only one possible good answer at any time or in any situation, that answer being as heavily weighted with personal significance as was the question itself. There is one answer, it is felt, that must be so. I mean by this that all endo thinking is value laden, that nothing it touches is neutral, and that it begins and ends within an arena of personal significance. From Wittgenstein's statement above we may venture that he had a clear sense of this mode of thinking and that his own may often have resembled it.

Endo thinking involves circling an area of thought, as it were, then allowing the thought to grow and develop within its area. The central word here is "grow" and the images are of development rather than of either reflection or activity or movement. For all the great changes it finally brings about, growth is silent; it is neither busily chattering in self-reference nor noisily acting in the world. In endo thinking a set of general notions is first known or held, and these are then developed. They are held initially because of a faith in them, which in turn flows out of one's known orientation in a situation. Endo thinking, then, takes place only on the basis of an earlier established foundation; it is never free to wander imaginally, as is thought in the ecto style. What is lost in regard to the free play of possibilities may then be gained in regard to personal significance. In place of that sudden flash of insight that so often starts off the process of ecto thought, there occurs first a situating of oneself. One experiences no sense of novelty and none of the surprise as in the case of the ecto leap or the meso breakthrough. When it occurs, endo thinking becomes the growing experience of some surety that evolves itself into a form, like a groundswell. At the end one has the feeling of a job well done.

LEARNING: THE ENDO MODE

In place of the rather general discussion of thinking that was presented in the preceding sections, I should now like to turn to a more specific kind of activity, learning. I will review learning in the three modes, beginning with the endo. As a general introduction I will first present some figures obtained in the early 1950s by R. W. Parnell, a British psychologist. He had developed an objective method of rating the physical characteristics of bodies (height, weight, and body fat combined by formula) so that he was able to arrive at the equivalent of a Sheldon somatotype without the use of judgments based solely on observation. Using this method he accumulated measurements and other data on a total of 2,866 male undergraduates at the University of Birmingham (see table 2). For each subject he transformed the rating of each component (ecto, meso, or endo) into a percentage of that subject's total rating. For example, if a subject was rated at 4 on the endo component (on a scale of 1 to 7), 6 on the meso component, and 4 on the ecto component, the subject's total would be 14; transformed into percentages, the subject's endo rating would then become .2857 (4 divided by 14), the meso rating would be .4286 (6 divided by 14), and the ecto component also .2857. Once all the subjects' ratings on the components had been thus transformed, Parnell averaged them across groups of subjects, with the results shown in the table. The subjects have been grouped according to their educational specialties (or majors, as we would say in the United States), and for each of the majors there is presented the average percentage of total score assigned to each component.[17]

It is apparent from these figures that students who choose different majors, at least in Great Britain and among males, also differ in soma-

Table 2   Relative Emphasis on Three Body Components in Male College Students

Academic Major	Average Percentage of Group		
	Endomorphic	Mesomorphic	Ectomorphic
Mathematics	31	22	47
Physics	20	37	44
Chemistry	43	26	31
Law	47	25	28
Mechanical Engineering	24	44	32
Medicine	31	37	32
Arts	38	26	36

$N = 2,866$

totype; in addition, these differences are not random but seem to be what would be predicted on the basis of common sense. For example, it seems reasonable to find that mechanical engineers are more practical and less theoretical than are mathematicians, and, as the table indicates, the former score higher on mesomorphy and lower on ectomorphy. Mathematicians and physicists, just as might be expected, score the same on ectomorphy but reverse on the other two components. Chemists, lawyers, and art majors rate highest on the endo component while engineers and majors in medicine rate highest on the meso. And this reasonable set of results holds true in spite of some cultural differences between American and British college students. The objective data thus indicate that there may be more than chance relations between one's physical structure and one's choice of academic discipline and career. To the degree that these disciplines also differ in content and in demands they make on the learner, the data have interesting implications for a psychology of learning. I begin the discussion of three styles of learning with the endo mode.

If my style of learning happened to be primarily endo—and under the assumption that learning is a process of change—I would probably change in such a way that I would not know about my own process of change. It would therefore be quite different from a series of acts that constitutes a performance, for in the endo style there is no actor to do the act and no audience to attend to the doing. Rather, as an endo learner I would unreflectively do what I do while satisfying some of my ongoing needs in so doing. If I play in the water at the seashore because this is what I want to do, I may then in the course of this activity "learn" not to be afraid of the water, or if I then move around in the water because this is what I want to do, I may "teach myself" to swim after a fashion. Other methods and other approaches are of course also possible for me, for the simple reason that by the time one is old enough to benefit from such learning there are meso as well as ecto components developed. Thus, the common practice of dropping a child into the water so that it then quickly "learns" how to swim is surely not, as in the endo style, based on satisfying one's ongoing needs by engaging in a desired activity. Rather, a survival need may come into play to energize the child and lead it to struggle rather than lie passively; and in addition, meso-style activities immediately take over. The child learns through a process of rapid movement, achieves an immediately desired goal, and then finds itself using the newly gained skills to do more of the activity, in this case staying afloat or swimming to shore. In endo learning, by contrast, there does not occur a clearcut point in the process at which the learner can say, "Hey, I can swim!" as might, for example, occur if the method of dropping the child in the water has a successful outcome.

For reasons that now begin to be evident, endo learning is often hard to see. Consider the case of the infant babbling all the sounds that are physically available to it, a total corpus that usually far exceeds the limited set required by a particular language. The babbling arises from something like a biological urge that is probably part of the set of such urges that accompany being a member of our species. Certainly the babbling is not done in order to achieve a goal. It is, so to speak, a result of being pushed from behind rather than pulled from ahead, for the endo style is all past and no future. Even congenitally deaf children go through an initial period of making babbling sounds, providing evidence that the need-satisfying activity of babbling does not require what is usually called reinforcement. If any learning comes out of this babbling, it is in the form of a socially meaningful by-product, as a consequence of which the young child is enabled to become engaged in still other need-satisfying activities.

If we now ask specifically what it is that is learned in the endo style, we come up against some of the important ways in which learning styles differ. First of all, the very question of what is learned may be one that is appropriate primarily to the meso style—this being one more example of the fact that questions are often loaded so as to provide answers limited to only one or two styles. There may never be an identifiable *what* in the case of endo learning. In trying to discuss it, we may perhaps more appropriately refer to a kind of process, a shift in faith, a discovery or loss of important modes of feeling, perhaps a peak experience or a moment that is memorable as distinct from remembered. In all of this we seem to be referring not to learning in the experimental psychologist's meaning of the term but to a period of growth that is then immediately buried in the person's ongoing development.

There is an important consequence of this fact of being buried in one's development. What has been learned and is now known in the endo mode is, then, known as though it were in the bones, rather than, as in the usual (ecto) case, as though it were stored away as a memory trace of the learning. We know many things in this endo way, although we somehow ignore the important kind of learning that made it possible. For example, if you are asked which of the following alternatives is a correct phrasing in English: (A) a rural little cozy community, (B) a cozy little rural community, (C) a little cozy rural community, or (D) a little rural cozy community, you would probably have no trouble selecting B—but the way you make the choice might escape your attention. Most persons find that they have to say the phrases aloud, perhaps listen to them being said, or whisper them, or perhaps even taste them, before being sure. I suggest that resorting to these hidden sources of knowledge, as in their very taste in the mouth, suggests they are stored in hideaways other than neutral memory traces. It is as though we had learned them and now know them in our very vitals.

It would follow that in order to teach in a way that is appropriate to an endo style of learning, one has to give up the idea that there is some identifiable goal to the learning. Along with this one has to give up the even more prevalent idea that the teacher is in possession of some packet of information or skill that is to be passed from one person to another. In place of these dogmatic propositions derived from other learning styles, one starts with a quite different proposition: endo learning means not trying. Teacher and learner must now become jointly engaged in situations that satisfy the learner on grounds other than learning or reaching a goal. In effect, the teacher disappears or at the very least becomes absorbed into the whole situation, as in the common example of one's learning a new language by the immersion method; here there is no teacher as such, only a learning environment in the form of a different culture and language community. The learner then becomes continuingly engaged in situations belonging to the new culture, and the teacher appears only as someone playing an appropriate role within the environment.

If we were to design a learning method that is as completely endo as we can manage, we should not prepare some identifiable material, or test the learner in order to be sure the material is not already known, or organize the material according to some rule-directed scheme that is already known, or present the material under conditions neutral to it. Rather, we might first provide an appropriate, living model, then bring the learner and the model into significant contact, preferably a physical contact, and try to have something relevant to the learning happen between them. We might have them both participate in an ongoing situation, preferably with the learner so situated that the model's teaching would be absorbed unreflectively, almost as a by-product of some other activity. It would not do for the teacher to tell the learner what to do or not to do or even to talk about what was being done, for the *what* of the learning should not be abstracted from the situation and displayed to the learner as a kind of independent entity. That would only call forth activity of the person's ecto style.

As a result of this approach, we would have involved the learner in a kind of learning by doing, but unlike similar learning in the meso style, it would be restricted to the doing of what is naturally performed from the beginning. Endo learning is an outgrowth of what is ongoing. For this reason it is not usually well suited to the learning of artificial skills, although some aspects of the endo style may for certain persons be appropriately applied in learning any kind of skill. In endo learning both the way the learner is initially involved and the way the person is then engaged on a continuing basis are uniquely personal and must remain so. Neither part of the learning conforms to an independent *what* that is externally defined. In endo learning the learner and the teacher will define in different ways what has been learned; in ecto learning they will both know it, and probably agree on it, because it has been externally defined; and in meso learning they will come to a consensus on what has been learned in the course of working on it together. It is just because the definition is so uniquely personal in endo learning that learners will come to their own definitions. Skills that can be defined or explicated only in some artificially new way may simply not be learned. For example, material that can be defined only in abstract and nonpersonal terms, such as arithmetic operations, may be learned only with great difficulty and even accompanied by anxiety.

Consider the following example. If it happened that my father walked in a slow and stolid manner, I might grow up to walk in a very similar way. The phenomenon is familiar to students of human development under such names as imitation and identification, and it may occur with adopted children as well, that is, in the absence of genetic influence. The essential point hidden under all the labels is that as a child I would somehow have learned to walk as my father did and then would have remembered it. When I was subsequently called on to walk—that is, whenever I was in a situation appropriate to walking rather than running or sitting or standing still—my memory would serve me well, and I would then walk as my father had. I need not anticipate at this point what I will say later about the characteristics unique to endo remembering, but they surely apply to this example: the circumstances under which the original learning probably occurred, the absence of any formal teaching, the resulting inability to recall the learning process itself, the fact that at no point can I talk about what I had learned, the continuing unintended rehearsal of the act as it was learned, and finally the fact that both my original learning and any subsequent rehearsal of it would be in terms of my uniquely personal version of the model. It should also be evident that not only activities such as walking but in fact most of our customary instances of expression as well as many of the enduring aspects of our personalities, are formed and maintained in the endo style of learning and remembering. Indeed, they are often more memory than learning, for in the endo style the former is usually more potent than the latter.

Some interesting consequences follow from the characteristics that I have just referred to. For one, the results of endo learning can only with great difficulty be unlearned or forgotten or even changed in the way they are customarily carried out. In some respects they function as though they were biologically fixed action-programs—what is sometimes termed instinctive behavior—in that the mode of executing patterns is relatively fixed and unchangeable. This is why the early stages of learning a physical skill such as swimming are so important; one's mistakes tend to get built in and are often difficult to eradicate at later stages. Psychoanalytic theory of development, because it deals primarily with what is learned in the endo style, has arrived at the same conclusion. William James may have had something like this in mind when he made his famous statement that one learns to ice skate in the summer and to swim in the winter. He may have been suggesting, as I am here, that following the initial stages of endo learning one goes through ensuing periods of silent, unintended rehearsal in the body, in this way "fixing" what has been learned. In any case, since what was once learned in the endo style has become so tightly integrated with the experience of ongoing situations in which it is rehearsed, the specific form in which the learning is demonstrated cannot usually be altered unless its naturally occurring situation is also altered. Only in this way could there occur a change in feelings, motives, and experiences that have become associated with the learning. The example of learning and retaining one's particular language accent is a case in point: I could probably learn to speak Russian more easily than I could learn to speak English "naturally" with a Russian accent.

Understandably, it is very difficult to devise an approach to learning that deliberately emphasizes the endo component. On the face of it we seem to have an insoluble problem: how to get someone to learn without learning, to do without doing. The small number of instances in which something like this has been accomplished are therefore of more than passing interest. In the next chapter I will discuss a method of teaching languages that seems to be modeled rather closely on a sense of the endo learning style, perhaps the only teaching method in any discipline of which this can be said. Here I describe, not a method but a more or less accidental finding that helps us understand the endo style. Some years ago Charles Curran, a counselor interested in new approaches to helping college students, devised a method of group therapy based on classes in language learning. Reasoning that the beginning language student was in a psychological situation quite similar to that of someone beset with common neurotic symptoms—anxiety, feelings of helplessness, some depression, low self-esteem—he set up language learning groups as a simulation of the neurotic situation. One finding that emerged unexpectedly from his original study was that students who try to learn more than one language at a time are not thereby penalized but rather seem to do as well as, and often better than, those who learn only one new language at a time.[18] Since this finding runs counter to what is generally accepted in the psychology of learning, it may merit closer examination.

Evidence from many decades of learning studies supports the general proposition that two bodies of subject matter, as long as they are sufficiently similar and are learned in the same way, will provide interference if one attempts to learn them both at the same time. One's performance on both will suffer. For this reason students are usually advised not to begin the study of two new languages at the same time. Since the learning style usually studied in learning research, and certainly the learning style that is emphasized in school settings, is some combination of meso and ecto, with very little admixture of the endo, we may accept these findings as applicable to meso-ecto learning. What is meant here by interference, then, is a cognitive interference, in which discrete elements from one source cannot be made to occupy the same position in an overall plan as elements from another source. What this immediately suggests is that if you want to assist learning in the endo mode, you should make ecto-meso learning difficult by creating interference or by some other method. This is, in fact, what the linguist Stephen Krashen has proposed, although not in exactly this terminology. He distinguishes between a mode of language development he calls learning, by which he means rule-directed, cognitively organized, ecto activity, and another mode he calls acquisition, which is much closer to what I have been calling endo learning. He then suggests that the simplest way to "enforce" acquisition is by presenting material too fast for normal cognitive skills to be used,[19] that is, by inhibiting the use of an ecto learning style.

To return to Curran's finding, we seem to have here a situation that makes possible the student's use of an endo style of learning. In the sense that we usually understand it in learning theory, interference probably cannot occur in the endo style. The style does not concern itself with elements that are systematically arranged according to some independent and rule-determined plan, but rather enables the learner to become immersed in a meaningful "soup" of impressions. These will reinforce each other rather than interfere, at least as long as their significant aspects all share the same feeling tone. If Curran's approach produced this sort of result, aiding rather than inhibiting learning in what would normally be an interference situation, we might suppose it was because the approach emphasized an endo style of learning.

And this is what we see on examination. Curran's learners are accepted into a highly supportive group situation in which their anxieties, individual as well as common, become a focus of concern. In their initial stages of learning they rely heavily on the services of a "guide" who remains behind them, ready to supply translations of what they hear as well as appropriate responses that they may then imitate. The guide is a skilled and helpful alter ego who takes up their burden and provides the cognitive skills they may need, thus removing from them the pressure to gain these skills or to reach a goal. By virtue of this arrangement, they can at the beginning remain comfortably floundering in a situation in which they simply absorb the atmosphere of the new languages, with the situation fitted to them rather than the reverse. If they now experience at the same time more than one such atmosphere, so much the better for their learning, for their immersion experience will be that much the richer. In many ways, theirs is the pyschological situation of the infant learning its native tongue.

In addition, as we can now see, the key element is the goal. It is the very lack of this element that distinguishes endo learning from other modes, for in endo learning there is no goal as such. If you are dropped into the water as a child in the rather unfortunate method sometimes used to "teach" you how to swim, you do not adopt as your goal the swimming of a hundred yards, nor do you try to do any particular thing as such. Rather, you flounder until you either panic and cry for help or, if the learning is successful, you find yourself feeling more comfortable, more at home in this swimming situation. To fully understand endo learning we must give up the notion of directed, goal-oriented activity, and we must attend more carefully to the meaning of the term *situation*. In the present example, what it means can be expressed only in a hyphenated phrase on the order of agglutinative languages. It is: being-in-the-water-unsupported-and-having-to-remain-afloat-and-breathing. The first stage of endo learning, then, consists in the person feeling temporarily at home in this or an analogous situation; normally the other stages of endo learning will then flow organically out of ongoing activity and satisfaction in the situation.

LEARNING: THE MESO MODE

The meso deed is always a fight for space, for like an object, one meso deed cannot occupy the same space as another. Ecto events, being immaterial, can and do occupy spaces together; they appear and disappear at will. Endo acts will fuse together and be mutually absorbed. But the meso "kill" that occurs

on their meeting is not a form of aggression and may occur without anger—
unless the meso actor's tie to deed and target is broken. Then the warrior's
kill turns into sadism, in which the target is experienced as no more than an
object.

Meso learning is done through physical action or an analogue of action—through practice, through forcing the issue continuously by means of direct questioning, often through concrete demonstrations to oneself and to others as to what has been learned.

From the point of view of the learner in the meso style, the critical issue is: How can I find out? How can I master this question, overcome this gap in my knowledge, or get through this obstacle of not-knowing? The unknown is not sensed as a provocative puzzle, as in the ecto mode, nor as a mysteriously ill-defined boundary area, as in the endo mode, but as the literal presence of a block, a hindrance, or a gap that can be overcome with some effort. The common expression "writer's block" derives from the meso style and may in fact be incorrect as a description of the situation of many writers. The answer that comes back to the meso learner will be something like: I will work at it. I will try to find out. I will search out the answer. I will make a greater effort so as to pass through the gap. Behind such answers is the conviction that if the question was asked, it was because there was indeed something "out there" to be worked at in this manner. If it is there, waiting to be encountered, I will manage to attain it through my effort, my will and persistence, through the grit and striving that always overcomes known obstacles.

In the meso mode there are therefore no unanswerable questions. If a question can be phrased sensibly, it can be answered; which leads to the typically meso advice to frame one's difficulties in the form of questions so as to be able to overcome them. One consequence is that those who typically learn in the meso style are unable to question their own questions. They take their methodology for granted and are unable to grasp the possibility that other methods, hence other questions, might recast the problem in quite different ways. Often they appear to ecto learners as relatively simpleminded and unsophisticated. One model of the meso learner is the prisoner trying to break out of jail. Here the emphasis is on *it*, right there, which because it is there can be breached.

The emphasis is not on *I* coming to terms with the problem in all its ramifications, as it would be in the ecto mode, nor on the self-object situation as in the endo mode. For the meso an important part of this *it* is the specific activity that gets the learning done. This is what the meso learner is most often aware of, the active process by which the learning takes place. Thus, the meso learner is able to demonstrate his or her learning to the teacher as a concrete fact, and so this style of learning lends itself well to periodic examinations. One of the meso's most important ways of learning, of course, is by means of rehearsal; therefore, practice is heavily emphasized in this style.

An equally important aspect of meso learning is the clear presence of an end or goal that attaches to the conclusion of the learning and is an integral part of it. Meso-oriented theories of animal learning, for this reason, refer to goals as a central aspect of the learning process, even though such theories are usually unable to conceptualize the organization of behavior around an event that has not yet taken place. If the endo learner is driven as though in the teeth of a wind, the meso learner is occupied with a goal that is immediately up ahead. We should note that meso goals are not grand, overarching, or in the distant future but relatively close, well articulated, and both practical and attainable. They serve as focal points around which the learner may organize what it is that is to be learned, hence what the learning is all about.

This in turn tells us something about how meso learners may act in concert. Whenever the situation is so organized that its meso aspects— for example, the goal or what is to be achieved—predominate, meso learners can get along well. What happens is that they find they can work together, which is what the meso style primarily demands. Recently Ted Turner, a millionaire American entrepreneur, and Fidel Castro, the revolutionary Cuban leader, found that they got along together famously, which is understandable since both are predominantly meso in orientation and style. Just as mesos like each other if they can work together, so ectos like each other if they discover a community of ideas and endos like each other if they appeal to one another personally. The moral would seem to be that if the need is for workmates, meso should mate with meso, but if the need is to get along with one another, meso or endo should team up with endo. The ecto may well cause trouble in almost any personal arrangement unless it is structured as less of a relationship than a partnership—for example, of two scholars.

Since the meso style is so heavily involved with doing, I seem to be discussing that activity rather than learning in its own right. This cannot be helped, since the endo and ecto styles are so much more attached to those first stages in behavior that we call learning. Thus it will happen that learning takes place in other than a meso style but that the activity or performance itself, through which the continuing presence of the learning is demonstrated, remains meso. We can see this in the case of animal learning, which as I have begun to suggest is probably endo, whether the learning happens naturally in the wild state or artificially in the laboratory. However, once the activity has become established as a performance, it will continue to be practiced unless it drops away from disuse; it will become in effect part of the animal's repertoire and habitually performed. As habit, it is then behavior in the meso style, and this is probably what sustains it.

To sum up, meso learning is one form of energetic work, and so it happens best when circumstances favor the expending of energy in rapid or intense bursts. Every aspect of the situation is then turned into what is immediate, concrete, and real, rather than what can be thought or talked about or what can be absorbed at the personal speed of the participants. Meso learning, like all organized work, can and should be fitted to the requirements of a known schedule. Because it is most effective when it is thus engineered, the meso style need not depend on the effect of a human teacher. Hence the great success of teaching machines or computer programs, at least for material that can be fitted to the machines' demands and restrictions. The teaching machine, which if not Skinner's invention is at least Skinner's child in education, turns learning into a well-engineered program for carrying out small jobs. Each of the jobs is organized, labeled, and fitted into its proper logical and temporal niche in a schedule. Each must then be completed successfully before the learner proceeds to the next job, exactly as in the case of putting a car together on an assembly line or building a house with the skills of different craftsmen.

Scheduling, in the manner that the teaching machine enforces it, in turn permits one to set up concrete and realizable goals and to provide feedback at each step. The notion of feedback, especially in the guise of reinforcement, is of central importance for the meso learning style, as Skinner has been at great pains to show. It is of minimal importance in ecto learning, for there is not much here that can be fed back—not results, because more often than not they simply lead on to further issues and problems, and not satisfactions, because these are rarely either intense or significant in the ecto style. Nor is feedback of great importance in the endo style, for the process is not known reflectively to the learner and the results would therefore be meaningless rather than helpful. But the meso learner functions best under conditions of knowing where in relation to a known goal the process of learning is situated at each moment. It is the goal that organizes meso learning, as distinct from the situation and the feelings or memories it evokes in endo learning, or the knowledgeable teacher and the coherent set of ideas in ecto learning.

For the true meso learner, then, teachers work best when they are either equivalent to the learners—as in the case of the peers who function as instructors in the Dartmouth language learning system discussed in chapter 4—or when their equivalence is irrelevant, as in the case of the teaching machine. But the teacher, peer or not, is neither responsible for nor a model of how the material is organized. That model follows the simplest of all abstract principles, the idea of unity. All the steps in the meso learning process are, as nearly as possible, arranged so as to be equal units. It is then assumed that the simple additive sum of the units of learning, the steps toward the goal, equals the goal.

For all the reasons I have been discussing, meso learning works best when it takes the form of drill and practice, just as though the learners were already in the grip of a learned habit. It may be for this reason that the military, built almost entirely around meso ideals, is so enamored of repetitive drill in all its activities. One-shot meso learning is for obvious reasons rare, just as it is in the learning of a physical skill; on the other hand, the idea of a learning curve in the case of meso learning makes sense, with its gradual accretion of equivalent units toward an identifiable end point.

In all these respects as well, meso learning conforms to the picture of the learning process that we can abstract from work in experimental psychology, from the time of Ebbinghaus[20] to the most recent laboratory studies. According to this picture, learning is based on units and comes about in the manner of a physical skill, with repeated trials leading toward the gradual elimination of errors and the achieving of a smooth, unthinking performance. Once this point on the learning curve has been reached, the performance may be repeated indefinitely and will not change in any appreciable degree. It then functions like a long-established habit whose origins are now forgotten.

Once the goal has been reached, meso learning can be interfered with in three major ways, each of the ways corresponding to a characteristic of one of the learning styles. It can become rusty due to lack of practice, which is the equivalent of a meso lapse; or it can become less useful or even fail if one thinks about it instead of doing it (as in the well-known instance of the centipede that began to think about which leg to move first), which would constitute an ecto lapse; or it can fail because the learner has become overinvolved in the doing of it, as when one tries too hard, which would be an endo lapse.

LEARNING: THE ECTO MODE

A Harvard physicist named David Nelson had this to say when asked what he got out of working on a project: "The main satisfaction we're getting from this crystal work is the intellectual excitement. For me that's plenty. Isn't that really the driving force of science?"

Any treatment of ecto learning is bound to be redundant. Because the heart of the ecto style resides in such mental processes as thinking and knowing, both learning and remembering have usually been considered merely as subcategories included within ecto thinking and knowing—whereas what I am saying in this book is just the reverse, that the processes defining the ecto style make up only one of the possible subcategories of learning and remembering. The generally accepted view, that learning is self-evidently an ecto function, is deeply embedded in our culture and is in fact one of the foundational assumptions of the discipline of psychology.

At the risk of repeating what I have said in earlier pages, I may present a general statement about ecto learning. It begins with some question about ideas or concepts and not, as in the endo mode, with a personally felt riddle or problem or, as in the meso mode, with a goal that is sensed as somewhere up ahead. In the ecto mode one starts with what is appropriately called an intellectual concern; it might often be called, as well, an intellectual delight. At times the question arises because of a gap in one's thinking, as in: "But if this is so, how can it be that . . . ?" The question, as we see, may be of interest for its own sake, since it may have its own niche in the organized structure of one's thoughts and ideas.

These characteristics arise in turn out of a basic feature of the ecto style, that in it one thinks "at a distance" rather than in immediately concrete terms; that is, by way of symbols, abstractions, or other forms of mediation rather than being in touch with a presented world of action or a surrounding world of felt situations. Ecto learning, like other activities carried out in this style, is learning through the central nervous system and so takes on the characteristics of that system, a major one of which is to work with secondhand data. Our external sensory organs are in firsthand contact with energy sources in the physical environment, but the central nervous system is a once-removed processor of that energy. In this sense we say that what transpires in the central nervous system or on the model of its functioning is always at some distance. Another consequence of this arrangement is that the central nervous system is, so to speak, neutral in respect to its information. Whatever passes through it is processed in the same terms, in more or less equivalent bursts. For the ecto style, then, there are no wholes but only neutrally ordered parts, and for the person behaving in the ecto style, the whole is always subject to analysis; the global always carries some implication of being vague.

Lacking a means of direct contact, the ecto style involves one in dealing with representations of the world, in contrast with, say, being actively involved in the world. Even in meso learning there occurs a true activity of learning, and even in endo learning some activity in the form of change and growth follows on its engagement with the felt consequences of situations. But in ecto learning one first knows about something even before one may have actually dealt with it—a curious state of affairs that is difficult to explicate. We notice, first, that because there is no somatic investment when one learns in the ecto style, the ecto learner is not changed by the learning. This is in direct contrast with the other styles: the endo, in which learning is almost identified with change, and the meso, in which change gets built into the body in the form of habit patterns. Because there is no direct contact with what precipitated the learning and subsequently no change in the person as the learning takes effect, it can be said that the ecto learner does not actually deal with what is learned. The situation may be described in these terms: in ecto learning one leaps ahead in order to learn about something, this being followed in turn by a kind of "certification" in retrospect. If there is a motto that applies to this procedure, it would be "Leap before you look." That is, the way to learn something in the ecto style is to report to yourself what you already know that you know, and then tell yourself how you know it. Let your body catch up with your mind.

Only if one begins in this way is it possible to be faithful to the central ecto feature of keeping the question at a distance. One first transforms the question situation into symbolic form, then manipulates the symbols. But we should keep in mind that my language here is less than precise, since the term "manipulate" implies a kind of direct contact. Although contact is absent, one manipulates the object of thought— and note that in the realm of concrete action there can be no analogous manipulation without contact. The ecto realm is not one of such concrete action, of the physical in contact with the physical, but rather of the symbolic and the unreal, a realm of abstractions that at best represents the real world. In such a realm it is possible to leap ahead and have hold of some target that is not yet grasped.

Learning in this mode is truly an exercise in unhampered control, much in the manner of the pure brain so often depicted in science fiction fantasies or in newer versions in which the bodiless artificial intelligence of the computer is hooked up to substitute for the bodiless artificial intelligence of the pure brain. Control in the ecto realm is absolutely limitless. In the meso realm, as we well know, the world is ever present and is experienced as resistive to our biologically determined limits. In the endo realm one pays a price for control in the necessity to first absorb whatever one has to deal with. Indeed, the ecto learner is so far removed, at least in principle, from the real world of what is encountered and overcome, absorbed and rejected, that it is hard for us to conceive of ordinary behavior being done in an ecto style. It may be hard, too, for the person whose style is predominantly ecto; such a person tends to be awkward and uncoordinated in physical actions.

Adrift in a realm of unfettered control, there then occurs, as a matter of cold, hard fact, no control at all, and so the ecto is usually a poor learner, often a learner who is derisively called a dreamer. The major problem facing an ecto learner is an inability to let things in. Such persons therefore make poor waiters or waitresses, because this is an activity that urgently requires an openness to others' demands and needs. The ecto learner might easily grasp rules of grammar in a new language but would not "hear" the new sounds that make for an appropriate accent. In general, immersion situations, in which one is dropped into a novel setting and literally forced to learn rapidly, would be felt as an unpleasant nuisance, whether in regard to language learning or swimming. But give the ecto learner a chance to grasp material in what is felt as an appropriate manner and, as we see in school classrooms, learning can be most impressive. This will be true even in situations that one might not ordinarily connect with ecto concerns, such as food preparation. Some of the best chefs are ecto; only their clients have to behave endo.

In an ecto mode, to know is to have learned. This phrase may require some additional explanation. I have taken it from Gilbert Ryle's[21] discussion of perception, in which he makes use of Aristotle's observation, "To see is to have seen." The observation refers to the fact that if I see something, the act of perception is completed in the very act of seeing. There is no ongoing process I can identify that then culminates in an act of seeing. That act is itself an endpoint, or a completion without a prior process leading up to it. To see is simply to have finished seeing. In an elaborately developed example, Ryle compares the act of perception with the apparently similar act of running a race and then shows that they are very different. To win a race is to complete the process we call running a race, and there is no way that one can do the former without having at an earlier time been involved in the latter. His point is that we can distinguish two major categories of acts. The first, of which perception is the prototype and ecto learning an excellent example, consists of a terminus without a prior process leading up to it. The second, of which memory is the prototype, consists of a process leading to its conclusion; running a race or a judge trying and then deciding a case are excellent examples of this category. Ecto learning, then, is more like perception than like memory, and endo learning is just the reverse. Meso learning partakes of some of the elements of both categories.

It follows that the ecto learner can *un*-learn as easily as the original act of learning and that forgetting is a legitimate aspect of all ecto remembering. In the endo mode, on the other hand, and in the meso mode to a certain degree, forgetting really has no place. The ecto learner *has* some new knowledge and therefore can lose it, whereas the endo and meso learners *are* their new knowledge, for they represent it and have been changed by it to become the persons they now are. And since ecto learning is a form of perception, it is often heavily influenced by history and culture, as is perception, whereas endo and meso learning are more apt to be influenced by the circumstances of an individual life, just as is memory.

It is understandable that ecto learning is most relevant for organizing ideas. The ecto realm is where theorizing begins and ends. In endo learning, by contrast, an overarching structure is not possible, and there will be little expectation that the results of one's thinking can be brought together in one coherent whole. In meso thinking one's efforts are organized around goals, usually immediate or relatively short-term, and only an ecto effort, superimposed on the meso activity, will enable the goals to be organized into some larger structure. It is therefore ecto learning and thinking that provide us with structures of thought. Ecto thinking is really about such structures, and ecto learning then becomes the activity of filling in gaps in the structures.

Like all ecto processes, ecto learning takes place in terms of symbols and in this sense is unreal. We can perhaps understand something of the status of symbols if we consider briefly some products resulting from the three styles—words and thoughts in the ecto style, acts in the meso style, and expressive movements or gestures in the endo style. All are alike in that they are transient. They appear briefly, for the purposes of the moment, and then are gone forever once the purpose has been taken care of. All occur quite rapidly as well, and their recipient does not usually have time to consider them carefully. But although they are similar in these important ways, they also differ. Two significant characteristics are to be found only in ecto words and thoughts. The first is the intangibility of thoughts, and the second is the arbitrariness of words; both the ecto characteristics tend to make ecto activity less "real," less easily grasped or handled in a physical sense.

An example that may highlight this point is given in Roger Shattuck's moving account of the education of the feral child Victor, the so-called Wild Boy of Aveyron.[22] Shattuck notes that the boy's chief teacher, Dr. Itard, reports that he could never get Victor to understand a spoken word. This failing was particularly significant since Victor clearly understood the meaning of a tone of voice and of many bodily actions and gestures. It appeared that Victor had an intelligence of the body, and so it may be asked: what did he lack beyond this? What was it that Victor would have needed in order to understand spoken words? I suggest that in order to be able to make sounds into words, to receive sounds and process them into words and so perceive them as verbal communications, one needs the capacity to go beyond the given, the concrete, the immediate. The spoken word, in and of itself, carries no meaning-content. It is only a brief and arbitrary sound that we humans, by virtue of our being members of a particular language community, can know as one or another meaning.

B. F. Skinner has often referred to our shared realm of meanings as a "verbal community," and this touches precisely on the point. It is our membership in a community of shared meanings that makes it possible for us to know, on apprehending a certain sound, that this sound "is" this or that word, carrying this or that meaning. Unless we are able to take the first step of making contact with a community of meanings— that is, unless we succeed to some ecto grasp of these unreal entities— as Victor, for whatever reason, was not, we will not come to make linguistic use of the sounds that we hear. They will not be carriers of meaning for us but will remain merely the sounds of the world coming at us and often intruding on us.

We cannot usually access the moment or the situation in a young child's life when there occurs the first grasp of the notion of meaning, as distinct from the idea of sounds. Fortunately, we have a report of such a moment in Helen Keller's[23] account of that day when, as she says, she first realized that the "things" of the world, everything she could feel and sense, were linked, one by one, to representations in words. As sighted and hearing persons could tell her, the link resides in the bonds of meaning between thing and word. In Keller's story, she felt the cold water on her face at the moment her teacher spelled out the word on her palm, and in that instant she realized that the movement-word *was* in some way the water—or, as we would say, the symbol or representative of the water. More important, and even world-shaking in its significance for her, was her sudden realization that there was such a movement-word for everything that could be discriminated in her world. This was the moment she first stepped into the ecto realm, the truly human realm.

Another example concerning Victor, from Shattuck's detailed account of his learning struggles, will indicate the way the boy failed to achieve an ecto style. (We should note that ecto thinkers are as well able to learn from failures, from negations, from lapses and absences as they are from victories, from gains, and from what is indubitably present.) On one occasion Victor did actually manage to articulate the French word *lait*, meaning milk. But in reporting on this incident, Itard, who was a very perceptive observer, noted that the achievement was by no means as striking as it seemed. The reason, as he pointed out, was that one may use a word in two different ways, relating to two quite different modes of behavior. One may say the word in advance of the act, "signifying a need or desire," that is, talking about something that is not actually present. On the other hand, one may say the word at approximately the moment the act occurs—in this case, at the moment that Victor received the milk—which would signify at best a "happy association." As we know, many animals are capable of making connections between a discriminable event and an otherwise arbitrary signal, as for example to bark when the trainer's hand is raised or when someone says the word "Speak!" Some animals can go one step more and seem to "ask for" something by making their own sounds. The family dog, for example, may train itself to produce its specific "I want to go out" bark in order to get someone to open the door.

But there appears to be a point beyond which this connection between sound and event cannot be stretched. The dog, no matter how intelligent or well trained, has no way to indicate that it will be wanting to go out a few hours later—even if we could assume that it was capable of holding such a thought. In order to produce its bark as a message, the dog must already be close in time and space to the act of going out, for example, being blocked only by the temporarily closed door or else being attracted by some sound or smell on the other side of the door. A number of writers have made the same point in regard to the level of language available to chimpanzees in the wild. They appear to be capable of standing around in a group while sharing a meal and, by means of their vocalizations, saying something to each other that is the equivalent of, "Oh, this is good. These are certainly tender shoots." However, they appear to be incapable of standing in a group and saying to one another, "That was a good meal of shoots we had here last week," concerning an event now distant in time, or else, "Do you suppose the shoots are more tender up around the bend of the river?" concerning a possible event that is distant in space. Their "talk" is very much like their breathing—a complex responsiveness to the major features of an immediately present situation. Unlike human speech, which is largely ecto and may serve as a distancing mechanism, the speech of these animals is usually a device for bonding the group together. It is an endo and not an ecto function.

It is a small gap but one that is impassable for some creatures, between a kind of sound-making or vocalization and true speech as it is shown in humans. The former is often seen in the case of the pet parrot that can elaborate its vocalizations into sounds that resemble those made by humans; this is what Victor did when he mouthed the word *lait* on being presented with a glass of milk. But performance of this sort is limited. Its boundaries are determined as a function of the endo mode, then marked out by the attentional processes that underlie perception. The function of such processes, in fact, may be to establish the limits of situations within which associations can be formed and the animal's intelligence then exercised.

This set of limits is set by the animal's immediate responsiveness to a felt situation. But as the case of the family dog shows, more extended limits may be set by the use of meso functions, and the endo boundaries will then be stretched beyond the perceptible. For example, the dog that is eagerly waiting, even straining, to go outside for its regular evening walk appears to be pointed at the door, even "through" the door. In this instance a more extended boundary, embracing more time or more space, has been formed as a consequence of the animal being caught up in an action sequence whose end result or goal it already knows. One might say that an intelligence of action, a meso function, has extended the boundaries of the animal's situation. Its bark now refers, not only to what is within the limits of the perceptible, but beyond that to limits of an action sequence with which it is now occupied. But as Victor showed, the important difference here is between situations or modes of activity that are limited to endo and meso functions, and symbol-using modes of activity that give rise to ecto intelligence. Only the latter are excarnated.

To think and especially to learn in the ecto style, one must keep a distance between one's conduct and the target of one's learning. The target may perhaps be bathed in the cold light of "intellectual curiosity" but nothing more of the human or the personal. It is as neutral and separated as it can be, in a space in which any movement or even nonmovement is possible, in a time that is timeless and ahistorical. Where anything is possible, nothing has value. The entities populating such a space and time are called *facts*, which are the ecto equivalent of what in our everyday world of action we call things. The fact is child of the theory, which is the major structural member out of which the ecto realm is fashioned.

In the pure world of the ecto learner and thinker, this is all there is to work with: theories, their related propositions, and finally decisions concerning just what, in a world in flux, are to constitute the units called facts. Manipulated in their own unreal domain, the facts if organized into a coherent pattern are then assumed to make up a true picture of what things are like in the world. What the ecto learner has learned in this way is now known *about*, in contrast with the learning that occurs in the meso style, in which one can immediately repeat back what has been learned as though it had been practiced, and in even greater contrast with the endo learner who knows in a dogmatic sense and whose knowing is therefore a form of prejudice, a completed passion.

To conclude this discussion of ecto learning, we may ask whether it has anything to tell us regarding animal learning, particularly learning that is experimentally manipulated and studied in the laboratory.

In the normal development of a predator such as a lion, the cub begins its life with ready access to nourishment that is brought to it or that requires very little movement on its part. Then as it begins to grow, the food that is available to it may only be obtained at greater and greater distances. The cub must bestir itself, move toward its mother, follow her, sometimes race to get ahead of the other cubs in the pride, and finally walk appreciable distances in order to get to the carcass that is the pride's food for the day. In the cub's experience locomotion thus comes to be associated with the obtaining of food and the satisfying of its hunger, just as though it now had a motto, "If you want to eat, you have to walk." The results of this associative learning are quite evident in the hunting behavior of the adult lioness and in the pacing of the hungry lion in a zoo when its hunting movements have been aborted.

Associative learning forms a major part of the normal experience of every motile animal. Curiously, however, it remained for a scientist at the end of the nineteenth century, Ivan Pavlov, to turn this fact to theoretical advantage. In his well known experiments with dogs he began with an associative connection already in the animal's repertoire—in this case, salivating at the odor of food—and arranged that a quite different and arbitrarily selected event would occur at the same time. In the vocabulary of learning psychology, he paired an unconditioned response, the salivating, with a new stimulus, the ringing of a bell. The result was that the dog now salivated to the ringing of the bell, just as it would normally salivate to the presentation of food— and just as the lion in the normal course of growing up in the wild learns to substitute patterns of hunting for earlier activities of walking for food.

When we describe associative learning in this way, its resemblance to endo behavior comes clear. Like all endo behavior it arises naturally out of the arousal and satisfaction of normally occurring needs. Within the situation in which the need is satisfied, day after day and year after year in the animal's life, more and more events or aspects of the environment may become encompassed within the animal's sphere of relevance, some of them perhaps arbitrary or even unique to the individual. This is certainly how the family dog learns that its daily meal is forthcoming when a specific human comes through the front door in the late afternoon. But what never changes as far as the animal is concerned is that a need is satisfied within a familiar situation.

We see this in the behavior of animals that have been conditioned according to the Pavlovian paradigm. Their behavior remains directed primarily toward what satisfies the current need, in this case the food, with the result that the behavior associated with the new stimulus remains, as it were, on the periphery of their action. The dog conditioned to salivate at the sound of a bell attends to the possible presentation of food, not to the bell, and the chimpanzee conditioned in a similar fashion to make certain sign language movements with its hand in order to "ask for" a food reward attends to the reward, not to the hand or to the donor of the reward. Just as the hungry lion, pacing in its cage, is abortively engaged in obtaining food, so the trained dog or chimpanzee is attending to and aiming toward the food. Pavlov's great discovery, it would appear, was simply that behavior in the endo style involves a complex intelligence and so is susceptible of far more elaboration than had ever been thought. In the experimental paradigm it substitutes for ecto learning, as it may in the wild as well.

4

Remembering Language

Ecto buzz words include: creativity, stimulation, imagination, theoretical, fantasy, inner life, causality, and such phrases as: Is it possible? What if? Meso buzz words include: will, initiative, action, grit, persistence, effort, determination, goal, ingenuity, and skill. Endo buzz words, harder to find, might include: passion, global, accept.

MEMORY IN PSYCHOLOGICAL THEORY

The treatment of the topic of memory in modern psychology has, I will argue, followed the sequence: ecto, then meso, then endo. That is to say, from the time of Aristotle until the beginnings of experimental psychology in the late nineteenth century and then into the 1950s, psychological theory concerning memory has concentrated on its ecto characteristics. During this period the meso or endo functions that might have participated in activities of remembering were simply ignored. Then, in a surge of interest that led to the reevaluation of old problems, memory was rediscovered during the 1950s; or specifically, the meso mode of remembering was attended to for the first time. Still more recently—and thus far only minimally explored—the possibilities of the endo mode began to enter psychological theory.

My discussion of the three modes of memory in this chapter will therefore begin with a brief history of the traditional (that is, ecto) investigations, then summarize some of the work within the meso mode, and finally try to spell out some of the implications for endo memory to be found in the most recent work. I will apply these conclusions to the topic of how one learns one's native language and remembers it so well and what this has to tell us about learning a second language. The chapter will conclude with a section on the use of the three styles in teaching second languages.

It is generally agreed that the modern experimental treatment of the topic of memory began with the innovative and ingenious studies of his own cognitive processes by a German teacher and amateur scientist, Herman Ebbinghaus, in the 1880s.[1] He found a practical way of studying what had seemed until then an ineffable subject matter, his own memory processes. To do so he had to devise a method, invent his own measuring techniques, and even create a new unit of measurement. His approach consisted, in brief, of memorizing his material while keeping track of how many trials this required, and then at some later time testing himself on what he had retained by ascertaining how many trials were now required to re-memorize the same material to its original state. If, for example, he had originally needed twenty-two trials to memorize certain lists to a given standard—such as being able to recite the lists three times without error—he would then wait one hour, or one day, or one week, and attempt to re-learn the same material. If he now needed fewer trials to memorize the lists to the same criterion of performance, the improvement could be assumed to be a consequence of having remembered the original lists. He called this the *method of savings*. By its use he was able to show that the curve of forgetting, in which the amount of material retained (or "saved") was plotted as a function of the passage of time since its first learning, dropped off sharply at first but then gradually leveled out at some minimal level. The seemingly ineffable process of remembering, presumably hidden in the mind's operations, had now been subjected to exact and objective measurement.

One of Ebbinghaus's most valuable contributions was his invention of the "nonsense syllable" as the unit of material to be retained, or lost, and counted. Reasoning that if he used meaningful material as the subject matter for his studies, there would be no way to chop it into equal units nor any way to assure that the material would not vary in familiarity and affect his results, he invented a kind of artificial word. It consisted of a consonant-vowel-consonant combination randomly put together—for example, *zog* or *tis*—to resemble a word in structure yet have no apparent meaning.

These experiments produced, to psychology's great benefit, a number of important conclusions regarding memory, as well as establishing the possibility of studying such processes in the manner of the natural sciences. Much of the theorizing about memory that has taken place since Ebbinghaus's day has consisted of attempts to explain these and more lately acquired facts. But his findings were necessarily constrained within certain assumptions, for as we are all now aware, and as Thomas Kuhn[2] has shown in elegant fashion, theory as well as method is always founded on some form of implicit proto-theory. The latter is then revealed to scientists of a later era as a collection of unspoken assumptions, self-evident precisely because it is known unreflectively. This has been continuingly and almost painfully true of the past century's work on memory, beginning with the contributions by Ebbinghaus.

The unexamined assumptions concerning memory and how it functions were those inherited from the commonsense wisdom of his day, going back at least to the writings of Aristotle. In this view memory consists of the reception, the storage, and the later recovery of material. Something is impressed on us, it is stored away as an impression, and it is then recovered by being brought out from storage when needed. The most familiar situation analogous to this arrangement is the library and its workings. Here a book is received by the library, put in its proper place on a shelf, and at a later time brought out when requested by a patron. In all, this proto-theory accords perfectly with our commonsense view of how remembering operates.

In the terminology favored by contemporary theorists, this sequence consists of, first, a process of encoding (or information processing), then storage, and finally retrieval. The two major forms of retrieval are recall, in which one deliberately brings something to mind (or remembers in an active sense), and recognition, in which one identifies the memorized material when presented with it. Recognition is appreciably the more sensitive method of the two, as we demonstrate for example in our ability to recognize a familiar face after a lapse of decades. Recall, on the other hand, is the more useful of the two methods since it can be brought into action almost at will.

As psychology has always recognized, memory and learning are closely linked. If we learn something, we usually remember it, so that learning then serves as a first step in the process of remembering. If we do not remember it at all there is then no evidence we have ever learned it, since the only test of whether learning has occurred is some evidence that what was learned was subsequently remembered. However, even though learning always has to be assessed through some form of memory, the test is not yet logically complete. If memory is demonstrated, learning must have occurred, but if memory is not demonstrated, the question of whether or not learning had originally occurred remains unsettled.

Because of the close links between learning and memory, much of what was said in chapter 3 concerning modes of learning is also applicable here. Thus, we may say that the proto-theory of memory that one finds in traditional psychological thinking consists of a description of the ecto style. It is concerned entirely with neutral units of memorized material in the form of value-free content closely resembling the symbols and abstractions of ecto-type thought. The currently fashionable concept of *metamemory*[3] takes the similarity one step further in postulating "mechanisms" that enable one to interrogate the contents of one's own memory, much in the manner of ecto thought processes that manipulate various mental content. Just as in the case of ecto learning, what I have remembered is what I now have, not what I now am, for I am no more defined by the contents of my memory store than a library is defined by some of the books on its shelves.

Another Style of Remembering

Within the last few decades this emphasis on an ecto mode of remembering has come under very serious criticism, particularly in regard to the aspect of encoding. Much evidence has accumulated to indicate that encoding is not simply the passive reception of stimuli but is rather an active process of organizing incoming material. A first step in this active process is what is called "chunking," in which the input is "naturally" broken into meaningful parts. In addition, as Tulving and his associates[4] have shown, these chunks are usually formed of "associative clusters," or groupings of items and details according to their similarity of meaning. As an example, if subjects are given lists of ordinary words to remember and then recall at a later date, they can be assisted in their later recall by the use of other words as cues.

If the word to be recalled from a list is "chair," the subjects will be better assisted by a word associated with it (such as "table") than by a word with no such associative connection—even though the word "table" was not on the original list to be memorized. What seems to happen, at least in one explanation, is that the word "chair" is not just passively received and stored away but is somehow processed in terms of its belongingness in clusters of meaning.

A more direct demonstration of what goes into the encoding process was furnished in the now classic study of Bransford and Franks[5] in which subjects are presented with a string of simple and unrelated sentences such as: "The car climbed the hill" or "The big cat jumped through the window." Subjects are not told that some sentences are related in the sense that they form parts of the description of a complete event, or that other sentences are unrelated to the events and may even be contradictory to the events. But even though they are never given this important information about the individual sentences, subjects have no difficulty, nor hesitation, in figuring it out for themselves and then making use of it. Instructed to do no more than listen to the sentences, they appear to "naturally" organize them in the ways just described. As a result, they correctly identify those sentences that "belong" to the larger events, the sentences that might logically belong even though they were never given in the original list, and the sentences that could not logically belong—and all this without having been instructed to this end but simply asked to listen to the sentences. Apparently what we hear when a string of details comes to us is not a sequence of unrelated, meaningless, or neutral units—as one theory would have it—but a progressively built, coherent, and meaningful composite. In this way we make sense out of what we hear even when the experimenter has arranged that there be no sense in the material.

Such experiments give subjects a chance to do what earlier experiments on memory never allowed them to do—to construct events and situations rather than simply memorize details. It turns out that Ebbinghaus had not only restricted his own remembering processes but had arranged to have generations of experimenters and subjects restricted in the same way. Thus, in studies with children in Russian schools the following arrangement was designed:[6] a first group of children would be observed while on the playground and the different activities in which they spontaneously engaged would be recorded. Later in the laboratory setting, these children would be tested for recall of the activities by asking them to repeat what they had done earlier. A second group of children would be given a list of the activities done by the first group and, having memorized the list, would be taken out on the playground and asked to do all they remembered from the list. Given this distinction between doing-followed-by-redoing and memorizing-followed-by-doing, the advantage in terms of memory was significantly in favor of the former; and a similar advantage was shown between a group tested by doing-followed-by-doing *versus* a group tested by memorizing-followed-by-verbal-recall.

These studies, taken together, begin to suggest that another mode of memory, if it is only allowed to appear, can operate efficiently in its own right. It is an active mode, similar to the processes that take place in the course of developing a motor skill and perhaps underlying the acquisition of such skills; it may therefore appropriately be termed meso memory. Like the meso style of learning, this kind of remembering requires that the person be actively engaged in an ongoing situation and be permitted, even encouraged, to make sense out of the situation, to become involved in it, even to take some first steps toward constituting the situation as personally significant.

TWO KINDS OF MEMORY

If you have misplaced something, send the endo to look for it. The ecto will look all around it and even through it but, guided by an image that may not be correct, is just as likely to fail to see it; whereas the meso may look too hard and so overlook it. But the endo will be able to pick it out, if it is there, in part because the endo's perceptual processes do not imply a context or surround. For this reason the endo is not distracted by context or by intrusive details; and also for this reason may appear in other situations as stubborn.

Developmental Studies

As these developments in memory research were occurring, another set of writers, these of a more clinical bent, seem to have arrived at a convergence of views regarding two major categories of memory.[7] In spite of pronounced differences among them in terminology as well as in theory, they agree that in normal development the child demonstrates in sequence two kinds of remembering activities. One of these writers,[8] using psychoanalytic terms, describes the earlier appearing form of memory as a direct outgrowth of deeply felt and affectively charged experiences. It arises in the course of experience in unsocialized behavioral events, and it involves close links between felt bodily states, occurring at the time, and the particular memories that are laid down.

When the child remembers something in this way the remembering necessarily occurs in the absence of a socialized scheme for organizing the experience, that is, in the absence of what I have earlier called an independent schema. As a consequence the memory would be held in such a way that the child could not easily share it with other persons, either then or later. At some other time in childhood, however, a different sort of memory system arises, based on a scheme of logical organization that enables sharing with other persons. It is an outgrowth of the child's socialized experiences, as distinct from the earlier preponderance of personalized and body-centered events. I suggest that the parallels here are certainly striking enough to merit comment—between an earlier or primary mode of remembering in the endo style and memory activities that can be ordered and shared in the meso and ecto styles. This is to say that the early form of remembering, as described by McGuire and other writers, is close to the endo mode and the later form of remembering to the meso and ecto modes, as I describe these styles below.

This point has been made by others as well, notably Freud. From these independent accounts in different sources we may derive a consensus on the features that mark the early style of endo memory, or what has been termed the style of a "private" memory system, as distinct from a "socially addressable" system.[9] In the private system of remembering, experiences become attached to situations in which the child is, for the moment, strongly or deeply involved. The situation need not be exceptional but rather the kind that occurs repeatedly in the child's ongoing life, with the result that there then occurs a kind of "unintended rehearsal," as it is often called: the child does the same thing, under the same powerful influences, in a more or less regular and repetitive way. However, the memory that is then built up in connection with this situation is experienced in an individualized way, for the child has as yet no framework that is consensually shared by which to organize the experience; the features of the experience are not yet, for the child, socially defined, and so if the child did have a vocabulary by which to refer to these features, the words might well be personal and individualized rather than consensually useful.

One important consequence is that these memories, although they become familiar to the child, are known and held in a nonreflective way. The child holds them but does not think or know about them and, indeed, could not do so. They are merely there, as they are, just as familiar and just as much a part of one as, say, one's skin color but for this reason not experienced self-reflectively. In order to become self-reflective or self-conscious about what is experienced, a child has to be able to hold it off, so to speak, as one does when making a comparison with other experiences, and this would require, in turn, some independent schema within which both experiences could be similarly arrayed. That would require having developed some elements of the ecto style, whereas in this account we are still deeply in the endo style.

By contrast, memories that develop and find their place within the system that develops later are known to the child in a different way. When they originally occur as well as when they are recalled, they are more logically organized, within some schema, and so they are to some degree held by the person in a consensually recognizable form. They are known to the person, or could be known, in as abstract and reflective a mode as may be necessary. And since such memories are experienced as elements of some schema, they have the great advantage that they can be stored; they are not global wholes but discrete parts, therefore open to being manipulated as units. They do not have to be rehearsed in order to be retained as part of one's memorial stock but as units can be passively retained. The analogy of the library fits them as it does not fit the earlier endo memories of the child. This is meso-ecto memory, in contrast with endo memory; it is the kind that has been the topic for study by experimental psychologists since the time of Ebbinghaus—and for most of that century it has been considered the only kind of remembering there is.

The Gap

One of the central characteristics distinguishing early and late developing forms of memory is rehearsal. Much traditional thinking in psychology, since the days of Aristotle, centers on this characteristic, even though it is not always referred to explicitly. As we noted earlier, in late appearing memory the person acts as a neutral carrier of memory elements, serving as one who is changed locally but not significantly when certain data are fed in. One of the oldest conceptions in regard to remembering is related to this point. It is the idea of the memory trace, which goes back at least to Aristotle. He stated that the brain receives impressions—the Greek term in this connection, engram, was in fact for many years the psychologist's technical term for the memory trace—which are retained and then read off as required at later times, in a process that we term recall. In Aristotle's view the fact that we have retained so little conscious memory of our earliest years is due to the fact that in early childhood the brain material is too liquid and unformed, like water, and therefore cannot retain impressions; while the related fact that in old age persons find it difficult to retain new impressions is explained by their brain material now being too hard.

In all, the notion of the memory trace represents a major triumph for an ecto emphasis. A small alteration in some impressionable portion of the brain or central nervous system suffices to preserve memories implanted through the years, and since the brain has some four billion separate cells, whose interconnections provide an almost infinitely larger set of elements, it would appear that there is more than enough space for all the locations needed in a lifetime. The theory of brain traces implies, in addition, that memories retained as traces have the same status as books stored in a library. All the activities of the larger organization—the library, or the central nervous system—go on without disturbing the single stored element, which waits on a shelf or as a trace until it is called out as a consequence of the act of recall.

This arrangement calls for another important feature, that there occur a gap in time between the occasion when the memory is first impressed as a trace and the later occasion when it is called out to be experienced as a recalled memory. We all know what happens. Suppose you open an account at a bank and one of the items you are asked to furnish, as a way of confirming your identity, is a personal detail such as your mother's maiden name. When you are asked, a curious thing happens. You may not have thought of this item for years but with very little effort it is brought out to be displayed on your personal screen of remembering and read off. Like your other stored memories, it is identified by the fact that some period of time elapsed between its being stored and its being recalled. If you had just learned your mother's maiden name as a new fact a few moments earlier and had then been asked almost immediately what it was, you would hardly refer to your act as "recalling" it, nor would psychologists feel constrained to develop a theory explaining how you managed to retain it.

In short, it is the fact of this gap in time between initial impression and later recall that is one of the central elements in the process of ecto memory. To this we now add one other consideration, that if at the moment of recall you experience this item as one remembered rather than one currently perceived or thought, it can only be because you are able to perform a kind of comparison. You hold this item, and perhaps some of its associated images as well, against a logically organized and consensually known sequence of events in the real world. At the moment of recalling the item you know that, placed against this sequence, the item comes from the "then" and not from the "now." For the memory itself, although it is an artifact out of your own store of personal experiences, is an artifact of a special and limited kind. Like certain objects that are found in an archaeological dig, it itself carries no identifying characteristics that might tell how old it is or where it might belong in a temporal sequence. That inference has to be made by reference to other data that are themselves separately ordered—for example, the way that a series of strata in rocks might be organized. Like other stored items of this sort, the memory is neutral in regard to time, being neither in the past as a memory nor in the present as a perception or thought. In the terms of the argument that I have been pursuing in these pages, it requires an independent schema in order to be held and known as a memory, and therefore it can be considered a memory held in an ecto style.

Facts and Skills

A related distinction that has recently entered the research literature on memory is that between what is called "declarative memory" and "procedural memory." The former is concerned with the knowing of facts such as names and dates, whereas the latter has to do with the knowing of skills, of how to perform in certain ways. The two forms of memory may be mediated by different nervous system structures. The essential characteristic of declarative memory is that it can be recalled at will and that it can be "declared" or talked about; equally important, it can be lost, as by a stroke, or can be forgotten. As regards procedural memory, on the other hand, it is not really recalled but rather re-expressed or brought back into play, as we do when we use a cognitive or motor skill or behave in terms of a habit that may have become rusty from disuse. The procedural memory thus cannot be forgotten in the same sense, and it is rarely lost in the usual course of injury. Procedural memories are brought back by a kind of recognition process, declarative memories through a process of recall.

It has been suggested that declarative memory is unique to the human species and may have arisen quite late in evolutionary development. Evidence for this claim is in the finding that persons whose amnesia is a consequence of brain damage may have lost much of their memory for facts such as names and dates but can still perform in terms of learned skills although they are unable to explain how they do it. That is to say, they seem to have lost memories that show either of the major characteristics of what I have called ecto memory: memories consisting of neutral and isolated items of fact, and memories that require that one can talk about or refer to the memories. Further, such patients lose their capacity even to reenact learned skills if they are required to do them in a different way—whereas one of the marks of ecto-style remembering is that its memories can be manipulated endlessly. It seems very clear that the work pointing to two distinct styles of memory fits well with some of the distinctions that I am making here. Declarative memory, as it has been defined in this research, looks much like what I have called ecto memory; as we shall see in the following section, procedural memory has many of the characteristics of what I call endo memory.

ENDO MEMORY

Another line of research now being actively pursued in regard to human memory has suggested the importance of the "self-referential" character of one's remembering. Classically, as in the Ebbinghaus experiments, the material was deliberately made as neutral, as non-self-referential as possible, in order to study what was assumed to be some pure process of mechanical association, unsullied by associations linked to the individual subject. However, when self-references are brought back into the experimental situation, in a deliberate attempt to assess their influence, they are shown to have an important effect. Since remembering in real life is often linked in important ways to one's ongoing interests, attitudes, motives, and personal feelings, this new tactic is no more than an attempt to make up for what was lacking in earlier investigations.

One way the effect of self-reference has been tested is to present two kinds of remembering tasks to subjects, one in which they simply read what is presented to them and the other in which they generate their own material according to some instructions. The general finding, over a wide range of procedures and materials, is that self-generated remembering is more effective in terms of the amount recalled. Equally significant is the finding that self-generated errors have an effect exceeding what might be expected from the magnitude of the error, again suggesting the importance of personal significance in regard to material to be remembered. What is held to be related to one's ongoing experience as a person, in contrast to what is isolated by means of distancing skills, forms a distinct category of memories, remembered with surprising strength. In reviewing studies in this area, Anthony Greenwald[10] proposes the interesting hypothesis that the distinction between two types of memories, those self-generated and those not, helps us to understand the common finding that reward makes repetition of behavior more probable whereas punishment does not necessarily have the opposite effect. He offers the hypothesis that when one tests for the effect of reward, the logic of the situation requires that one put the subject in a situation calling for a specific kind of behavior: behavior that the subject will, on a later occasion, regenerate. It is the fact that the subject later generates the originally rewarded behavior, not the fact of some imprinted Thorndikean associations or connections, that explains the effect of reward on behavior.

To his review of an impressive body of studies supporting the general principle of the significance of ego involvement in remembering, Greenwald has added another concept that is relevant to our inquiry in these pages. In effect, he redefines the essential characteristic of ego involvement as "engagement in a persistent task."[11] By the term "persisting task" he means one to which the person is committed, together with some complex of belief, attitude, and feeling, over some period of time. This definition relocates the phenomenon of interest from the person's experience to the person's behavior. A related pair of concepts, introduced by Nuttin and Greenwald in earlier work, concerns "open" and "closed" tasks, that is, tasks that do not seem as yet closed as distinct from those regarding which the person has a sense of closure.[12] It is clear that if a task is experienced as open, and if circumstances make it possible, the person is likely to keep engaging in it; it will then be definable as a persisting task, whereas if for the subject it is closed, it will not show behavior related to persistence.

The importance of these concepts for our purposes here is that another body of experimental findings shows clearly that more is remembered in reference to tasks experienced as open than closed.[13] If this is so, it suggests that there is more than one way in which remembering goes on. In addition to remembering as traditionally conceived, which I have discussed earlier under the category of the ecto style, that is, a neutral remembering of facts in which there is a gap in time between storage and recall, we have here a form of remembering that is not at all neutral and to which the person remains committed and involved. I suggest that the latter is close to endo memory, and that the experimental results briefly reviewed in this section, although meant as support for quite different concepts and models, may reasonably be used in support of my argument in these pages.

Endo Memory as a Distinct Style

Remembering that occurs in the endo style has unique characteristics that can be identified. The process appears to occur in the following way: that initially some aspect or "member" of an occasion is singled out, not as a discriminable element but rather as a defining characteristic. The occasion itself would have to be an event in which the participant is significantly engaged, not merely present while engaged in something that is of more importance than the event itself. Something of the event is then caught by its participant; it becomes memorable. The event itself is not an isolated or unique thing but belongs to the naturally occurring sequence of its participant's life. Examples might be the way people tend to let their voices rise at the end of a sentence; or the custom of standing when a person with grey hair enters the room; or the practice of planting each foot solidly when one walks.

As a result of these features, endo memories, once created in this way, do not happen on single occasions, to be stored away as isolated elements in the manner of ecto memories, but rather occur and then reoccur. To put it another way, there is a "remembering" which is then followed by a series of naturally occurring and unintended rehearsals of the original remembering. There is then no gap in time between an initial implanting and later occasions when it is recalled, but rather a natural flow of events and repetitions within which the memory is repeatedly re-experienced as a "member" of ongoing occasions. "Membering" becomes re-membering. As a further consequence, the fact that the memory belongs to the past is built into it as an aspect of the way it is known; it could not be experienced as temporally neutral, as an artifact with no particular identification in time. It needs no external, consensual schema by which to identify it as a "past" item, for it has always been known only as a part of one's personal history. In all these respects the endo memory differs from the ecto memory.

Because it is buried in this way in the very texture of one's past, the endo memory in fact helps to form those consensual schemes against which ecto and meso memories can be placed for temporal identification. The endo memory, serving as an artifact against which other memories can be dated, thus underpins all our remembering. If on a particular occasion it is also experienced in its own right, its specific characteristics will indicate the way it is buried in the person's history. It may surface with more or less emotional charge, in more or less detail, or in connection with this or that other particular, all of its characteristics then serving as evidence of the depth and nature of one's investment in it.

Like other major processes in this style, endo remembering takes place in the form of cycles, the model for which is the familiar hunger cycle. In the meso or ecto styles, by contrast, the temporal dimension of processes is a straight line. Each instance of a hunger cycle is normally complete in itself, occurs in its own time, and happens at its own speed. The human, even the animal, caught up in this cycle is for a time engaged in it, certainly to the exclusion of other cycles of engagement. As a consequence, the characteristics of one endo cycle are experienced as unique to that instance, and time is not experienced as a linear unfolding, stretching backward into one's known past and forward into one's probable future, within which one feels located in relation to other times.

In an endo cycle, to put it in other terms, there are no "times," only Time. There is thus no past as such. There is, rather, the paradoxical situation of being caught in time but not experiencing time. To be truly hungry is to have the experience of being driven onward by hunger, even of time passing too fast, but equally that one has never been hungry before—or stated more precisely, it is to have the experience that the hunger that is going on now is all the hunger one can know, and that the question of other hungers is, right now, irrelevant, even meaningless. If we try to assure the ravenously hungry person that, after all, this is just one more instance in history of a normally occurring hunger cycle and that they have all been satisfied on former occasions—as indeed they must have been, or else the person would not be here now, proclaiming today's hunger—and that this hunger too will be satisfied, our assurances will have an effect only if the hungry person is able to shift out of the endo mode. Infants cannot do this; a great part of their early growth, in fact, consists in just this learning to live in some combination of all three styles. In this mode in which the endo cycle holds full sway, one acts as though one had no personal history, even though one's personal history is in fact built on layers of such endo experiences. It is a paradox that is at the very heart of endo memory.

The endo experience does not fit into that mode of linear time in which we usually remember something. Rather, the endo style provides an endless revolving of cycles in a pattern very similar to that of the wheel of fate in some religions. The very notion of Fate, in fact, belongs in the endo style. Experiences that we have in the endo style seem, therefore, to be outside the province of memory in its ordinary sense. They are experiences that require us to redefine both memory and learning, as I have tried to do in these pages. We need to understand them in the special sense of something being laid down beyond recall, leaving behind as an effect only a remembrance of something alive, underpinning everything we do or recall later.

A Case Study

The neurologist Oliver Sacks[14] has reported on a case he calls "the lost Mariner," a man whose condition was diagnosed as Korsakoff's syndrome. This is a neurological disorder, often a consequence of long-term alcoholism, in which the person seems to have lost any capacity for recent memory. If he is introduced to someone and then brought face to face with that person only a few minutes later, he will have forgotten that they had ever met. If he writes something, by the time he has finished a sentence or two he will have forgotten that he wrote it. Yet together with this loss of recent or current memory there is a retention of the contents of personal memory for details and events in the past—in the case of the mariner, an excellent retention of everything that occurred before 1945. In addition to the loss of recent memory, an amnesia for the moment by moment occurrences of his existence, this patient also showed what Sacks aptly terms an amnesia for his own amnesia—which is to say that he lacked an awareness *that* he had a memory defect. In current psychological terminology, he showed a loss in short-term memory coupled with an unimpaired long-term memory.

Equally interesting is the question of what he did remember. If he saw what he had just written on a piece of paper, he would, as we said, have no awareness, because no memory, that this was writing he himself had just finished. At the same time he would know that it was his own writing, and he would confess to a "faint echo" that he had in fact written it. In addition, of course, he had not forgotten how to walk, to talk his native language, to act as the kind of unique individual that he was. When his brother came to visit him they would have an affectionate reunion, and of course the brother would not have the experience of greeting a stranger but someone who was the person the brother remembered.

And he did appear able to learn, that is, to begin to acquire a new store of memories, in this way seemingly contradicting the limitations imposed on him by his condition. In the course of time he gained "a sense of familiarity" with the institution in which he was a patient, knowing, for example, where certain rooms were located. He came to be able to recognize some of the staff members, in particular the voice and even the footstep of one of the nurses (although he often confused her with someone he had known in high school). And he was able to become bored, leading to a "fretful and restless" wandering through the corridors, an emotional state that we feel is somehow linked to the processes of memory.

Finally, there are his achievements during the years he spent as a patient. He came to be a regular disciple of church services, in his attention showing an "intensity and steadiness of attention and concentration . . . wholly held, absorbed, by a feeling" that was perfectly fitted to "the spirit of the ceremony."[15] He had no problem at all in attentively following musical performances or plays. And after some preliminary practice he became an excellent gardener, patterning his on those he remembered lovingly from his own earlier years. In Sacks's view, this man had learned a new kind of time, a new way of ordering his world: "what was fugitive, unsustainable, as formal structure, was perfectly stable, perfectly held, as art or will."[16] As a consequence of his participation in nature, in art, in music, and in religious observance, he became a changed person, "deeply attentive to the beauty and 'soul' of the world," showing thereby "the undiminished possibility of reintegration by art, by communion, by touching the human spirit."[17]

It is of some interest to pull out of this case study the evidence for two kinds of memories, two kinds of learning, two styles of ordering one's own experience, and then to see if these two modes can be fitted to any that I have been discussing in these pages. First, what the patient had lost, apparently irretrievably, consisted of the ability to order his experiences self-reflectively and against a "map" of a systematic series in time. This is what we do all the time. At one point Sacks offers, by way of contrast, the view first expressed by the British philosopher Hume, to the effect that normal experience consists of nothing but "a bundle or collection of different perceptions" strung together without a bond holding them together or linking them into a unity; to this Sacks adds that his patient was, in a sense, reduced to such a Humean creature. The person who lacks the capacity to map ongoing experiences onto some independent schema will be reduced to being victim of an unending flux of impressions, far too many to order in a selective and useful way. Such a person, also, will have lost the capacity to entertain, as an item of experience, any fact about his own experiences; he will be amnestic for his own amnesia.

I suggest that what Sacks's patient had lost was the ability to act in the ecto style or to use that style as an aspect of his ongoing experience. The various kinds of evidence that Sacks presents appear to support this way of summing up the patient's deficiencies. However, he had not lost completely the capacity for behaving; therefore the way he now acted would reflect the endo style at least and possibly some aspects of the meso style. He showed, for example, that he was capable of learning a whole way of life as long as his learning and his remembering were permitted to be based on his strongly felt participation in concrete situations. The locations of rooms, the features of some staff members' faces, the voice and footsteps of a nurse to whom he was deeply attached, the deeply felt details of a religious ceremony or a musical performance or even a dramatic stage presentation, and the simple skills associated with growing things (a pattern of activity going back into his own childhood)—all these aspects of a life, so strongly reminiscent of the important experiences of childhood, remained within his capacities and formed the endo basis of his reconstructed existence. I am suggesting here that the patient's condition consisted of the loss of ecto capacities coupled with the retention of endo capacities and perhaps of meso as well (although this was apparently not tested and is not referred to in Sacks's account). His "recovery" consisted of rebuilding an existence on an endo foundation, a feat that may be feasible within the very protected environs of an insitute for the neurologically impaired.

THE MEMORY OF LANGUAGE

The extended example to be presented in this section is one that I have discussed elsewhere[18] in connection with certain aspects of childhood development. It is the phenomenon of learning one's native tongue.

Observe someone who is in the act of talking spontaneously with a friend, in the course of an exchange in which both are conversing in their native language. The speaker will be engaged in the situation in an unselfconscious manner while making a series of very rapid movements with the lips and tongue, movements that are remarkably subtle and complex. To see how difficult it is to manipulate the facial muscles so as to make the sounds of a language, one might try reading aloud as rapidly as possible in a language that is strange.

In addition to the sounds and movements accompanying ordinary speech, we should also note the ongoing play of expression on the speaker's face. In parallel with this ongoing speech and its expressive counterpart, too, we will note other acts occurring if the speaker is even ordinarily expressive: the hands may move to emphasize or underline a point; the eyes may be directed at the other person or not, toward details or toward a totality; the head or shoulders may tilt, turn, move forward and back, in a pattern of bodily "communication" of feeling and meaning. All of this is likely to occur while the speaker is engaged in still other actions, such as setting a table, knitting, playing cards, walking, or keeping a balance in a moving bus. As a total performance it is quite remarkable, especially since it does not seem to require the speaker's conscious attention.

This may be the most remarkable aspect of the performance, that normally a speaker is only minimally aware of the set of actions connected with ongoing speech acts. Yet perhaps we should not be too surprised to be reminded of this characteristic of normal speech, for it occurs in other spheres of action as well. As a number of writers, beginning with Heidegger, have pointed out,[19] we may distinguish two modes in which something is present to us. It may be merely an object, which we observe or perceive in a neutral manner as having no connection with our concerns—in Heidegger's terminology, *vorhanden* or at hand. It may also be present to us as usable, useful, a link in our own chains of instrumental concerns, or in short "handy"—in Heidegger's lexicon, *zuhanden*. Whatever I can attend to can be known in one of these two ways. The cloud may be merely an object available for my contemplation, merely at hand, unless I am a farmer for whom the cloud carries the meaning of a link in a significant chain of weather events, in which case it will be perceived as an indicator of tomorrow's rain.

An important feature of phenomena that are experienced as useful, instrumental, or handy is that they usually escape our notice. The pencil in the writer's hand is not part of the writer's attentional field, for the writer is attending to what is being written, not to the writing of it. Only if the object should fail in its instrumental function, as when the point of the pencil breaks or the pen runs out of ink, will it then appear in the writer's consciousness as an object for contemplation. Otherwise one might write for pages without noticing what color the pen was. This may be the phenomenon described by some novelists: persons who are very accustomed to one another may fail to notice one another until one changes or leaves. To restate the matter in the terms being used here, it is a central characteristic of the meso style and to actions carried out in that style that insofar as they can proceed without interruption they sink below the level of awareness. If I have learned to play tennis well, the actions I engage in when serving are no longer experienced at the level of my conscious awareness nor is the tennis ball that I play with in my field of awareness. Both action and object, being handy or a link in my instrumental concerns as a tennis player, are "forgotten." I recapture an awareness of the action or the object only if something goes wrong—if the ball rips and is no longer usable, if I strain a muscle and must then attend to the arm that hits the ball, if my serve is of so little use to me that I must begin to improve it.

Consideration of this characteristic of phenomena experienced within the meso style may help us to understand the behavior described above, a multitudinous complex of actions and subactions carried on seemingly without accompanying awareness. We may also be helped to understand a phenomenon commonly experienced by adults who attempt to learn a second language. If I am faced with an object—this blue colored writing instrument, let us say—I may or may not have a word for it in a second language that I am learning. If that language is French, I may or may not have available the noun *la plume*. But in regard to my native language, the word is not only available to me but more than available; I use it with no sense that I am using it, automatically, as it were, on being presented with the object. And I express this availability, or my experience of it, in a way that is unique to language usage. I find myself unable to separate the word from the object for which it stands. If my native language is English, I will look at the object and immediately, unthinkingly know that it is a pen.

It seems so simple, but like all of our common acts, it hides a mystery. Note that in the example here, it is not the case that I know it is a small blue object and also know that it is called a pen. Not at all. Rather, for me the object and the word are fused into one, or the word has disappeared into the object, with the result that I simply know that this object before me *is* a pen, not an object for which the word is "pen." Try to look at this object and convince yourself that it *is* a "mirk," or try to convince even a very young child that an animal for which it already knows the name, such as cat, is really called a "house." Only when we attempt to learn a second language, usually at some age well past early childhood, do we experience word and object as separate. For example, we may say that in French a *pen* is called *la plume* but never, at this stage of language learning, that in English *la plume* is called a *pen*, unless we are trying to explain the matter to someone whose native language is French. With the exception of the rather infrequent instance of the balanced bilingual, we will all report the same experience—that each referent will immediately and automatically have its appropriate term in some native language, a term from which it cannot be separated, and that certain terms in other languages will come to be known as standing for these named referents. Like the pen that disappears into my action as I use it, so that I no longer notice it as such, the words of my native language disappear into the fabric of my action and the order of the world that I create. They are available for use but not normally available for conscious inspection as nameless items in their own right.

Some curious phenomena make sense when considered in these terms. If you overuse a word, repeating it over and over, far beyond the needs of any normal reference in speech, you may then break the tie that links word and thing. As in the common instance of repeating the words "looking glass" a hundred times, the meaning drops away from the sound and we are left with what this collection of sounds might seem like in a little known second language. Or to take another phenomenon, the tip-of-the-tongue experience, it may happen, for reasons still not known, that in the course of normally saying a word— almost always a noun or a name—we find the link broken and so are unable to say what we would like. We know what we are referring to and can even find other ways to describe the missing referent, indicating that it is the word and not the thing that is absent for us, and we can in addition capture and express certain nonlexical characteristics of the word, such as how many syllables it has or what sound it begins with.[20] But this is true only of words on the tip of the tongue in our native language or else in a language that we know almost as well as our native tongue. If the phenomenon occurs in a language we do not know well, we will not report the tip-of-the-tongue experience but rather that we simply cannot recall the word for this or that referent. The reason is that normally it is the referent that is held and known in our native language, thus making it possible, and indeed rather common, for us to have the referent at the same time that we are lacking the word for it. The experience of tip-of-the-tongue occurs when, unexpectedly, the link between word and referent in our native language is somehow broken; the meso component of our knowing lapses, leaving only the endo component to supply certain nonlexical features as well as the feeling that we "really" know it but at the moment cannot think of it.

If we now sum up this discussion, it appears that in our use of our native language much of the content is buried in our actions, which in turn are buried in our bodily existence. As a result we can know most of the words in our native tongue in a manner that is below our conscious awareness. The hiddenness of our language extends even to some aspects that might normally be open to reflective consideration. For example, we cannot tell someone the meaning of the "little words" of our language, words such as "and" or "but" in English, even though we use them flawlessly. Nor can we say, and even might be surprised to learn, many of the rules that from an early age we seem to have used without error, for instance, the rule that in the

English sentence beginning "The little yellow house" the color name follows the other adjective but in the sentence beginning "The yellow brick house" the adjective for color comes first. In this instance the rule is not universal across languages—which might have provided us with a convenient explanation a la Chomsky—but differs from one language to another. Thus, in many of its most important characteristics our native language is known and used as though it were a habitual motor skill—instantly available yet necessarily out of awareness. Speaking a native language, then, is at least in this respect action in the meso style.

But it is more than this. Our native language is not simply available but, as we noted above, superavailable. It is as though it were buried in our very bones, a characteristic that we express when we say that some native ways of expression simply "feel right." In these respects our native language is not so much a possession we have as a set of personal characteristics that help to define what we are. It functions not as an instrument, but as more than a skill: an expression of the kind of person we are. In his work on perception, Merleau-Ponty[21] discusses at some length the case of a brain-damaged patient, one Schneider. He was unable to use his arm "automatically" as an expression of how he was situated in space—for example, to point at something or to draw a circle in the air—without first figuring it out as a kind of problem in geometry. What seems to have ruptured in his case was that vital connection through which each of us is able to know, without being aware of the knowing, where we are for practical, functional purposes. Because we are non-brain-damaged we are able to express ourselves through the use of arm, torso, whatever, whereas Schneider was reduced to using a limb that happened conveniently to be attached to him and so could serve as a tool. Schneider's arm, the pen that runs out of ink, the second language that we have only partially mastered, all are examples of the tool or instrument that is not a part of us as individuals but simply belongs to us and so cannot function as expression. Here we refer to aspects of language, or of action, that call on the endo style.

When an endo component enters into what we do, then we belong to it and it belongs to us. We then *are* the doing or the knowing, or, as we say, the doing or the knowing expresses what we are. For this reason it is fitting that one does not say, "I remember the words of my native language," a statement that would only be made by someone who has been away from the use of their native tongue for many years and now begins to experience it as a non-native. The reason we do not make such a statement is that in the ordinary, ecto sense of the term our native vocabulary is not remembered by us. That would be true only if the vocabulary had the status of discrete, neutral items stored away and awaiting recall, only if the vocabulary were a set of possessions, tools that one happened to have at hand, like Schneider's arm, rather than living aspects of ourselves as persons. Language as it is known and spoken by a native is a meso-endo accomplishment, minimally ecto.

Our continuing knowledge of our native tongue, a knowledge that we refer to quite aptly as "known in our bones," is remembering in the endo style. It is a kind of knowing that was originally acquired in our participation in significant situations and almost as a by-product of the ongoing activity within the situations. Each aspect of it, once grasped, was immediately and continuingly placed into practice in a form of unintended rehearsal. It was never taught in an ecto manner. For example, no one instructs an infant by saying, "Now, this animal is a dog. Remember that word *dog*. Store the word away so that if ever again you come across a similar four-footed animal of about this size, you will have the word available. Tomorrow we will learn the word *cat*." We do this with many elements of our ecto memory, as for example when we teach long division with the proviso that students may not need the knowledge today but will now have it available for use on future occasions. Rather, in the case of an infant learning, or rather growing into, its native tongue, it gains the word *dog* as part of one or more ongoing situations in which it is engaged with a dog and needs to fill out the engagement and complete its own participation in the situation by making a vocal reference to the animal. Very young infants, we say, are not ready to talk, by which we mean that although they may perceive the dog and even be fascinated by it, their participation need not as yet extend to the point of referring to the dog in some way.

The curious phenomenon of one's language accent deserves comment in this connection. Although in a restricted sense it can be said that you learn an accent, it can hardly be said that you remember it. Rather, what you do in the course of speaking a language, especially one that is native to you, is simply and unthinkingly felt as right, and the idea of accenting your language in alternative ways might at most be entertained as an ecto possibility, no more. Your experience of your own accent is so much a matter of embeddedness in what you are that if you are like most persons you will say that you have no accent in your native tongue. As an example, I speak English as a native language, perhaps with an accent that results from having grown up on the Atlantic seaboard of the United States—that is, in my case with some mixture of what is called Pennsylvania Dutch and a touch of New Yorkese—but as far as I am concerned I have no perceptible accent in English. My view is that I speak English naturally, as I unreflectively feel it "has to" be spoken. I would, however, speak English with a different regional accent if circumstances had arranged it that I had grown up in another part of the United States, that is, if I had had a different personal history, if I were a different person than I now am. In this sense my accent is an integral part of the person I am, and should it change I would be a changed person. My use of my accent, then, is behavior in the endo style, and my unthinking knowledge of it is an example of endo memory. The suggestion that I forget or change my accent strikes me as meaningless, akin to suggesting that I forget I am male rather than female. It is not a matter of forgetting, not even a matter of remembering in the ecto style, but a matter of what I am.

TEACHING A LANGUAGE

When rating oneself one tends to overrate the ecto component and to underrate the other two components. This is in part because rating is itself an ecto procedure, and in part because the ecto style is related to the kinds of valuation prevalent in our culture.

The discussion in the preceding section concerns learning one's native language. In it I have tried to make the point that this is a meso-endo function—grounded in the endo style and exercised in the meso style. Learning a second (or third) language later in life, however, may be accomplished in any of the three modes or in any combination of them. To demonstrate this I will discuss three successful methods of teaching and learning a second language.

To begin, we should bear in mind that learning a language that is not one's native tongue is a difficult, complex, and time-consuming endeavor, almost always involving many years of training and practice. It is therefore understandable that no methods are wholly satisfactory and that all sorts of training systems have been tried, most of them achieving at least some partial success. But given these disclaimers, we may still be able to make distinctions among major teaching approaches so as to show their relations to our three behavioral styles. The most familiar of these by far is the schoolroom approach in which pupils are taught a language in just the same way as they are taught any other subject. In this approach educators take for granted that learning a new language is not essentially different than learning European history or long division or even carpentry. The features of this approach are familiar to all and I need describe them only briefly.

The teaching method is in large measure a function of the individual teacher and to some degree of the tradition or practice of a particular school or school system. The learning takes place in a group, resulting in the element of competition playing an important role. The prevailing assumption is that something specific and identifiable, and often quantifiable as well, is there to be learned, from which it follows that one can test whether the learning has occurred. The ecto character of both subject matter and teaching procedure is further emphasized by the kinds of tests that are usually used. They do not take the form of personalized interchanges, even when the class is small enough to permit this, but consist of depersonalized instruments either in the form of objective tests or essay-type assignments. Such tests imply very clearly that what is to be learned can be found in the test items, thus emphasizing the point that what is to be learned can be defined independently of the learning process and consists of impersonal data that can be organized and administered by any person trained in the required skills, that may then be transferred unchanged from the teacher to the pupil(s), and that does not require as tester someone who knows or has learned what is being taught. Nor does this approach accept the learners' own judgments as to whether they have learned; that can be known only to the wielder of the test instrument.

Understandably, emphasis is placed on those neutral and independent rule systems that govern correct usage in a language—rules that in sum are called grammar—thus constituting another important ecto feature in the teaching situation. The teaching itself is divided into arbitrary time periods that are scheduled for reasons of administrative rather than personal convenience. Given these characteristics of the teaching approach, it will follow that good students will do well in language classes, just as they do well in other academic subjects. And since long hours can be spent at the task, during a period of life when learners have a great deal of energy to expend on such chores, the ecto approach can claim its share of successes in teaching language at the high school and college level.

Practical considerations of time, budgets, and staff time largely determine how subjects are taught in school. This precludes exploring the important question of whether individual students might differ in the teaching and learning styles to which they are best suited. As long as ecto methods predominate in language teaching, the kind of student who can best mobilize ecto resources will flourish by comparison with others who might do better as meso or endo learners. Yet the heavy fire of criticism directed in recent years at public schools and universities, from students, their parents, and even the teaching profession itself, has resulted in significant changes in language teaching. So many variations have been introduced into the traditional classroom setting that it may now be difficult to find examples of the pure ecto style; it has been infiltrated, so to speak, by elements of the meso style.[22]

As the ecto approach emphasizes the neutral character of course content, the meso style stresses the presence and the continuing activity of a teacher or an adequate teacher substitute. In the meso approach, the material is broken down almost mechanically, rather than according to an independent set of rules, for it is assumed that one chunk of material is the equivalent of any other. The meso method is modeled on the structure of a decisive motor act in which a directed movement is begun, carried out to its end, stopped, and then checked as to whether it has achieved its aim. A series of such acts, as many as possible, arranged in a sensible sequence is presumed to give rise automatically to learning.

The familiar device known as a pinball machine is a good example of a meso learning method; its embodiment in the teaching machine—or in the approach developed by Fred Keller that is based on its use—fully exemplifies the meso style. The main features are its clearly stated, short-term goals, its prepared package of materials broken into short, manageable chunks, its emphasis on practice and drill, and its use of immediate feedback concerning results. The method assumes that the learner need only do each part of the task over and over, constantly forgetting how many mistakes might have been made before at the same point, in order to become as skilled as need be; errors are forgotten and only successes count, just as in an athletic contest all that counts is to come out ahead at the end.

In language teaching the method developed by John Rassias at Dartmouth College comes very close to a pure meso approach. This approach, which has been extremely successful, involves a corps of enthusiastic and well-trained students who themselves have been through the course and who then serve as drill instructors in some sections of the course. In addition, more traditional classroom sections are taught by regular faculty members. The drill sessions consist of rapid-fire, repetitive practice on a few points of grammar or usage, accompanied by immediate and positive feedback. The group of five or ten students is directed by a drill instructor who is a peer of the students and encourages a strong group feeling, who is very active and enthusiastic, and who assures that by means of a fast-paced sequence of questions and answers each of the group members has on the average forty or so chances to participate during one session.

Learning by doing is heavily stressed, the assumption being that understanding will then follow. All the characteristics of the meso style seem to be operative here—language being turned into a form of high-energy work, in an arrangement fitting very well with the preferred action style of young males. The drill instructor is required to be as active as the students and in fact to serve as their model. He is energetic and in constant physical movement, making brief but frequent contacts to ask questions and to hand out small rewards, and is friendly and encouraging but neither intimate nor emotional. The students are pressured by the atmosphere, the setting, and the procedure to become similarly involved in an active, physical, enthusiastic yet emotionally neutral way. Everything about the situation is meant to be immediate, practical, and turned toward practical ends rather than being contemplated or talked about. The sessions remind one of athletic contests or manual crafts, all in the hand and of the hand, to be worked at for quick, certain, known purposes. Finally, it all takes place in efficiently organized small groups, which comprise the ideal settings for meso learning. The ecto works best alone and the endo with a small number of others to whom there is an emotional attachment.

The pattern may be described as a work-learn arrangement in which the work aspect takes on as much importance as the learning aspect. In all these respects the pattern has also been successfully applied in a number of other settings, all of them competitive, high-energy, and oriented toward the style of the young adult male. These include engineering firms, research laboratories, and small, technologically advanced businesses. Organizations of this sort seem to have developed a novel and effective combination of the best features of meso and ecto styles of teaching and learning.

As for the endo style, it may seem almost a contradiction in terms to suggest that it might be put to use as a basis for a system of second-language teaching. The endo style is on principle nonsystematic and in its pure form it rules out an independent schema that might organize its own naturally occurring events. It may be for this reason that the only system that comes even close to representing an endo style, one developed by Georgi Lozanov,[23] contains many elements of the meso style as well. Lozanov is a Bulgarian psychiatrist and educator who was strongly influenced by his studies of Buddhist practices of meditation in India. His method of teaching languages, more recently adapted to other subjects such as arithmetic, is in wide use in his own country, particularly in the lower grades, and has also been used with some success in Austria and Canada.

The central concept in the Lozanov approach, which he terms "concert pseudo-passivity," refers to the learner rather than to the teacher, the material, or the situation. The term refers to a specially induced state, akin to an experience of light meditation or perhaps autohypnosis at a concert, that the learners must first become able to attain at will. It may be described as a state of listening attentively and with absorption yet not with any goal or intent consciously in mind. The image suggested here is that of the involved concertgoer, who is deeply and intently absorbed in the music, not for any purpose outside of the ongoing experience itself and not with any reflective awareness of a possible goal, but who is also alert enough to detect deviations from an expected sequence or routine. It is a curious form of automatically controlled attention without a goal.

Lozanov brings about this state in his learners first of all through training and then by the use of a number of devices—the strong, authoritative, yet friendly and supportive figure of the teacher (for whom the model is, perhaps, the good parent) who is perceived as more personally powerful than in ecto or meso teaching styles; impressive background music that has been carefully selected from the classical repertoire; a great deal of repetition, done in an insistent rather than an intrusive or energizing fashion; and the practice of fitting the presented material to an almost hypnotizing rhythm. With the learners very comfortably positioned in postures that are conducive to relaxation, usually in fairly large groups so that a group atmosphere of participation can have its effect, and with individuals guided into a semi–dream state that is midway between passively absorbing and actively apprehending, a very large amount of rote material, such as hundreds of words of vocabulary, is then presented over and over against a musical background.

This appears to be all there is to the method. Lozanov reports rather astonishing results in regard to the amount of material that can be learned: in some instances as many as five hundred new words of vocabulary per day, with as much as 90 percent retention for periods of up to one year.[24] The theory he develops to explain such feats of memorization centers on the descriptive notion of "peripheral perception," by which he means absorbing at the margins of one's perceptual field rather than grasping at its active center. From his results it would appear that a continuing state of minimal engagement in one's own activity, freed from possible goals or achievements—assuming one can sustain it while remaining involved—is helpful in learning material that itself is not systematically organized.

And this may be as close as we can get to a description of learning in the endo style—in sharp contrast with the rather extended descriptions available to us in regard to the other two styles. Endo learning is difficult to describe because on principle it denies what it is supposed to be about, some organized and goal-directed activity. Thus we end up without a specific verb to use in talking about what happens in the process. For example, we cannot properly say that the learner "gains" anything. Rather, it appears that the learner somehow comes into possession of some digestible material, absorbs it, and then comes to feel comfortable with it. One may then look back over the completed process and perhaps even point to what was learned, but in truth the seeming accomplishment was a by-product of the situation in which the learner was occupied, nothing more.

The examples that I have discussed in this section, taken from a variety of approaches to language teaching, may serve to indicate how individualized the learning process could be if it were possible for educators to give learners some choice about their learning. The lesson is especially clear in regard to the learning of motor or athletic skills. When an adult tries to learn a complex skill such as playing golf, a teacher's intrusion is usually assumed to be necessary, in the form of observation, criticism, instruction, or at the very least the learner's own intrusion in the form of self-awareness and self-criticism. Yet it does not seem to occur to such learners or their teachers that individuals may differ in the learning style to which they are suited.

Professional sports teams, for example, often depend heavily on the use of training films. Team members as well as the members of other teams are filmed during practice sessions and games, and everyone is then required to study the films of themselves and others in order to "learn" about their styles and their mistakes, presumably to be able to cope with the former and correct the latter. This may be the best approach to use with some athletes, but it may well constitute a form of interference with the naturally occurring learning process in others; which is best in the individual case can only be discovered by a process of trial and error. If a player's natural learning style is mostly endo, self-observation—particularly observing oneself as a neutral object on a screen—and subsequent self-awareness during play will constitute more of an interference than an aid. If the natural style is mostly meso, the player will learn more by doing than by observing or thinking about doing.

An interesting example is provided in the personal technique developed by the well-known baseball star Mickey Mantle. His method of learning from his mistakes was this: following each game, and while he was still dirty and sweating from the game, he would sit alone for as much as an hour and slowly review in retrospect each play of the game just concluded, remembering and thinking over his own movements in relation to each play. During this process he would take the same amount of time for his personal review as the play itself had originally taken. It is noteworthy that he was able to retain—almost as a by-product of his playing activity during the game—a complete memory for each of the dozens of plays that had just occurred. Equally noteworthy, he seemed to know that for him the best approach to learning was not to see himself on a movie screen but to become immersed again in the remembered, ongoing situation and to participate bodily in its reoccurrence. This was not so much recalling it as reliving it. In short, he seemed to have sensed that for him the use of important elements of an endo style was necessary in order to improve his skills.

ON TIME AND SPACE

Memory is the living creature's way of recapturing time and space. It is therefore appropriate that I conclude this chapter with some remarks on time and space in the three behavioral styles.

Time and space are experienced very differently in the three styles. The ecto style is strongly linked to time, for that is the ecto domain. Theories, the great by-products of ecto-style behavior, really conquer time, not space, which is why they can be cast in the form of logical predictions. The prediction in science is atemporal; time is conquered by acting in spite of time.

Both endo and meso styles, on the other hand, are tied to space, although in quite different ways. In the meso style space is the literal space of action: real, measurable, closely corresponding to the geometer's results, for one has to depend on the reliability of this space as an arena for all one's meaningful actions. Behavior in the meso mode serves to conquer space.

But for the endo the slow move from impulse to consciousness is not in time. It may, rather, be immediate and all of a piece, or more commonly it will be cyclic and literally timeless. Space may then be relevant in the endo style, or rather spaces—those places where one or another value finds a home.

There are differences as well in regard to the tenses of time. For the meso, the past is experienced as a simple past, or a preterit, extending only minimally backward from a known present. Short-term goals in the direction of a future close at hand are balanced by small chunks of a simple past. For the endo the past is experienced as extending through past time with the meaning of "it has been" or "it used to be," while the future is vague, even endless. The future belongs to the ecto realm and the true past to the meso realm; therefore the future is always invented and the past only discovered.

In the endo style, time is not marked out but is rather homogeneous, extending in all directions from the person's center. For the ecto, the image of time is that of time unrolling or running on in an endless series of equal, meaningless units against a void. True ecto statements are therefore in the nature of predictions rather than of propositions related to the present or the past. The ecto-dominated person is nowhere in relation to time, except perhaps in a void. The meso exists in a time that is always marked off, usually by the doing of things and the reaching of goals.

Endo time may be the most difficult to explicate, though perhaps we can if we try to get a feel for it. In the endo mode, time is simply everywhere or wherever. There are no crescendos, no buildups, no climaxes that might be predicted. Time simply proceeds, and it is experienced as a moment that enlarges until it enters the body of the person who is caught in that moment. The person is thus changed, in celebration of that moment. If a form of social time, a time beyond the person, should arise in the endo mode, it will be because some links have been forged between the person and the equivalent social life of others in a community of times.

5

Varieties of Individual Development

The three styles may be distinguished in terms of how far they have wandered from the earth. The endo style keeps the individual "glued firmly to the earth," with the person dependent for very survival on absorbing nourishment and maintaining strong ties with powerful others. The meso makes up for distance from the earth by the development of "powerful equipment of both offense and defense." The ecto has wandered the greatest distance, in some cases too far to return, and "seems to have sacrificed both visceral mass and somatic strength."—w. h. sheldon, *The Varieties of Temperament*

In this chapter I will introduce the topic of "forming the body," using that phrase here in the sense of one's individual development over the life span. What I present here is not a theory of development but rather an overview of individual change through time, emphasizing in particular sequential changes that occur in regard to the three styles of behavior. My discussion will center on key aspects of the work of Piaget and Freud.

AN ACCOUNT OF CHANGE

Imagine a sequence that extends through some years and involves a change in an individual's life; it is summarized in table 3. Such a sequence would begin with an *event* that is associated with some *process* in the person, the consequence of which would be some nontrivial *historical change*, that is, some change in the person's history or life pattern. In some instances this change will die away without leaving an important aftereffect; this sort of change is not our concern. In other

Table 3   A General Pattern of Change in Human Life and in Its Three Behavioral Styles

	Marker	Endo	Meso	Ecto
Step 1 ↓	An event, associated with:	A situation	A social occurrence	Conscious fantasies; perceived events
Step 2 ↓	A process in the person, resulting in:	Incorporation; "unconscious" perception	The person's act or movement	Perception; attention; other cognitive act
Step 3 ↓	A historical change and:	Continual doing/living	Motor "memory"	Encoding into long-term memory
Step 4 ↓	A life-change in the person:	Continual doing/living	Practicing the act	Retrieval from (long-term) memory
Step 5	The enduring consequences are:	To be identified with certain deep-rooted values; character neurosis	To have learned an act	Subsequent attitude or memory; symptom neurosis
	An example:	Learning one's native language; developing one's personality	A developed motor skill	Nontrivial learning or remembering

instances, with which we are concerned here, the change will act on the person as a *life-change,* so that we may properly talk about some *result.* The five terms I have emphasized constitute in the most general terms a significant sequence in an individual's life, and I suggest that the outline is general and neutral enough to be applicable no matter what the person's behavioral style. In column 1 of table 3 there are listed, reading down, the five general "markers" that I have just defined, constituting a sequence of significant change. In the other three columns of the table this sequence is traced in terms of each of the major behavioral styles. Finally, I have added, at the bottom of the table, a prototypic example of a change in each style.

The table may be read from top to bottom to trace a sequence within one style, or it may be read across columns, within a step, to compare the styles in regard to each of the markers. The ecto column may perhaps seem the most familiar, since it is the ecto style that we customarily associate with such sequences. However, one part of the ecto column may give rise to some misunderstanding. The entries in the first and second steps of this column may seem to imply that the event or the process are unreal. Indeed, it is a common misunderstanding that ecto-type phenomena are unreal, that they are exemplified by such events as thoughts or perceptions or fantasies. I should therefore emphasize that this is a misunderstanding, that the phenomena referred to all across steps 1 and 2 of the table are equally real. The difference as we read across a row consists rather in how the person lives the event and how the person is "connected" to an ongoing sequence.

In the endo mode the person is connected fully, and usually emotionally, in an activity that in the table I have called incorporation, which occurs in reference to the occurrence of a meaningful situation. In the meso mode one is connected with an identified part or aspect within a situation by way of a motor act directed toward the event. But in the ecto mode one is connected at a distance, neutrally, preserving the distinction between self and surround, in touch with a discriminable unit out of some less sharply apprehended whole. It is an activity that Werner and Kaplan,[1] in their valuable discussion of the process of symbol formation, have called *decontextualization*, meaning by this term a way of distancing between the vehicle of activity and its referent. Thus step 2 of the sequence may take the form of endo participation or meso act, but also of ecto perception—or, of course, some mix of the three. It should be noted that which style predominates at this step of the sequence will probably determine in large degree what the ensuing steps will be.

This is because the style in which step 2 is carried out will be determined by the way the person is typically behaving in regard to this sort of event. For example, in early childhood when meso and ecto styles are as yet in early stages of development and therefore less likely to predominate, it is likely that step 2 of a significant sequence will be in the endo mode. This means that whatever the actual event or process that occurred, it will be expressed by the individual in the endo mode. Once lived through as a form of endo activity, it is unlikely that at a later time (or at later steps in the table) this occurrence will take the form of a remembered idea. If the mother repeatedly conveys rejection to the baby who is feeding, these events will be grasped (step 1) by the infant in the endo mode and will then produce changes that may last a lifetime (steps 2 to 5). Is it likely that years later this person will merely have an opinion that people are not to be trusted, as though this were simply a memory held in the ecto mode? No, it is far more likely that this consequence, if the person holds it at all, will be held as a deep-rooted knowing in the very bones, a conviction so fundamental that it serves as a foundation for important aspects of the personality.

As the meso mode begins to assume a greater importance in the life of the growing child, endo and meso styles interpenetrate so as to provide the individual with socially more effective ways of responding to events. As I will show in a later section of this chapter, this seems to be the sequence that Piaget formalized as a theory of childhood development. The task that Piaget set himself may be described as explaining the normal course of development from a non-ecto to an ecto being. Freud's task, on the other hand—to state the contrast immediately between our two major theorists of child development—seems to have been somewhat more complex. He dealt primarily with clinical data, material which so often speaks of the endo style, and so his task was to explain its persistence beyond childhood and into adult life.

The difference between these two theorists is evident if we consider again the example of the rejecting mother. In Piaget's scheme there is no need for any "mental" representation to occur as such during this first stage of development. In his view this does not occur at all until the child has gone through other stages of mental life. For Freud, however, even the earliest stages of childhood development were complete, although perhaps miniaturized, versions of adult mental life. Thus in my example Piaget would see the infant's subsequent behavior (steps 2 and 3) as simply reflexive, not yet "intelligent," for its intelligence, now as well as later, is to be defined in terms of how closely it corresponds to ecto thought. Freud's view was that at this instant (step 2) the infant would hallucinate the absent breast, thus beginning a life of thought, a career of mental representations, even within a stage of development that is entirely endo. It was precisely because he discovered so many ecto-type activities within earlier, endo stages that—as we will see in a later section—Freud was compelled to make so many important changes in his account of development. In the terms of table 3, we may say that Freud's formulation was to attach endo steps 1 and 2 to ecto steps 3, 4, and 5, and that it took him another fifteen years to unravel the skein of difficulties that resulted.

A major theoretical problem for Piaget, on the other hand, concerned the reality status of events and objects in the world of the growing child—which is a kind of problem that arises only within the ecto realm of activity. It appears, for the child, as the question of how the child knows that something is or is not real. Once the question is raised, the ecto answer is—as I showed in chapter 3—that something is real if I can make it disappear. Piaget is able to locate the first signs of a true ecto style toward the end of the child's first year, when there develops what he calls "object permanence." The situation, in the form of a little test of the child's capacities, consists of the experimenter showing the child an attractive toy and then placing it out of sight, for example, under a cloth. Children of less than a year (all these ages are, of course, approximate) will usually accept the "disappearance" of the toy without getting upset and will turn to whatever else may capture their attention. At some time during their second year, however, children will respond as though the toy is still "there." They will show surprise or distress at its disappearance and may even search actively for it at the place where it was last seen. In Piaget's terms, they have achieved "object permanence," or the ability to retain an idea of an object even though the sensory and perceptual cues to the object's existence have radically changed. This, according to Piaget, is the earliest indicator of that mode of intelligence that defines the adult. It is ecto intelligence, in which one is capable of maintaining a world of ideational representations whose very first instance may have been an image of a toy that an adult hid beneath a cloth. Earlier manifestations of activity similar to intelligence are at best what he calls "sensorimotor," and "even though it involves the attribution of meanings, sensorimotor intelligence . . . does not involve representations, and does not qualify for Piaget as 'thinking'." "Since this intelligence is not reflective, being closely tied to perceptual and bodily actions, it cannot make judgments in abstraction from the sensorimotor milieu."[2]

PIAGET: DEVELOPMENT IN TWO MODES

On a television show concerning a group of men who gather at the Bonneville salt flats to race their cars across the desert, one of the participants, a beefy man approaching middle age, is asked why he goes to all this trouble, expense, even danger, just for a few minutes of flaming excitement at the wheel of a car. He has no hesitation in replying: "So that you do something more today than you did yesterday." Not "the same as yesterday," we note, but a little bit more. Here is the voice of the meso style, at any age. Each day, often each moment, is constituted as a small obstacle to overcome. We should not be at all surprised at the classic answer of the meso mountain climber to the ecto-style question: But why do you do it? The answer, "Because it is there," means that from the meso point of view, it is in fact concretely there, today's obstacle to be overcome.

Piaget took as his life task the elaboration of a theory of the growth of intelligence, rather than the study of behavior, as with Skinner, or the study of personality and psychopathology, as with Freud. In a brief statement about his work a few years before he died he referred to "the only field I know: cognitive psychology," and asked that the field be developed in the direction of two of its "extremes . . . its sources, which are biological, and its outcomes, which are epistemological."[3] In my summary below, where I refer to the well-known Piagetean "stages," I mean my discussion not as a full exposition of his many contributions but rather as highlighting some major points for their relevance to my thesis.

As can be seen from his reference to cognitive psychology and to epistemology, Piaget's emphasis was on the ecto style of behavior. Yet as he always insisted, the sources of this behavior lay in biology. He saw himself, true to his own origins in zoology, as one who would be able to forge links between the biological and the logico-mathematical sciences. Human development, he said, occurs as the consequence of an interplay between two adaptive "movements" in the individual's ongoing behavior. One of these movements is *assimilation,* in which the individual apprehends and deals with the world in terms of whatever cognitive organization has already been achieved; the perceived world is assimilated to whatever understanding is already present. The other movement is *accommodation*, in which the individual's cognitive organization is changed to fit the world as it is met; the individual is accommodated to whatever the world presents.

The broad biological program of the human species, as it is played out through the interweaving of these two movements, results in four major stages of development that appear sequentially: (1) the sensori-motor stage, from birth to about two years of age, in which initially diffused activities come under the control of schemas that are built up out of sensory and motor processes. This makes possible complex behaviors that then lead to (2) the preoperational stage, from age two to age seven, in which cognitive activity first appears and in which socialization proceeds while the foundation is laid for the full development of cognitive abilities; (3) in the ensuing period of concrete operations, lasting until the age of eleven or twelve, the cognitive schemas that develop are precursors of fully attained cognitive skills which appear at (4) the final stage of formal operations, when whatever may be available to the individual is achieved.

In Piaget's terms the growth of the mind involves changes, taking about ten years to accomplish, from the practical action-world of early childhood to the world of representation, symbolizing, and information processing that characterizes the fully formed intellect of the adult. The sequence begins with reflexes, turns to habits, and then grows into cognitive representations, in a "remarkable continuity with the acquired or even inborn processes on which it depends and at the same time makes use of."[4] In the terms I use in this book, Piagetean growth consists of a change from behavior largely in the endo and meso styles to behavior dominated by the ecto style. But since Piaget was occupied with ecto activities as signs of true intelligence, and viewed meso and especially endo activities as at best a useful foundation for the mental growth that came later, he had trouble seeing the earlier stages as evidencing intelligence. He did recognize that intelligence must extend "an organic adaptation which is anterior to it," and that this adaptation must rest on an "organizing activity inherent in life itself," yet as far as he was able to see, "the primitive stages of psychological development only constitute the most superficial acquisitions of awareness of this work of organization."[5]

Compelled as he was to see intelligence only in forms of "awareness," Piaget had to deny a true mental life to the world of the young child; at the same time his descriptions fully revealed intelligent modes of adaptation prior to awareness. Thus, in discussing the organization of the pattern of infant sucking, particularly when it shows the ability to adapt to the position and shape of the nipple, he cannot admit that there is any "recognition" of the object; at most the infant "rediscovers a sensorimotor and particular postural complex . . . (and) this elementary recognition consists . . . of 'assimilation' of the whole of the data present in a definite organization which has already functioned"[6]—a description, I suggest, which is all that we need to sum up the activity of an endo intelligence. And immediately, because such a statement might imply that he is permitting recognition of a form of intelligence at this level, Piaget adds in a footnote of warning: "Let us repeat that we do not claim to specify the states of consciousness which accompany this assimilation. . . . What this behavior simply reveals is the groping and the discernment which characterizes the use of the reflex.[7]

To the investigator who, in the powerful tradition of modern thought, ignores the living body in favor of an abstraction called mind, psychological development can consist of nothing other than improvements in ways of ecto thinking. By contrast, the view I suggest in these pages argues that all three components are active in each of our activities all through the life span. What changes, then, is not simply one component but the way they are combined in behavioral expression; therefore, intelligence of one kind or another—and there will then be many kinds—is manifest at every stage of development. It may well be true, as Piaget showed in a series of classic demonstrations, that the preschooler who is just making the transition from the sensorimotor to the preoperational stage has yet to gain a level in which ideas can be manipulated so as to act upon ideas or the even more advanced level in which there is available a system of abstract rules directing how such symbolizing operations can be carried out. But it may equally be true that the child at this age possesses other kinds of intelligence that enable it to accomplish tasks that, if tackled as intellectual puzzles in the manner of adults, might never be achieved. The chief of these tasks, the learning of one's native language, I have already discussed at length in an earlier chapter and will not repeat here. Another such action, the imitating of another's action, is of equal interest.

Imitation: The First Level

It is well accepted that human infants as well as monkeys and apes of all ages are capable of imitating discrete acts. Only recently, however, has it been shown that imitation in human infants may occur as early as a few weeks after birth. In carefully designed studies, Meltzoff and Moore[8] have shown that infants who are less than three weeks old, and in one instance an infant only an hour old, are able to imitate a variety of different mouth movements—protruding the lips, sticking out the tongue, and opening the mouth. This finding raises fundamental questions about the organization of behavior from the very beginning of postnatal life.

We should note first of all that the infants in the Meltzoff and Moore study were not demonstrating the kind of imitation that Piaget has called the earliest, in which one imitates oneself, so to speak. This consists of performing some small movement and then repeating it, often many times, just as though each doing of the movement is imitated in the next doing of it. Rather, these infants were permitted to observe an experimenter demonstrate the mouth movement while they had a pacifier in the mouth, and only after the demonstration was concluded was the pacifier removed so that they might imitate the movement.

A first question that is raised by this finding is one that runs through all studies of imitation. From the point of view of the imitator, what is happening is that some part of another person's anatomy is projected forward, that is, toward the imitator. To follow such an act precisely, then, the imitator ought to try to project the tongue toward the back of the mouth so that it moves in the same direction as the tongue that is being imitated. To respond to a movement in one direction with a movement in the opposite direction would seem to be an appropriate imitation only if the imitator is able to grasp the guiding conception extend-the-tongue—but how is a newborn capable of doing this? A related issue poses the same problem but in even more serious form.

If the infant's stimulus for imitation is the sight of another person's tongue, and if the infant cannot see its own tongue, how is it to know that the seen object over there is the same as this felt object in here? Again, this would seem to be possible if the infant already has some knowledge about tongues as objects and where they are generally located. We are brought back to concluding that imitation is possible only if the infant has already achieved a level of cognitive development for which imitation is supposed to be the first stage.

A final issue is equally troubling but of broader biological significance. We may ask: Why does the infant imitate? It may be argued that this capability has some biological utility, perhaps in the form of survival value, yet there is the counter argument that such "prewired" programs for behavior are for practical reasons usually restricted to narrow and tightly controlled, rigidly executed kinds of action. The number and variety of infant imitative movements that have been demonstrated, as well as the persistence of the ability into developmental periods well beyond infancy, argues against a claim on these grounds. We are therefore left, as before, with the conclusion that in human infants and perhaps in the higher primates as well, a form of cognitively developed behavior occurs in the absence of prior cognitive development.

This is, in fact, the explanation that Meltzoff and Moore offer for their results, that the infant possesses an "abstract representational system" which enables it to match the observed action against some built-in image of an expected act. Unfortunately, such an explanation demands that the infant possess capacities far exceeding those that, as far as we know, are available to it. Indeed, if it were capable of such ecto performances practically at birth, we would have no problem of development to explain. A similar kind of explanation is offered in a popular text in psychology. According to this author, the child "can only copy her elders if she has some rather well-developed notions of the what and how of her own facial anatomy, and of the correspondence of her own anatomy to the anatomy of others."[9]

On the face of it, the problem of early infant imitation would appear to have no reasonable solution. Every explanation seems to call for developed capacities in the infant that we are sure do not yet exist. But on the other hand, this may just be the point. So long as we insist on restricting our understanding to one and only one kind of intelligence, we will be trapped in a dilemma—that the first stage of ecto intelligence seems to require an already highly developed level of ecto intelligence. But if we are willing to accept the possibility of other styles of intelligence, the problem may become solvable.

Recall our earlier discussions of the endo style and how performances in it are carried out. The infant behaving almost entirely in the endo style, or under the influence of the endo component, is first of all not engaged in building a world out there by means of perception. What is perceived, in whatever modality, is not projected out into the world—as we do, for example, in our every instance of visual and auditory perception—but rather incorporated. Analogies that make sense in terms of adult experience are difficult to find, but perhaps we can come close with the example of smelling something. If you bend close to a flower to sniff at it, and if you close your eyes so as not to see it, your experience when the fragrance fills your nostrils will not be the experience of "creating" an object in space, at some location near your nose. That experience is, truly, inescapable if what you are doing is seeing the flower; that is, you unthinkingly and inescapably experience, not your seeing, but the object of your seeing somewhere in space near you. But when you smell the flower, at least with your eyes closed so as not to see it, you experience something in you rather than something in the world. What you create is a change in you, not a change in the world.

In this sense we may say that, in at least some instances of smelling, and in all instances of pure endo behavior, you incorporate the perceived object. I suggest that this is the experience the infant has when presented with a human face, an experience that is rather clumsily described with the word "participation." For it is not that the infant reaches out, so to speak, to participate in what is seen as happening out there. Rather, the infant draws the stimulus in and effects a fusion with it or, if you will, mouths it and absorbs it. Infant and other become one; therefore, they perform the same act. In this light it is as correct to say that the other is imitating the infant as the reverse.

I suggest that this explanation, or rather, this way of viewing the matter allows us to answer the seemingly unanswerable questions we raised above. There is now no problem of the infant translating the object that is seen pointing toward itself into another object that points away from itself and no need to postulate that the infant has any of the knowledge of anatomy needed to accomplish this, nor the cognitive ability required by other explanations. The other question, as to why the infant imitates, is also answered as soon as we identify imitation with the pure endo act. This is, in fact, the infant's repertoire of action, the endo style, with very little admixture of other styles. When it acts in the endo style, it acts in such a way that, given the right circumstances, it is seen to imitate what others do.

Imitation: The Next Level

Very early in the infant's life there begins to occur the development of the meso component, a process that Piaget has traced in great detail. The advantage to the growing child is that to the relatively passive and absorptive character of endo activity there is now added a set of activities in which the infant actively attempts to master the world through physical manipulation. Imitation now occurs at a more complex level of development.

The most important of the endo-motor schemas of the young infant is, of course, the set of movements organized for sucking. It involves not only the mouth and face and digestive apparatus but also, as observation clearly indicates, the breathing apparatus and the musculature of the arms, the legs, and the trunk. This sensory-motor schema, as Piaget calls it, is one of the action patterns forming the first content of a developing endo-meso intelligence. Very soon thereafter there appears the set of movements organized for grasping, within which one may distinguish the hand-grasp movement, the arm-reach movement, the eye-focus movement, and a number of others, all of which eventually coalesce into a larger schema of look-see-grasp-hold. By the time the infant is ready to sit unaided, at about six months of age, the major sensory-motor schemas of the upper half of the body have come into place. Together they form the foundation through which the infant comes to situate its body in space. At this point imitation at a higher level can occur.

In this new form of imitation, the child no longer has to become completely absorbed with every instance of what is to be imitated—a capacity that is perhaps useful in basic survival instances but that can hardly serve as a basis for an endless variety of moment-to-moment learning activities. In place of this endo mode there develops a new, meso style of imitation, in which the child imitates the act. But this is possible only if a new foundation has already been established for any motor act. I suggest that the great advantage to the growing child of the meso style is that by its practice the child comes to experience itself as situated in space. This could not occur in the endo mode. But as sensory-motor schemas develop and finally coalesce into a functioning whole, that whole is experienced as a known and controllable set of functions with its own "home base" and its own capacity to carve up the spatial surround into arenas of familiar action. It is on this basis that all subsequent action becomes possible; one always moves *from* one situation *to* another, for example, from a specific situation of rest to a different situation of rest or of movement. One moves from-to; one never simply moves, because in movement or not one is always in a movement-determined situation.

The child at this stage, then, is imitating the act, that is, imitating an organized movement in space in reference to its own movement-determined situation in the same space. If the intelligence guiding this act were not meso but ecto, as it would have to be if the child solved the problem by some procedure of recognition or matching, we would have to presuppose just the developed capacity that Piaget is at pains to tell us does not yet exist.

There is a charming anecdote that Piaget recounts concerning his daughter Lucienne, then sixteen months old. She observed him place a necklace that she wanted into a small box and close it almost entirely, leaving only a slit to suggest how the necklace might be reached. To solve this problem she first looked at the box "with great attention"—an interesting instance of the ecto style beginning to influence her behavior—and then as though in preparation for dealing directly with the box, she opened and closed her mouth a number of times. To this Piaget comments, "Apparently Lucienne understands the existence of a cavity . . . and wishes to enlarge it," but because of her lack of words she is forced to the use of "a simple motor indicator as 'signifier' or symbol. . . . [It is] a phase of plastic reflection."[10]

A number of comments are in order here. Piaget sees the mouth movement as indicating her understanding of "the existence of a cavity," whereas in the argument I am pursuing one would say that it indicates, rather, that she has grasped the nature of a specific act. In a similar episode when she was eleven months old, Lucienne had done the same thing: in imitation of her father's opening and shutting his eyes, she clasped and unclasped her hands, then opened and closed her mouth.[11] The similarity here strongly suggests that what the child masters and expresses is essentially a class of movements, in this case the class that we would call open/close. Her performance is largely in the meso mode. Although Piaget's apt phrase "plastic reflection" does capture much of what I am saying here, his reference to a "simple motor indicator" as a "symbol" seems to me to indicate that he persists in viewing development even in these early years as unidimensional, as a matter of a greater or less lack in the single capacity for (ecto) symbolic thinking.

It is not always easy to tell from Piaget's writings what place he allots to sensory-motor schemas in the course of development. He is apparently willing enough to credit the place of action patterns, or motor intelligence, in the first year or so of life. To this he adds that with the onset of language toward the end of the second year, the action patterns become "internalized" and true thought patterns then grow out of them. Like the messenger who gasps out a message before dying, it appears that the purpose of overt action patterns is only to carry on the developmental sequence until more appropriate (ecto) modes of behavior can take over. It is noteworthy that Piaget gives almost no place to such significant meso milestones as the development of an upright posture. In any case, the last three of Piaget's four stages of development, and the concepts on which his reputation is largely based, concern what I call ecto functions, which come to dominate the growing child's behavior. Indeed, major criticisms of Piaget's work[12] have consisted largely in arguing that his emphasis on the ecto style was not carried far enough, and that significant ecto-style behavior may appear even earlier than Piaget had thought.

Some Other Attempts: Mother and Infant

Recent sophisticated attempts to re-evaluate the course of an infant's development of "intelligence" seem to have foundered on the same point—an insistence that there is only one kind of intelligence and that development consists in attaining this intelligence. A statement commonly found, for example, is that at the very start of life the infant forms a kind of symbiosis of consciousness with the mother and between self and world; it does not distinguish self from "out there," and only gradually is this distinction formed, or to put the matter in the more elementary terms that may be found in some texts, the infant experiences and acts as though it and the mother occupy the same body. In a recent discussion of the matter, Kenneth Shapiro[13] quotes a number of writers to this effect (Merleau-Ponty on "the syncretic system of me-and-other," analytic writers on "symbiosis," and Harry Stack Sullivan on "prototaxic" experiencing) and he refers to the phenomenon as a functioning "child-world."

But clearly the infant is not in fact joined to the world or to any part of it. If not, does the infant then experience itself as joined to mother or to world? I suggest not, for at least two reasons; first, it does not experience itself, as we would all agree, therefore it cannot experience itself as either joined or not joined. Second, and more important, if its complete experience consists of a seamless whole (in which, as we but not the infant know, it is in fact present) then on principle it cannot "know" that this is so, no matter how we define that verb. It is in the position of the fish that cannot ever know that it is in water. If this is all there is, all there ever was, and all there could be, then this is not knowable. The structure of infant experiencing is simply not concerned with the joining or not joining of self to other.

All these writers seem to be trying to create an emergence of a self that has not yet emerged; their case rests on such an assumption. I suggest that the trap is unavoidable if one is convinced that in describing ways of knowing and forms of intelligence we must from the beginning refer to some variant of ecto functioning. The self, as the core of all self-reflectiveness and of distancing, is the central construct within ecto functioning; therefore these writers must perforce include some beginnings of self at the earliest stage of development. Shapiro does at one point quote with approval Merleau-Ponty's description of "an un-differentiated group life . . . an initial community,"[14] but this attempt to explain such phenomena as infant imitation falls short. It admits a Piagetean-type motor reaction in "the affected body" but will not ground the infant's intelligence any more securely in the body. If we are to accept the evidence, from Piaget to current investigators, concerning the varieties of infant competence, we will have to recognize that like other species of mammals, the human infant demonstrates varieties of intelligence, some of them describable only as an intelligence in the endo style.

FREUD'S TWO CRISES

As I have tried to show in the preceding sections, the theoretical system of Piaget, although it purports to deal with human development from birth to late adolescence, makes no place at all for the endo component and de-emphasizes the meso component in regard to all but the first year or two. Intelligence is defined in terms of the capacities of those persons we call intellectuals, who are predominantly ecto. In these respects Piaget's thinking follows the mainstream of Western psychology. I am aware of only one group of investigators in developmental psychology who are an exception to this tradition, those at the Gesell Institute of Child Development at Yale, whose publications were most influential during the 1950s and 1960s. Their analysis of the development of behavior in children was based explicitly on Sheldon's work on human temperament, hence their premise was that "we behave as we do (that is, our personality is what it is) because of the way our bodies are built."[15]

Within Western culture, Sigmund Freud's life work represents the other major contribution to the understanding of life-span development. Because my purpose is not to survey his monumental achievement but to explore some aspects of it, I will concentrate on his earlier work; that will give us an opportunity to consider the issues as he first saw them. Interestingly, this will also give us the chance to touch on such questions as his "seduction theory," which in recent years has exercised scholars of psychoanalytic thought.

My account of the first half of Freud's career will present the thesis that Freud's major writings from about 1893 to 1906 comprised an attempt to build a theory of personality development along completely ecto lines, and that in pursuit of this aim he surmounted two major crises in his thinking. The expression "along completely ecto lines" should be read as a reminder of the two ways in which a theory may be an expression of the ecto style. As I have noted earlier in a number of places, all theories can to some degree be considered as activities in the ecto style. This is because of the nature of theories and their logical structures. But in addition, any theory, no matter how it is structured, may embrace *content* that refers primarily to one of the three styles. For example, it is possible to use an ecto style of thinking to derive an abstract theory that is entirely in reference to meso activities, or even a theory that claims that all thinking activities are done in a meso style. This seems to be just what we see in the case of McGuigan's[16] impressive research on what he calls the psychophysiology of thinking.

This is to say that the ecto component may appear either in the formal structure of a theory or in regard to its content and emphasis. A theory in which both structure and content are predominantly ecto would, I suggest, be one that is "along completely ecto lines." This appears to be what Freud aimed to do, at least during the very productive first half of his career. I believe that much of the biographical evidence, as in his letters and in his self-analysis, indicates that he was never completely an ecto-style thinker. Like many creative persons as well as like most neurotics—and Freud was surely both—he did not always effect a good match between what he was and what he did or tried to do. His expressed aim was to explain all human development, all personality change and its aberrations, in terms of the play of ecto-style entities and processes. In this the influence of Darwin was almost overwhelming and the early influence of such scientists as Helmholtz was very strong. His great dream, therefore, was to construct a science of the human personality or, as he soon came to conceptualize it, of the human psyche. This required, in his eyes, a theory in the ecto style, and it has served until today as a model of the type.

From 1892 until the early part of 1895, Freud and his friend Josef Breuer worked together on a book that was finally published as *Studies on Hysteria*.[17] It consisted of their theoretical speculations on the problem of hysteria plus a number of case studies, the latter written from the summer of 1892 to the end of 1894 even though the clinical work with these patients had in most instances been completed some years before. From the beginning the question they faced was how to explain the origin and course of development of the array of symptoms presented by these patients. The problem was by no means straightforward, for in the case of the syndrome called hysteria the patients' symptoms were without demonstrable physical cause even though they were mostly physical in nature—for example, stammering, tics, pains, disturbances of the senses, cramps, or uncontrollable movements.

The Case of Frau Emmy

The patient whom Freud pseudonymously called Frau Emmy von N. will serve as a first example. A forty-year-old woman whom he treated during 1888 and 1889, she presented specific pains that he interpreted as of two kinds. One "set," as he called them, appeared to be determined organically, probably by rheumatic changes in muscles, tendons, and fasciae and subsequently exaggerated by her in neurotic fashion. The other set, he said, "were in all probability *memories* of pains," referring to periods in her life that had produced "agitation."[18] Of this latter set Freud commented, "These pains, too, may well have been originally justified on organic grounds but had since then been adopted for the purposes of the neurosis."[19] In his discussion of another patient he makes the same point, this time in answer to his own question: "Why was it that the patient's mental pain came to be represented by pains in the legs rather than elsewhere? The circumstances indicate that this somatic pain was not *created* by the neurosis but merely used, increased, and maintained by it."[20] Further, even motor symptoms—an uncontrollable exclamation, for example, or its "degeneration" into a tic, or its development into a spoken formula during a delirium—"can be shown to have an original or long-standing connection with traumas, and stand as symbols for them in the activities of memory."[21]

The point, then, would be to track down the moment of trauma; as it turned out, this was rather easy to do once Freud had perfected his anamnestic technique. But this in turn only raised an additional question: "Why had not the whole thing remained on the level of normal psychical life? . . . Why did she not always call to mind the scene it-self?"[22] The answer he arrived at repeatedly, in one patient after an-other, was that what identified the moment of trauma was there having occurred some event or perception that, though neutral in itself, aroused in the patient some incompatible idea or feeling. Some aspect of the original experience then mastered the subsequent discomfort by split-ting off and becoming unconscious. It remained in this state, often for years, until it surfaced again under appropriately stimulating conditions.

In his case of Elisabeth von R., Freud was able to obtain from the patient some direct evidence on just this point. Warm feelings had been aroused in her for a young man, on the occasion of a party—but this was a party she had been able to attend only because she tempo-rarily left her sick father whom she had been nursing. Arriving home "in a blissful frame of mind, she found her father was worse and re-proached herself most bitterly for having sacrificed so much time to her own enjoyment."[23] Understandably she experienced an "incompatibili-ty" or conflict between her happiness and her guilt, and this led to her repressing the erotic feeling from consciousness. Its emotional charge then became attached to some physical pain that was current at the moment, with the result that later reoccurrence of the pain reminded her of her guilt, and resurgence of the guilt brought on its accompany-ing pain.

When this explanatory scheme was applied to the patient's current hysterical symptoms, everything became clear and "the analyst's la-bours were richly rewarded."[24] An incompatible idea was "fended off," "psychical excitations" were converted into "something physical," and these then became her hysterical symptoms. Experiencing tender feel-ings toward the young man (who happened to be her brother-in-law) and resisting such feelings "by her whole moral being," she developed intense physical pains on numerous, seemingly unlikely occasions when she was in his company.

The First Crisis

Freud's achievements in this and similar cases are easy to recognize. To trace them out, we may refer again to table 3. The event starting off a sequence consists in these cases of a complex situation—for example, the presence and the company of her brother-in-law, which leads to her dawning realization that she is in love with him. In the terms of the table, the first and second steps are probably endo-meso. But at this point in his explanation Freud introduces new kinds of elements and in so doing shifts the account over to the ecto column. He speaks of symbolization, of charges of energy, of conscious and unconscious processes, that is, of those terms that for him are beginning to make up his new formal theory. At this point in his career his major achievement consisted in precisely this, that he was able to account for the last three of five steps by the use of elements of an ecto theory.

This explains why the physical pains offered to the analyst as symptoms are, in his theory, not "real" pains but merely symbols, for in the ecto realm there are no physical realities, only symbols of those realities, at one step removed from the world of bodily sensations or muscular movements. This, too, explains why in Freud's developing theory the conversion (of mental to physical pain) takes place not at the moment of original conflict but "in connection with her memories." For memories, like ideas, are elements in the ecto realm; they are irreal psychic entities that serve as representatives of some aspects of the real world.

At this point in his career Freud was little concerned with the nature of the triggering event (step 1) in our sequence. He was in fact willing to accept it as real and therefore as having been influential in precipitating ideas or feelings. As a consequence his case examples sometimes begin with a single traumatic incident such as an attempt at sexual abuse or even with a general situation that erupts into a distressing scene. In one particularly interesting case, that of Fräulein Rosalia H., the sequence apparently began with a single movement that she then preserved as a "motor" memory. The movement, which she presented as a symptom during treatment, consisted of a curious twitching of her fingers. It had been originally precipitated by a scene that aroused in her strong feelings of resentment, of needing to push something away or fend it off, and so Freud describes it in just these terms. "The movement of her fingers which I saw her make while she was reproducing this scene was one of twitching something away, in the way in which one literally and figuratively brushes something aside—tosses away a piece of paper or rejects a suggestion."[25]

Freud does not comment on the fact that what was preserved here as a memory was an expressive movement, the very activity of muscles, and not an idea, an image, a perception, or a feeling. Yet the patient was apparently not conscious of making the movement, either at the moment it was first made or later on reproducing it. Was it then unconscious? If so, can we then talk about unconscious movements? And finally, if we admit the notion of unconscious movements, how shall we reconcile it with the Freudian concept of Unconscious? In his description of the case, Freud accounts for the patient's symptom simply with the remark, "A mnemic symbol had been formed,"[28] which I think we may take to mean that an ecto-type element had been created and was then able to appear later in connection with a repetition of the original experience. As always, he was not concerned with the originating event (step 1) or even with the form in which it might show up, but only with what these events came to "represent" in the patient's psychic life.

It may not be inappropriate to refer to this development in Freud's thinking as his first major crisis as a theorist. Faced with an unprecedented array of clinical data in the form of feeling and ideation, direct experience and symbolization, among his patient group of richly talented women, he found a way to compact this diversity into a relatively simple formal scheme. It was surely a triumph of the scientific spirit he claimed to have inherited from his teachers, and it looked to be the start of what he now saw as his life's work: to spell out in one grand theory an explanation for all human development, normal and abnormal. If such a theory were to be true to its tradition in Western science, it would have to be entirely ecto; indeed, at this point Freud appeared to have pushed the ecto component as far back toward the origin of the sequence as seemed possible.

The Case of Frau Cäcilie

One additional example may show us both the kind of patient and the type of patient material that Freud was now able to comprehend by means of his scheme. The case was one he named Cäcilie M., a remarkably gifted woman who presented among many other symptoms all the indications of severe facial neuralgia. Freud was soon witness to many of her hysterical attacks, as he called them, and by now was able to spell out the presumed order of their parts. There was, first, a mood disturbance, which she usually tried to dismiss as merely the consequence of some recent event. There was then a "clouding of consciousness," which was followed by varied hysterical symptoms such as hallucinations, pains, spasms, and "long declamatory speeches." An experience from her past would emerge "in a hallucinatory form," explaining everything, and with this her "clarity of mind" was restored, at least until the next such attack, often only a few hours later. Given his scheme, Freud had no trouble understanding her newest symptom, the facial neuralgia. It turned out to be connected with a scene in which she had experienced "great mental irritability" toward her husband when he insulted her.

At precisely this point in her recital of the scene, Frau Cäcilie suddenly gave a cry of pain, put her hand to her face, and said, "It was like a slap in the face"—re-experiencing in this moment, in concrete somatic form, the pain that she had (symbolically) experienced at her husband's insult. The hysterical attack was now done with and the symptom, as such, was gone.[27]

In Freud's explanation, the patient had taken the route of "symbolization," in which the husband's insult was symbolized in a verbal expression that she then took literally. Freud could trace all of this back to an episode some fifteen years earlier when a conflict situation—just as in other instances—led to her forcing out of consciousness any thoughts about the situation; she then underwent a "conversion" concerning then-current experiences of facial pain based on a toothache. Still another of her symptoms, this one a sharp pain in the right heel, came about as a consequence of her fear when meeting new friends that she might perhaps not "find herself on a right footing" with them.[28]

We should note here that whether or not this patient fitted Freud's formal explanatory scheme as to the *origin* of her hysterical attacks, she was capable of a nearly endless variety of such "symbolic" expressions—a piercing look, it stabbed me to the heart, I'll have to swallow this, and so on. These and similar expressions are known to all persons in their own languages, for they are the ways in which we reveal through language the somatic basis for much of our experience. Frau Cäcilie was, it is true, somewhat unusual in this respect, for she thought and spoke in such terms much of the time, so much so that as Freud put it: "She had a whole quantity of sensations and ideas running parallel with each other. Sometimes the sensation would call up the idea to explain it, sometimes the idea would create the sensation by means of symbolization, and not infrequently it had to be left an open question which of the two elements had been the primary one."[29] She was a gifted poet, and it appears from this account that she customarily and spontaneously thought and even spoke as though she were composing poetry or as though ideas came to her in vivid, pictorial form with many facets of connotation revealed at the same time. Once she became angry at both Breuer and Freud, and as a result she had the "hallucination" of the two of them hanging on separate trees, the one next to the other. As revealed later, the explanation for this vivid image was in part that her anger had led to a wish they would die. But in addition, she had had the thought that they were so bad one could hardly choose between them, since they were each a match or counterpart for the other—and the link here was the French word for match, *pendant*, which has the dual meaning of "hanging" and "counterpart."

At this place in his thinking, although very briefly, Freud toyed with a notion that, if he had developed it, might have set him off on quite a different track. Musing on the evident possibility that these "symbolic" expressions—for example, to be stabbed to the heart—could not arise in any of us unless there also occurred some slight organic sensations accompanying the thought, he took a step toward a different conclusion. Perhaps, he suggested, it is not a case of hysteria taking common language as a model for the expression of sensations but rather "that both hysteria and linguistic usage alike draw their material from a common source."[30] But here he stopped, abruptly. What "common source" could he have had in mind? One cannot be sure, for he never again came back to this critical point. But let us keep in mind the kind of problem with which he was grappling at this time. The problem of hysteria raised some interesting questions concerning anatomy. The physical anatomy that was taught in medical schools, an anatomy of real bone and tissue, was clearly insufficient as the locus or cause of hysterical symptoms; for example, a symptom such as glove anesthesia was literally not possible, given the way nerve endings are known to be distributed in the body. As Freud put it, rather neatly, "hysteria behaves as though anatomy did not exist."[31]

He therefore turned to another kind of anatomy, his own invented or postulated anatomy of the psychic apparatus. He was now in the ecto realm. But very briefly, in his aborted reference to some "common source" for both ecto and non-ecto entities, he was pointing to a third kind of anatomy, the anatomy of the lived body. The hysteric who presents a glove anesthesia may be technically incorrect in terms of medical school anatomy, but she may well be correctly reporting her direct experience of her body as she lives it; therefore no third, postulated anatomy is necessary as an explanation. If this is what the patient is doing, she is behaving in a meso/endo realm, even though this may be inappropriate behavior for adults in modern Western society when they refer to their bodies. For one moment, at the very end of his lengthy case study, Freud toyed with but then quickly dropped a line of thought that might have led him to exploring somatic realms other than the ecto.

But he could not do this, for the pressures of a century of scientific development were at this moment pushing him in another direction. As Ernest Jones remarked, he was "on the brink of deserting physiology and of enunciating the findings and theories of his clinical observations in purely psychological language."[32] In the terms I have been using, he was on the brink of developing a completely ecto approach to the problems of normal and abnormal psychology and, quite possibly, at least in his own eyes, of becoming a new Darwin. As he reported at a later date,[33] it was just this turning from the physiological to the psychological that brought about his first serious disagreement with his friend and mentor, Breuer. A few years afterward he made one last effort at a theory that, while ecto in structure, was traditionally non-ecto in content. This was the famous "Project,"[34] a trial effort that he sent to his correspondent Fliess in the form of a rough draft but then dropped. In place of this scheme there appeared a nearly identical theoretical version, in the seventh chapter of his *Interpretation of Dreams*,[35] which was now ecto in both structure and content.

The Second Crisis

To reach his goal Freud had still one crisis to surmount. Referring again to table 3, we may say that Freud had thus far explained the development of a neurosis—motor or obsessive as well as hysteric—as composed of endo steps 1 and 2 followed by ecto steps 3, 4, and 5. Although the latter ecto explanation had been thoroughly spelled out in two papers on the neuropsychoses of defense in 1894 and 1896,[36] he had as yet not achieved an explanation within ecto terms of the first two steps in the sequence. A complete scheme involving all five steps did not appear in print until 1905, in the fifth chapter of his work on jokes.[37] It was there, according to his translator Strachey, that Freud "first explicitly repudiated all intention of using the term 'cathexis' in any but a psychological sense and all attempts at equating nerve-tracts or neurones with paths of mental association."[38]

What happened between 1894 and 1905 has recently been the subject of intensive study by Freudian scholars, both friendly and critical. As I have tried to show, Freud saw as his life's work the construction of a comprehensive theory of the human personality and its development—but a theory that would be true to the tradition of the natural sciences. This tradition has been within the ecto style, and because of his many contributions Freud has become one of that tradition's major modern representatives. But at this point in his career he had not yet completed the task he had set for himself. The problem of how a neurosis begins and then develops through the years, with all that this implies for the relations between children and adults, was in his view beginning to be resolved but far from complete. A major gap concerned the origin of a neurosis. Was it, as the clinical data seemed to imply, a normal perception of and then response to a real event? Or was it, as his theory seemed to demand, an irreal occasion in which the real event only symbolized a more significant ecto process?

The record of this period seems to show three things: first, that he waffled almost interminably over this issue before finally resolving it to his own satisfaction; second, that he was quite capable of holding to and playing with a number of mutually contradictory ideas at once; and third, that when he began to move in a specific direction, his announcements of the move were made at first privately, to his friends or correspondents, and only much later publicly. The relevant episodes at this time may be summarized as follows.

The Eckstein Affair

Beginning in January 1895 when Freud's friend and correspondent Fliess operated on Emma Eckstein's nose—she being a patient, disciple, and later psychoanalytic colleague of Freud—but botched the surgery so that she suffered severe hemorrhaging, both Freud and Fliess sought desperately to absolve the latter of blame for his ineptitude. Here was a clear instance of a "symptom," the hemorrhaging, which both knew had begun with the surgery and not earlier—but fortunately for their purposes, until some half-meter of gauze was actually recovered from her nose, the cause of the "symptom" could remain unclear. If it should turn out that the cause, and therefore the true origin, lay in a real event consisting of Fliess's inept work, both would of course be embarrassed and perhaps even feel guilt, but the case would then resemble others that Freud had known. But if they were able to discover a "psychological" explanation for the origin of Eckstein's "symptom," two needs would be satisfied at once. On the one hand, it would relieve the two overeager physicians of their guilt by shifting the blame to the patient, and at the same time it might provide a first model for the further development of Freud's theoretical scheme along completely ecto lines.

The evidence for Freud's almost panicky vacillation during this period and for his final opting for the latter explanation—that Eckstein's bleeding represented a "longing for love" and so was not precipitated by a real event, the surgery, but by a symbolization—has been presented in some detail by Jeffrey Masson.[39] Based on newly discovered data in the form of previously unpublished letters from Freud to Fliess, Masson has argued that this was more or less typical of Freud's personal style, to construct theoretical explanations that would glorify his own person even when this meant "assaulting" the truth and denying the reality of his own clinical data. Tracing a shift in Freud's thinking that was first evidenced in the Eckstein case, away from real events and toward psychological constructs, Masson accuses Freud of being false to his own data in order to curry favor with the medical profession, in order to save the reputation of his friend Fliess, and in order to preserve the image of his own father. In Masson's words, this shift was away from "the actual world of sadness, misery, and cruelty to an internal stage on which actors perform invented dramas for an invisible audience of their own creation."[40]

Masson's charge is not only in reference to the Eckstein case, although that is surely the most dramatic. It also concerns a number of other cases in which the point at issue is the origin of the patient's neurosis. To examine this, we turn to the second episode.

The Lecture on Aetiology

On April 21, 1896, only five days before a letter to Fliess in which he denied any "real" origin of Eckstein's symptom, Freud presented a lecture entitled "The aetiology of hysteria" before the Psychiatric and Neurological Society of Vienna.[41] It was an important occasion for the young Freud, an occasion when, with Krafft-Ebing in the chair, he could have the attention of his professional peers for the presentation of his newest and, he was convinced, his most significant discovery. He argued first from his findings as to the *course* of development of a neurosis, that "the symptoms of hysteria . . . are determined by certain experiences of the patient's which have operated in a traumatic fashion and which are being reproduced in his psychical life in the form of mnemic symbols."[42] Then he presented his bombshell: "Not only experiences affecting the subject's own body but visual impressions too and information received through the ears are to be recognized as the ultimate traumas of hysteria. . . ."[43] It is now no longer a question of sexual topics having been aroused by some sense impression or other, but of sexual experiences affecting the subject's own body—of *sexual intercourse* (in the wider sense)."[44]

His conclusion was this "momentous revelation" as he called it: "I therefore put forward the thesis that at the bottom of every case of hysteria there are one or more occurrences of premature sexual experience"[45]—which is to say that the origin of this neurosis lay in an *actual* seduction or sexual abuse perpetrated on the child. To Freud's great disappointment, his thesis met with an "icy reception," Krafft-

Ebing calling it nothing but "a scientific fairy tale." In terms of the account I am pursuing here, the first two steps of the sequence in table 3 had now been publicly identified as non-ecto, and this only five days before Freud's private statement to Fliess, regarding Eckstein, that the origin of *her* hysterical symptom lay in a symbolic feeling about a real event rather than in the event itself. Further, it was at this time that Freud was busy writing up material for his book with Breuer, in which he at least cast doubt on the notion of a "real" (or non-ecto) origin of neurosis. What the record shows, then, is that at this time Freud was holding fast to a number of mutually contradictory ideas.

Recent critics of Freud have focused on this lecture and on the cold reception it received, as the central fact leading to Freud's later change of heart. To examine this claim, we look at the next relevant episode.

The Self-Analysis

In June 1897 Freud began a self-analysis, based on material from his dreams, which was to form the basis for his great book on dreams as well as for much of his subsequent psychological theorizing. As recent research has shown, it is very possible that in his dreams Freud found at least some hints that his own father was guilty of the sexual abuse of his children. If Freud did uncover evidence of this sort, his desire not to believe his father guilty of such crimes would have added a compelling personal motive to his drive to construct a completely ecto theory, one grounded in "dreamed events" rather than "real" ones. He would then have felt even more strongly that his theory as presented in his 1896 lecture was not correct; that evidence from dreams and from analytic sessions notwithstanding, adult neuroses did not have their origins in real events such as parental sexual abuse but in children's fantasies *about* possible events, that is, as ecto in step 1 in table 3. This would at one stroke absolve his father and give him the complete theory he wanted. Further, if in fact adult neuroses had their origins in this way, one could conclude that children had a very rich imaginary (ecto) sex life, far richer than had ever been suspected.

To reconstruct the course of Freud's thinking during these years, we may say that once he had given up the theory presented in his lecture on aetiology, he was free to close the circle on a completely ecto theory.

Thus, in their sex life during early childhood, most of it in the form of wish and fantasy rather than real action, children may begin to imagine what they most fear and want, a sexual connection with the parent of the opposite sex. On this basis there begins to be built the child's personal character, and out of it will come that crisis of childhood known as the Oedipal complex; in many cases, out of this may also come "mnemic symbols" that can surface years later in the form of either neurotic symptoms or "memories" of having been abused during childhood. Anna Freud summed it up clearly in a letter to Masson, when he wrote her announcing his newfound conviction that Freud had been right in the first place (that neuroses had their origins in real events, not in fantasies about them). She wrote him that if his revisionist views were to be accepted, all of modern psychoanalytic theory would have to be given up.

The period we are discussing is 1897 to 1898, during which time, we may feel sure, Freud no longer believed in what has been ineptly called the "seduction theory"—the theory that adult neuroses have their origins in actual seductions in childhood. All that now remained for him was to announce publicly his change of view. This brings us to the final episode of the series.

The Public Announcement

In a letter to Fliess dated September 21, 1897, Freud confided his "great secret" that the tales of seduction he had been hearing from his patients were in his view nothing but "fictitious traumas," or what I would term purely ecto activities. In an ensuing letter on November 11, 1897, Freud repeated to Fliess the theme of his now developing ecto scheme: "In the collapse of all values only the psychological theory has remained unimpaired.[46]

It would appear that Freud was now firmly committed to a purely ecto scheme of the origins of sexuality in childhood. One more issue remains to be mentioned. Some critics have argued that Freud's compelling desire to redeem his father's good name and to ingratiate himself with the conservative medical fraternity of Vienna led him to change his views from supporting the idea of childhood seduction to opposing it. Yet the evidence does not support this interpretation of

Freud's motives. He seems to have changed his views as early as 1897, yet it was many years before he made the public announcement that one presumed he would have hastened to make if these were indeed his motives.

In early 1898, in a paper on the aetiology of the neuroses,[47] which he had delivered some months before at a meeting of a Viennese medical group, Freud ventured to speak publicly about infantile sexuality; yet in this quite frank paper, one of the early fruits of his abandonment of the seduction theory, there is no mention at all of his views, pro or con. Now there followed a period in which for more than four years after the publication of his work on dreams, there were no publications at all. If he had been so anxious to have his views accepted by his fellow physicians and so eager to save the reputations of Fliess and of his own father, he would hardly have waited until 1905 and then in three important works (his book on jokes, his "Three Essays on Sexuality," and the Dora case) have made only one brief reference to the matter. This reference occurs in the second of the three essays where he says, in what seems almost an offhand manner, "I cannot admit that in my paper on 'The Aetiology of Hysteria' . . . I exaggerated the frequency or importance of that influence [of seduction in childhood] . . . though I . . . overrated the importance of seduction in comparison with the factors of sexual constitution or development."[48]

Then at last, almost eight years after he had confided to Fliess the great secret of his switch in viewpoint, Freud finally went public with it.[49] The reasons he now advanced for changing his mind turned out to be less than dramatic or theoretically important. His material, he says, was "scanty" at the time and by pure chance they happened to include a "disproportionately large number" of instances in which a significant role was played by sexual seduction carried out by an adult or an older child. Since then, he adds—now in the full flower of his completely ecto scheme—"I have learned to explain a number of phantasies of seduction as attempts at fending off memories of the subject's own sexual activity (infantile masturbation)."[50]

I suggest that the explanation for this long delay is that his views were indeed changing, not for reasons of propriety or personal aggrandizement but because of the life task to which he had devoted himself. He had first of all to finish developing a comprehensive theory by which all of childhood development might be explained; and it had to be along purely ecto lines. In this theory the matter of origins may well have seemed only one element, hardly theoretically primary, in a large and complex puzzle. He therefore had to wait until the grand theoretical statement was laid out, as it was in the "Three Essays," before addressing himself to one of its elements.

There is little doubt, however, that his passage through these changes constituted a crisis. In his autobiographical account of the history of his movement, in 1914,[51] he notes that his original thesis concerning aetiology "broke down under the weight of its own improbability and contradiction . . . [leading to] helpless bewilderment." Out of this "came the reflection that, after all, one had no right to despair because one had been deceived in one's expectations; one must revise these expectations." His conclusion concerning his final, ecto theory is now that hysterical patients "create such scenes in *phantasy* and this psychical reality requires to be taken into account alongside practical reality."[52] The crisis, however, does not appear to have the issue of childhood seduction at its center. For example, in the important paper in 1914 on narcissism[53] Freud makes no mention at all of the seduction problem. Not until a complete autobiographical statement in 1925[54] does he refer to the matter again. In preparation for an extended discussion of infantile sexuality he mentions almost as a digression "an error into which I fell for a while" that occurred "under the influence of the technical procedure which I used at that time."[55] And just to show his readers that like them he is too sophisticated to give credence to such errors, he remarks, "If the reader feels inclined to shake his head at my credulity, I cannot altogether blame him."[56] The crisis having finally been reduced to the status of a foolish slip, we can all laugh at it together. "When I had pulled myself together, I was able to draw the right conclusions from my discovery: namely, that the neurotic symptoms were not related directly to actual events but to wishful phantasies, and that as far as the neurosis was concerned psychical reality was of more importance than material reality."[57] His purely ecto sequence is now complete.

LIFE-SPAN CHANGES

In regard to sexuality, the endo style is essentially androgynous. The orgasm is a meso function, as are so many of the complex acts linked to our survival—and so the sexually disposed meso is orgasmic. The ecto may be either ascetically sexless or a "textbook" performer although perhaps with a rich fantasy life. The sex-manual expert, then, is ecto; the routine performer is endo; and the pornographer is meso.

The story of Freud's development as a theorist during the decade from 1895 to 1905 concerns at most the first five years of a child's life. Like Piaget, Freud was convinced that the critical years are the early ones and that everything important in development occurs before the onset of puberty. To conclude this chapter, then, I will review these early years in terms of the theme of this book, noting how they express the changing interplay of three behavioral styles as one or another attains dominance. Following this, because the human life span does in fact extend beyond puberty, I will add some discussion of the expression of behavioral styles during adulthood and old age.

The Early Years

Although theorists do not usually state the matter in these terms, I think there would be general agreement on the predominance of the endo component in the months following birth. This is observable in many ways—the relatively large abdomen and the relatively short arms and legs, the excess of "baby fat," the clinging, absorbing quality of the neonate's orientation to the world and especially toward the mother, and the great emphasis on sucking. Freud's term "orality" captures much of what I mean here. Piaget, on his part, because of his primary interest in intellectual development, bypassed this phase of the child's life. Yet if this is in fact what occurs as a first phase, then it is predominantly endo in style and has to be considered a foundation for the child's subsequent development.

Some relevant evidence for seeing this as a phase predominantly endo in character comes from the baby's imitative ability, which I discussed in an earlier section, and from the area of language development, which occurs concurrently. As early as six weeks of age, the infant, who has already started to recognize the mother's face and who can already discriminate between a harsh voice and a tender voice or a frowning face and a smiling face, will also begin to respond appropriately to the rhythms of speech in its immediate vicinity.[58] All these developing skills (to use a meso term to describe an endo activity) consist of that engaged and participative connecting that is the mark of the endo style of learning. For example, if the infant at six weeks of age responds with pleasure to a smiling face or a friendly voice and with some distress to a frowning face or a harsh voice, this cannot be based on having already adopted a habitual response to such stimuli (which is meso) nor on having gained some knowledge about the meaning of the stimuli (which would be closer to ecto) but on another basis entirely.

What is required, I suggest, is that the infant (and here out of necessity I shift to a vocabulary of metaphors) grasp totally what is presented, absorb it until it is felt at the point of reception just as it must have been felt at the point of origin, and for the moment participate with the originator in a dance celebrating the moment, with whatever emotional tone is appropriate. When there is required of the infant some form of learning rather than simply an appropriate response, as occurs when the stimulus is the speech of older persons rather than their smiling faces, then the infant displays behavior best termed "participative grasping." As films of infants have shown, the baby now goes through a series of quite well defined movements—although they may be seen by observers as mere random thrashings—that keep time to the accented portions of spoken words. It is in this way that one begins, almost from birth, to build into one's body the very sounds and rhythms of one's native tongue.

These examples, as well as a host of other observations on young infants,[59] suggest that there is an underlying, foundational mode of intelligence in humans prior to what is termed the emergence of self toward the end of the first year. It grows out of that mutual interpenetration of movements and feelings, most often engaging mother and child, that constitutes much of the behavior of young children. This endo intelligence cannot be dismissed as simply an early phase through which the infant passes on its way to something higher or better, leaving the early style behind as the snake leaves the skin that once served it well. It cannot be defined as the absence but as the presence of a form of intelligence. How and when this endo intelligence forms, and what it contributes to the totality of the child's developing personality, are issues that can hardly be avoided in a comprehensive theory of development. Piaget began such a study, but he chose to begin with what really constitutes a next stage of development, which he termed sensory-motor and which I have called meso.

Following the earliest months of life, which constitute an endo burst, the child begins to develop and elaborate forms of motility and physical action. The picture during the second half of the first year as well as the twelve months or so that follow is one of an upsurge of the meso component. The child becomes semierect in a sitting position, learns to move volitionally by scooting or crawling and then walking, and becomes occupied, often to the distraction of parents and other adults, with moving, grasping, holding, pulling, handling, whatever can be accomplished motorically vis-à-vis the resistance of the world. In all, it is a meso burst that lasts, in individually varying form and emphasis, for the next three or four years and that will not again be experienced until the years of midadolescence. In Piaget's terminology we may say these are the sensory-motor years. In David McNeill's formulation of the language learning process, they are the years during which the child builds upon a primary "functional unity" that links Piagetean sensory-motor schemas with the movements involved in speech.[60]

To take another example from the field of language learning, the meso component is clearly evident when the child begins to produce "novel utterances." These are defined as combinations at least two words in length that the child begins to put together as its own productions. The first such utterances are almost invariably what are termed "performatives," or expressions describing what the child is doing at the moment. The speech consists of a track parallel to an ongoing series of motor acts. As one researcher describes it, "Both the speech and the accompanying bodily activity represent the same communicative act. The speech act is for the child indistinguishable from the act of reaching for the object."[61]

An interesting example of the degree to which one's first-learned language is embodied in motor patterns is given in the account by Volz of his son's partial retention of his first-learned language, which was Malaysian.[62] The child had learned this as a first language in Sumatra and then switched to German on leaving the first-language situation at the age of three years and one month. There was some difficulty in making the switch, but by the age of four the boy had begun to speak German as well as his native-born peers. However, although the boy could no longer speak Malaysian and seemed to have forgotten it, he still retained its meso component in the form of motor patterns, as though some aspects of the knowing had been buried in his muscles. When he spoke nonsense or gibberish while playing, or when he imitated his parents as they read aloud, his verbalizations were in the "sounds and intonations" of Malaysian.

The Taboo

Not all learning during childhood takes the form of learning what-is. There is another form in which the child learns, not "to do" but rather "not to do." As has been shown repeatedly in studies of reinforcement, however, one does not learn not-to-do simply by being told "no" nor even by being punished for doing it. Telling the person "no" will work only when a certain level of development has been reached, for it is a kind of ecto-style instruction. Punishment for doing something forbidden will usually serve only to teach the person either not to get caught again or not to do that thing in that way or place. True learning of not-to-do, of the kind that all of us experience in regard to unquestioned, often unmentionable proscriptions, has to come about in a special way. When it succeeds we experience it thereafter as a *taboo*, that is, as a proscription we hold so unquestioningly that we may be unaware of just what it is that we now forbid ourselves to do.[63]

How might such learning take place? If what we learn is not simply that something is forbidden, but more significantly, that we are now forbidden even to mention or think about what is forbidden, so that thereafter we are sure to obey the taboo automatically, we cannot learn it by instructions to this effect. The judge in a trial may attempt such a logically impossible maneuver, as in instructing a jury to disregard a remark that has just been made, but even judges know that it would be a waste of effort to follow this instruction with the further one: "And in addition, you are ordered to forget my instructions to you to this effect."

This example indicates the essential difference between what is learned by way of verbal communication in the ecto style and what is learned, necessarily in silence, in the endo style. If what is learned is, first of all, a proscription, and if it is learned by way of silence, it can be learned only by the learner closing off against what is to be learned. One learns, not to-do or what-should-be or it-is but rather not-to or it-is-not; one learns, in effect, that what one learns is not there to be learned. No such consequence can occur in either ecto or meso style, only in an endo style that as I have noted earlier is capable of functioning as though it were blind to the world. And once learned, the taboo that is now buried in endo behavior must operate in silence.

The taboo, once it is learned and then stored away, so to speak, is lived just as the body is lived in all its components. It is a mistake to think of the taboo as merely a passive resistance or as a boundary to other and more active elements of our experience. In a sense that is active yet is not conscious, we manage to keep ourselves from doing, even from thinking about doing, certain forbidden things. This can happen, of course, only to negatives, not to affirmatives, to what is proscribed and not to what is permitted or encouraged. If it should happen that we learn a taboo, any overt evidence as to its presence will then surface only under special conditions—for example, in certain responses resulting from activity of the autonomic nervous system, such as blushing, or in spontaneous sexual arousal or sudden emotional surges. But aside from such evidence, the taboo maintains its silent status, a tacit and hidden reminder of the limits built into our experiencing in those early years when the endo component was dominant.

Childhood

The learning sequence that I have described as typical of the preschool years of the child's life, from endo to meso to the beginning of an ecto style, is often paralleled by the spontaneous teaching methods adopted by human parents during this same period. Their efforts at first are not so much a kind of teaching as a kind of modeling and guidance—that is, in the endo style. At about the end of the first year of the child's life, parents start to shift over to a more active and directive teaching style, following the emerging meso characteristics of the child's behavior. They will now physically guide and even control actions, often repetitiously, and both parent and child become aware of the importance of explicit short-term goals, such as performing on the potty or finishing a prescribed quantity of food—behavior that is meso in style. It is only when the child has attained uprightness and is beginning to use language that parents begin to teach in the ecto mode, mostly by talking as one person might to another, about what is being taught and being learned. Since one can talk about what is not present in time or space, it becomes possible for the first time for the parents to introduce as props those two powerful motivators, guilt (in regard to what is now past) or anxiety (in regard to what will happen in the future).

In this way the child reaches that first major goal of childhood, the entry into school. Now for the first time there is made available a second career, one that is outside the home and family circle and runs parallel to what the child has always known. All through human history schooling seems to have begun at about the same age, which suggests that development in regard to the three components occurs naturally and at its own pace. Although many important changes in the school atmosphere have occurred recently, especially in the industrialized countries of the Western world, the school is still the arena in which for the first time a child is confronted with an ecto style in full bloom.

The major skills to be learned in this arena are formal, ecto-style skills, and this holds true even if the content comprising the learning is immediate, concrete, and practical. For example, if the child's first-grade class has a pet hamster, the children are quickly made aware that the animal is not really there as a pet. A pet is an animal you keep at home, whereas this animal is in the classroom because of what can be learned from it and from taking care of it. The children may fondle it or pet it, even entertain positive feelings toward it, but that is not why it is there. By means of the hamster as well as through the use of any other educational object in the classroom, they are instructed that the true significance of anything that happens is that all situations and events are part of some encompassing, and often abstract, body of knowledge. The good student is one who grasps this principle and is able to take advantage of it. Only this explains why a child will expend so much effort learning the sense of arbitrary marks on paper in an activity that is called reading or learning how to manipulate other arbitrary marks according to formal rules in an activity that is called arithmetic.

Schooling therefore demands from the very start that the child give up any emphasis on endo styles of behaving and learning, and that the ecto style be favored over the meso. Those who do not follow this directive, sometimes because they cannot, may come to be diagnosed later as hyperactive children, with too much emphasis on the meso component, or as immature and passive children who still emphasize too much the endo. For many, the transition will be felt as a wrench. A small episode, reported in a popular magazine, hints at the nature of the transition and of the child's experience when a last hold on an endo style of thinking is abruptly torn loose. A mother whose six-year-old son had learned to count well above one hundred was asked by him what would be the biggest number of all, "the very, very last number." Eager to take the opportunity to introduce him to the realm of mathematical abstraction, she told him that there was no last number, "that as far as you go there are always more numbers ahead of you." Having said this, she "was complimenting herself on having neatly slipped the conception of infinity into his consciousness, when she noticed that he was quietly crying."[64]

Admittedly the world of knowledge becomes attainable only if the child has access to an ecto style of learning and to the skills appropriate to that style. And as the world outside the classroom becomes more complex as it is manipulated to an increasing degree by commands from an ecto realm, this imperative becomes ever more compelling. Only the ecto learner is guaranteed the academic success that will promise life rewards after school is finished. But to the degree that some individuals or certain groups cannot accommodate themselves to a predominantly ecto style of learning, the population of students becomes categorized, even polarized. It soon becomes a matter, not of superior and inferior individuals or groups—although that is the way it is sometimes viewed—but of different kinds of persons, of individuals who differ in important ways within a society that rewards only one of those ways.

Adolescence

Toward the end of the years of primary schooling there occurs a second birth in the human life span, the upsurge and its accompanying changes known as puberty. During these years of early and midadolescence the adult sexual life begins, accompanied by a growth spurt so rapid that as much as 50 percent may be added to the child's weight and height within a few years. The somatic composition that results, however, is unique for each individual and is also differentiated by sex. The female burst involves largely the endo component, the male burst the meso, and both sexes may show an additional ecto burst with marked individual variation. Striking changes occur as well in every aspect of experience and behavior. It is during this period that the person's unique patterning of somatic styles becomes more or less permanently established.

Patterns of sexual behavior shown during this period provide a good example of developing somatic styles. Typically in males, and to a lesser but still evident degree in females, sexuality comes under the dominance of a meso component. The sexual "impulse" is now available for immediate arousal, that is, in the service of action and aimed at the orgasm as target. An accretion of smaller actions comes to surround the dominant one, with the result that sexual satisfaction comes to be pursued as a set of habits, usually carried out in the same way and with the same preferences. With practice the habits soon turn into skills. There are many persons who never grow beyond the point of repetitively practicing their sexual skills; their mode of sexual behavior as a dominating influence in their lives, once established in adolescence, remains with them into adulthood.

A thoroughly developed portrait of an adult male whose meso dominance was thus established in adolescence can be seen in the character of Rabbit, the protagonist of a series of novels by John Updike. In the story *Rabbit is Rich*, he is a father now in his forties.[65] In one scene he confronts his adolescent son with what he feels is a telling accusa-

tion: "How do you feel, about your girlfriend's going out with someone else?" To this the son answers, "I've told you before, Dad, she's
not my girlfriend, she's my friend. Can't you have a friend of the
opposite sex?" The father's answer sums up his meso stance: "You can
try it." For the father literally cannot comprehend the nature of his
son's sexuality—which appears to have elements of an endo style. In
Rabbit's view, a view that was once formed as an adolescent expression
but is now incontrovertible, the sexual urge if once (and ever so easily)
aroused, even minimally aroused, must then drive on to its climax. It
follows from this that no girl can be only a "friend" to a male.

We have here the image of an animal of sorts, an image that many
females quite correctly have regarding the typical male; the male is
seen as predominantly meso. Rabbit's son, on the other hand, seems to
be willing to live in terms of "urges" (although that is now not the
correct term) that may sometimes be diffused rather than directed like
an arrow toward their target. The two men might perhaps agree that
there is an urge involved and that in any case to have a female as a
friend is not precisely the same as having a male as a friend; however,
unlike Rabbit, for the son such urges, once aroused, may diffuse before coming to climax, almost as though the urge had lost its specific,
orgasmic end point. In this sense his sexuality shows some significant
endo characteristics.

Societies differ among each other, and even from one era to another,
in how much freedom they will allow individuals, particularly the freedom to express somatic components other than the typical ones at each
period of the life span. It is especially in adolescence, when the patterns of adulthood are beginning to be adopted and set, that traditional
societies seem to require that females adopt predominantly an endo
and males a meso style. Rites of passage, in one form or another, appear to be ritualized exaggerations of these two modes.

Adulthood

Much of one's adult behavior and experience results from an interplay
of life circumstances with the patterns that had been set in late adolescence. As important bodily changes begin to occur during the fifth
and sixth decades of life, the patterns may begin to weaken, resulting

in what appear to be significant changes in the personality. Evidence regarding such changes has been gathered in a number of extensive studies of older groups. In one such study, by Bernice Neugarten and her colleagues during the 1950s, healthy adults ranging in age from forty to eighty were tested on a variety of measures assessing their behavior as well as their experience during this period.[66] One major finding was that for both sexes there occurred an increased "interiority" of the personality: "The older person tends to . . . withdraw emotional investments, to give up self-assertiveness, and to avoid rather than embrace challenges."[67] This change may be in large part a result of a general decrease in energy as well as a product of changing roles with advancing years, but it also points to a sharp decrease in the dominance of a meso style.

Not only do both sexes show this kind of change, but they change in different ways. Another finding in the Neugarten studies concerned an interesting sex difference among the older adults whom they tested. On the one hand, the older women were judged as being "more tolerant of their own aggressive, egocentric impulses," suggesting an increased expression of the meso component, while the older men were judged as being more tolerant of their "nurturant and affiliative impulses."[68] Again, these apparent changes in personality may be a reflection of real changes in life circumstances and therefore individual behavior, but at the same time they strongly support a widely reported finding, that as they get older couples come to resemble one another. The women become sharper and more expressive of their own strengths, the men softer and more accepting of their own weaknesses. Each sex appears to turn toward the pattern typically associated with those of the opposite sex. In the terms I have been using, there seems to occur in the male an endo burst and in the female a meso burst.

In contemporary societies, older persons tend to be judged against the norm established by the behavior of younger, more active, more socially productive persons. Aging thus comes to be identified with loss, with the progressive loss of energy and "drive," a phenomenon that has been referred to as a "brownout." All the characteristics defining the age groups, either by their presence or their absence, are essentially meso. Youth is described as a period of energy and drive, and so by contrast the older age periods are described in terms of the loss of energy and drive. Whatever other characteristics may have developed as a consequence of the passage of years are simply ignored; we have no vocabulary for them, except a few terms—"wisdom" is one—that we have preserved from former societies. Older persons themselves, behaving like good citizens who pattern their self-concepts on evident social stereotypes, come to think of themselves in these same terms. In this way a myth is born that in the last quarter of the life span the major change consists of a variety of losses. Perhaps if age-related changes were studied instead as expressions of the interplay of three (or more) somatic styles, we would develop a new vocabulary and be able to discover unsuspected characteristics belonging to the middle and later years.

In terms of the three styles, it appears that human growth expresses itself in three great periods of growth. The first of these occurs during the first four or five years of life, the second in adolescence, and the third during middle and old age. Each of the periods of growth is introduced with a dramatic and radical shift in modes of somatic expression and follows immediately on a phase of rapid and deeply experienced transition—the first after the birth process, the second following the onset of puberty, and the third after what has been called menopause and might more accurately be termed "mid-life crisis." How the individual adjusts to this transitional period determines how subsequent years will be lived, whether as growth or as stagnation. Each of the transitions is marked by an outburst of one of the three somatic styles—an endo burst at the start of life, an endo or meso burst during adolescence, and then, perhaps in reverse, a meso or endo burst during late middle age.

Thus we have a cycle of human life, and perhaps of other mammals as well: growing from the inside out at the outset, and building first on the endo mode, followed by an instrumental meso mode; then settling into an individual pattern of styles for the major, "middle" years of one's life; and finally declining from the outside in during the later years, with the endo and meso modes establishing themselves in new patterns of growth.

6

Forming the Body

In earlier chapters I have used the term *body* as though its meaning were simple and clear-cut. To begin to correct this, in the present chapter I will circle back to consider in greater depth some issues related to the body that were left over from the discussions in chapter 1 and chapter 2. The central notion in these discussions is expressed in the term *forming*, which refers to the body as a continuously evolving set of processes and functions, and this in two distinct ways: first, from moment to moment in the course of an individual's life and, second, over the years and generations as bodies in general evolve as representatives of their species.

I will begin by considering the consequences of viewing the body as formed rather than forming, or, to put it in traditional biological terms, as nature's structural masterpiece and functional miracle. If we take seriously the notion of forming, howover, the body will have to be seen as continually "beyond itself." This may be what Sheldon was groping for, as I will try to show in an examination of his terminology. Following this, I will return to a discussion of the ecto style of behavior, since it is here in its mode of ex-carnation that issues concerning the body are raised most acutely.

THE BODY BEYOND ITSELF

Even simple actions may express one's behavioral style. In the first two decades of this century, before behaviorism in psychology and before the current interest in cognitive processes, psychomotor activity was a major topic of study. Enke[1] compared somatic types on a range of simple movement tasks and concluded that the endo is generally slower than the other two types, showing fluid, soft, and "rounded" movements by comparison with the "stiff and angular" movements of the typical ecto. Endo action is adaptable and easygoing, that of the ecto cautious and tense. These findings hold true whether the task is as habitual as writing, as simple as carrying a glass of water, or as complex as moving to music.

On casual observation the human body appears to be rather ineptly engineered. Perhaps nature, so often praised as the greatest of engineers, may really be a vast bungler whose mistakes, when they occur, are on a scale so huge that we fail to notice them. I say this because it often appears that the body cannot do some of the things that in fact it does. Like the bumblebee, its functioning appears to exceed the limits imposed by its given structure. It will be apparent that in this discussion I use the terms structure and function in the traditional sense meant by engineers and found in biology.

The Upright Posture

My first example concerns the fact that, alone of mammalian species, humans adapt an upright posture during their entire waking lives as adults. Even the chimpanzee, one of our closest relatives, is not two-legged and upright but a four-limbed animal that in its ordinary loco-motion chooses to walk as though it were four-legged, using its two arms and two legs. Humans, on the other hand, have utilized a true upright posture for at least the past million years. The advantages accruing to a species as a consequence of uprightness have been discussed by many writers—the freeing of the hands for purposes of manipulation, the development of a predominantly visual rather than auditory or olfactory access to information, and most important, the ability to take a stance at right angles to the world, with all that this implies for confrontation, for delay, for surveying, in short, for forms of looking as well as seeing, and for wisdom and insight as well as acuity.

It may be that the upright posture is of overwhelming importance in the development of the behaviors we consider uniquely human, but its importance may have encouraged us to overlook the great price we paid for these advantages. If we look at the way the body is structurally organized for uprightness, we see that it is built in the shape of three inverted triangles balanced precariously on top of one another. The inverted triangle at the bottom consists of the pelvis at the top, narrowing down to the relatively small feet at the bottom. Mounted on top of this is a second inverted triangle of the wide shoulder girdle that narrows down to the point of insertion of the backbone into the pelvis. The top triangle consists of the skull balanced atop the spinal column. As we are so frequently reminded by pains or discomfort in our sore feet, by our low back pain, and by the tension across our shoulders at the base of the neck, this is far from a satisfactory arrangement. Worse, it appears to be an arrangement that contradicts every principle of sound engineering.

Architecturally correct structures are built from the bottom up, the lower parts serving to support the upper parts within a gravitational field. Even a bridge strung on cables follows this principle; the cables are held up in turn by foundation pillars on which, finally, everything rests. As ancient buildings tell us when they begin to collapse, it is the top that gives way first, often leaving the pillars or walls of the foundation standing alone. By contrast, the human body appears to be built from the top down. Every major part—for example, the leg—is bigger around at the top than at the bottom. The origins of all the major muscles of the body are at the upper ends of the muscles.

Curiously, this reversal of the rules for structures does not seem to affect our ordinary movements, for we humans do share with many animals our patterns of movement. In general we move forward or up by pulling ourselves with the upper and front parts of the body, just as other land animals do, in contrast with amphibious creatures such as the frog or flying creatures such as the jumping flea. The horse, to take one example, jumps by means of its shoulders, its legs being quite weak for its size, as can be seen from the ease with which they may be broken. Similarly, human runners pull themselves along by a forward thrust of their chest muscles rather than by pushing with their legs. In function, then, we resemble other land animals, but in structure we appear to be very different.

It would seem that this can be summarized in only one way, that the human body is not pushed from behind nor held up from below but rather is pulled up from the top. In Erwin Straus's words, "In order to stand up, Man has to find a hold within himself."[2] This contrasts with everything we know from engineering, and we have to conclude that the body cannot do what it appears to do.

The Speed of Movements

It is known that the speed of the fastest nerve impulse in the body is about 100 meters per second. Since the distance from brain to finger tip in an adult is approximately one meter, the time required for an impulse to travel from brain to fingertips would be one one-hundredth of a second, or 10 milliseconds, and the round trip would require 20 milliseconds. This might be the schedule for a message to go down and deliver the order, "Move such-and-such," and then the subsequent "message" to return, as though saying, "Movement completed." In addition, the time required to activate a muscle, by an electrochemical process at the synaptic junction, is about 25 milliseconds. Thus, the total time for such a message to be completed and reported will be on the order of 45 milliseconds, and for a message to the foot, at a distance of about two meters from the brain, about 65 milliseconds.

Consider now some tasks or skills requiring rapid movements. The heel taps of a Flamenco dancer have been timed at 16 per second, which works out to 62.5 milliseconds per tap. A tap dancer has been timed at the rate of 24 per second, or 42 milliseconds per tap of the foot. A champion typist won first place in a contest with an "adjusted" rate of 250 words per minute, or, if a word is assumed to contain 5 letters, at 1,250 letters, or finger taps, per minute, or 48 milliseconds per tap. However, she must have typed faster than this, since her adjusted rate refers to the rate adjusted for errors, so many letters or words per minute being subtracted for each error that she made. Assuming an 8 percent error rate, which is not excessive for high-speed typing of new material, her actual rate of hand movements would have been 270 words per minute, that is, 22.5 letters per second, or 44.44 milliseconds per finger tap. To this we should also add the time required for her hands to move back and forth across the keyboard, since the different letters are almost randomly placed in respect to their frequency of use on the standard Sholes keyboard.

Sight reading of music at the piano furnishes still another example of rapid movement. At a moderate metronome setting of 110, each beat will take 545 milliseconds, a sixteenth note therefore taking 34 milliseconds. To this, again, would have to be added the time required for the pianist's hands to move from one place to another on the keyboard; and of course still less time would be available if the metronome were at a higher setting.

Bearing in mind the figure of 45 milliseconds for a round-trip message to the fingertips and 65 milliseconds for a round-trip message to the foot, it is evident that these various skills require time periods too brief to be carried out. It may be objected that some of these skills are simply repetitive, therefore requiring only that a general message be sent to hand or foot—something on the order of, "Carry out a repetitive string of movements like this one, all alike." However, this explanation will hardly hold for nonrepetitive movements such as are involved in typing new material or in sight reading unfamiliar music containing sixteenth notes. According to these calculations, we come again to the point that the body's behavior seemingly goes beyond all that the body is. If the body were to be known in the traditional sense as a structure involved in its functioning, we would have to conclude that it cannot do what it appears to be able to do.

Bilateral Symmetry and Asymmetry

Almost every motile creature, from invertebrates up the scale to humans, is built so as to have pairs of organs or organ systems that are bilaterally positioned on either side of a midline. Humans have two eyes, two nostrils, two ears, two lungs, two buttocks, two arms and legs, two kidneys, even two halves of the brain. The extra unit does not seem to serve the familiar engineering purpose of a backup system, for such a system would hardly call for two units in parallel, working together at all times. Nor can the arrangement be in the service of efficiency or power; indeed, quite the reverse. For efficiency you design a single probe rather than two eyes playing against each other in continuous binocular rivalry. For power, you design, for example, a crane with a single arm rather than two.

It has been pointed out, however,[3] that bilateral symmetry is found in almost all organisms that are not sessile because they must usually be streamlined. This provides the best structural arrangement for rapid movement, either to chase prey or to evade predators. Those organisms that are not bilaterally symmetrical in structure have either evolved from such structures by adopting a nonmotile existence or else have remained at a low level of organization. This argument undoubtedly explains the evolution of structure—but it does not explain the fact that in motile organisms the two sides of the body, in spite of their symmetrically paired organs and action systems, are almost never in a state of functional bilateral symmetry. In regard to function it is asymmetry that appears to be the order of the day, even though the structural order calls for symmetry.

The commonest example of our functional asymmetry is the condition we call handedness, or the dominance of one side of the body in initiating and then skillfully executing common actions. That handedness is not entirely a cultural phenomenon but appears with approximately the same frequency across many cultural millennia is shown in evidence from the cave art of northern Spain. A large number of prehistoric stenciled hands are to be found in certain of these caves, produced by placing one hand against a wall and then drawing a line around it or blowing pigment through a tube to produce a stencil. Approximately 85 percent of the stenciled hands are found to be of the left hand, suggesting that, just as we find today, this percentage of adults spontaneously use their right hands for such common actions as holding a brush or a tube. Humans (like elephants) show a general dominance of the right side in action.

Observation of everyday situations of rest, such as persons sitting in chairs, provides further evidence for the asymmetry of normal posture. Shoe salesmen will also verify this fact, that in the course of walking and wearing down their shoes most persons are asymmetrical to the degree that one heel becomes worn perceptibly more than the other. But perhaps the most telling evidence of all as to the normal asymmetry of function in human action is to be found in what might be termed, in Jung's sense, an archetype. Just about every culture seems to have developed one or more instances of a ritual pose that is bilaterally symmetrical. In our own culture, for example, there is the common position for prayer. In the Christian tradition one either kneels or stands with feet together and the hands pressed palm to palm at the midline, or in the Moslem tradition one kneels and then prostrates oneself, again with the arms and hands brought together at the midline. The usual position we call attention, as in the military, is another instance in which one stands still with the body positioned symmetrically. There is the position in which a corpse is often laid— on the back and with arms crossed symmetrically over the chest, and, finally, the full lotus position of certain meditative disciplines, with the legs symmetrically intertwined and the arms crossed in front of the chest.

Dissimilar as may be the purposes of these ritual positions, they have in common both a postural characteristic, that they are all examples of bilateral symmetry, and a general significance, that they are all ways of declaring that the person has for the moment given up the possibility of initiating any action. At prayer, at attention, in death, or in meditation the significance is the same: the body is, so to speak, prepared not to act. The universality of this archetypal pose suggests strongly that it means to convey an insight concerning symmetry and asymmetry—that a symmetrical structure implies nonaction just as an asymmetrical structure is characteristic of action.

Observation of infants at the beginning of their careers as initiators of action suggests the same inference. The infant begins life lying on its back, arms and legs akimbo, functionally nonmotile and positionally symmetrical. Its very first self-initiated movements in the world consist of "choosing" one side or the other, thereby beginning a lifetime of motility and functional asymmetry. In one of Erwin Straus's typically apt phrasings, he describes the infant at its beginnings, or the person at attention or in meditation, as "taking no sides." In order to envision a common, asymmetrical action such as walking as though it were carried out in functional symmetry, recall the remarkable performance of Boris Karloff as the monster in the original *Frankenstein* film. For normal walking is in fact asymmetrical from side to side as well as from front to rear, being really a form of protracted and continuously aborted falling—or, to quote Straus again, it is "motion on credit."

To summarize briefly, I have suggested three aspects of the engineering of the human body that support my claim to the effect that the body cannot do what in fact it does. In regard to the body's vertically organized structure within a gravitational field, it does not seem to be built so as to stay up; the most evidently upright of all living structures looks like the one most badly built for staying erect. In regard to the timing and speed of many voluntary movements, the body does not seem to be built so as to act as quickly as it does. And finally, in regard to the symmetry of structure and function, the two aspects are in conflict at the same time that neither in itself will explain the nature of ordinary movement; the body's bilateral symmetry of structure appears to be incompatible with certain critical movements and actions, while the body's asymmetry of function does not seem to arise from its symmetrical structure.

Body and Machine

These three sets of considerations seem to me to converge on a challenging hypothesis. In regard to three basic demands—to remain erect, to act rapidly, and to carry out a voluntary and goal-directed act—the body is always so arranged as to be other than in its present state. It is as though the living body is always ahead of itself, always acting beyond its present definition, therefore never simply what it is, and so never completely definable as a state or as the position belonging to a state. And just as we might expect, the living body is never truly at rest. Its every moment is an action, therefore a form of movement, even if that movement is aimed at the body being still. We have only to stand still and then close our eyes to have revealed to us the complex interplay of minute adjustments that we are normally engaged in, although out of our awareness, in order to maintain the position of "being still" or of "doing nothing." That this is real work, leaving its permanent mark on the body's structure, can be seen in the common observation that the dark meat on a chicken is on its legs, not on its breast, for the chicken must be constantly at work, using mostly its leg muscles, to "be still" aginst gravitational forces.

   It would follow from this that the body's functioning cannot be understood completely in terms of its definable structure or its observable states from moment to moment. Although the evidence I have offered is mostly in regard to human action, this inference would appear to be applicable, even if to a lesser degree, to action in other mammals as well. Function goes beyond the structure in which it occurs and is not simply structure in motion; it cannot be fully explained in terms of a biological structure and the influences on that structure. I suggest that in order to understand the functioning of a living body we may need a new *methodology of process* to supersede our conventional methodology of static objects and their momentary states. As a step toward such a new methodology, I turn to a comparison of the human and the machine in order to clarify the basis for our understanding of the human.

THE BODY IS . . .

A machine has no way to "be ahead" of its own state; it simply is and does just what its state is at any moment, its functioning being no more than the totality of its parts in movement. The structure of the machine conditions and determines how the machine responds to influences on it and so its functioning amounts to its structure-in-operation, no more.[4] A machine is not designed for a function, not in the sense that its structure and its function are conceptually distinct as they are in a living body. Rather, in a machine the structure and the function are simply two ways of looking at the same phenomenon, the causal connection between the two terms being from structure to function, never the reverse.

It may be objected that in at least one sense the machine's functioning may exercise an effect backward on its structure. For example, if the machine were overworked, this continuous functioning might lead to some part of the structure wearing out. In this sense, perhaps, function acts in a causal manner on structure. But it is clear that a backward effect of this sort is not a part of the machine's normal operation but rather a sign of the breakdown of the machine's function and then structure. In the ordinary course of events, as the machine does what it was designed to do, its functioning is caused by influences on its structure and not the reverse.

What the machine lacks, in a word, is an interior; and consequently it must also lack an exterior. At best the machine may be said to have an outside and an inside, that is to say, observable substructures within an overall structure. But the outside and the inside of a machine are not functionally distinct. They are two parts of a functioning whole that do not depend on whether they are, in fact, positioned in the inside or on the outside, for they may be positioned anywhere. In this sense their names are misleading. They may be structurally different, of course, but that fact is not intrinsic to a machine as machine, only to this machine at this particular time. Nothing but ingenuity is required in order to turn the machine inside out, as it were—for example, to take the machine's power source out of its inside position and substitute for it a wire running to an electric plug on the outside. As this example shows, what is inside and what is outside the machine are defined just as much by external conditions as by characteristics internal to the machine. Similarly, although an alarm clock has a face, a part that "tells time," on its external surface facing out, this is for reasons of convenience that arise out of external circumstances, not out of aspects intrinsic to machines in general. The face of the clock might just as well be positioned in the next room, spatially separated, or even at some future point in time so that the face would read, not what time it now is but what time it will be. Clocks in large airports, furnishing at one glance the time that it "is" right now in major cities around the world, have been thus manipulated and restructured in time and space.

We will need two different terms to distinguish between the place in which a machine is positioned and the position in which a living body is placed. Suppose we adopt the term *environment* to refer to that set of (usually) external conditions that impinge on the machine and influence it. The correlative term for the living body, pointing to a fundamentally different arrangement, might then be *situation*. Machines are in environments, living bodies in situations, and the term that I have chosen to use in the title of this book, *ecology*, since it is applicable for both situations and environments, now allows us to speak of the ecology of the body.[5] By my use of two different terms I also mean to imply that all the other words we might use in discussing these matters would ideally have to be different, although because we are generally lacking in an adequate dual vocabulary we may often have to make one word serve in two senses. The machine is, for example, *in* its environment in quite a different sense than the human body is *in* its situation.

The body's situation may be defined as the exterior expression of its interior, implying by this that unlike a machine, the body has not only internal and external faces but an exterior and an interior. These are not simply two of its parts but aspects of what it is and how it functions; hence the term "expression," a word that would hardly be used to indicate how a machine's inside parts are related to its surround. An expression is a voice, hence a sounding with an identifiable origin and an intentional direction. What is inner and what is outer are therefore not determined by conditions imposed externally but rather are products of expression arising out of the body's interior.

The effect of an environment on what it contains is to condition, to influence, to cause, ultimately to wear away and finally to change whatever it acts upon. This may occur over any time span, from the brief period in which a windstorm rips branches from a tree all the way to the millennial period, eons long, in which evolutionary changes are effected in living creatures. An object in its environment, whether body or machine, is always in an adversary relation with the forces acting on it. For the same reason, objects are always softer than their environments; that is what determines the boundary between them. In regard to the body and its relation to situations, on the other hand, there exists not an interface but an interaction, not a series of one-way influences in a causal chain but a mutuality of cause and effect in something more like a spreading network. In this relation all effective causes are also effects, all effects at the same time causes.

A first corollary, then, is that in the relations of living things to their situations there are no beginnings and no endings. Rather, living things grow out of their situations and then grow back into them, in an endless sequence of continuing life—from which we may draw the interesting cosmological hypothesis that life is coextensive in time, and therefore in space, with the physical universe. From this it must follow that living things are never built, not by humans and not in nature. They must always grow from other living things. This is to say that although machines are capable of making machines, and although humans can and do make machines and influence the making of other humans, it is not possible that machines can make humans.

The basic distinction between machine and living thing is that structure and function are related to each other in different ways. The structure of the machine is constituted of definable parts that in their interplay become determinants of the machine's functions. But in the living body, most particularly in the human body that we know best, asymmetrical function is always ahead of the body's symmetrical structure. Another distinction between machines and bodies arises as a consequence: whereas the structure and the environment of the machine comprise equivalent sets of causes—operating independently but, in their relation to the machine's functioning, acting simply as alternatives—in the living body the structure bears a different relation to its surround. The body is constantly engaged in situations that it creates and is created by, without beginning and without end.

In contemporary psychological thought there seems to have been only one writer who took even minimal advantage of this view of the living body. This was Jean Piaget, whose theory of child development is built on propositions similar to those I offer here. This may be seen in particular in the two kinds of interrelated activities that Piaget postulated as explanations of the growth process. They are assimilation, in which environmental influences are taken up into existing cognitive schemas, and accommodation, in which developed schemas are adapted to fit environmental conditions. Both activities, in their constant occurrence, take place together rather than in sequential cause-and-effect cycles, effecting an ongoing interaction without beginning and without end. The major limitation in Piaget's work was that he restricted his application of these valuable concepts to issues concerning the "growth of the mind," or to cognitive functions exclusively, rather than to the full repertoire of action in the body as it is lived.

In view of the distinctions suggested here, one cannot say that the body *has* a structure, not in the sense of a set of discrete parts influencing one another in one-way chains of mechanical causation. This is how we describe, quite properly, the operation of the machine, whereas the body as I discuss it here is a different kind of ensemble. Yet of course the body is an object and is put together in some way; it has its elements, these are organized, and so the body maintains its general shape—in all these respects corresponding to the structure of a machine. How are we to understand this structure that is similar to yet so different from what we know, and in what terms shall we describe it? One possibility might be that we describe not the body's parts, as though it were a machine, but its components, meaning something more dynamic or functional.

A New Typology

The term *components* brings us back to the work of Sheldon. He too argued against what I would call structure and ways of assessing it; he claimed that this would refer to nothing but "some fixed set of metric proportions, applying to living individuals but transitorily and under a specifically fixed condition."[6] The notion of structure would apply only if we were to allow a kind of freezing of the living body, stopping it in time and thereby subtracting from it one of the qualities that centrally define its aliveness. "One would not then be working with a taxonomy of somatotypes at all, in the proposed dynamic sense, but would have a taxonomy of purely static phenotypes . . . deprived of continuance in the time dimension."[7] Sheldon then raises the question of what one can do, given these conclusions. To describe the body as a static whole or in terms of any of the parts of that whole, as though it were a kind of machine, will not do. "The phenotype by definition has no fourth dimension, no continuance in time,"[8] yet it is just the phenotype that seems to be all one can directly deal with, or tangibly touch, measure, or weigh. There is on the other hand the genotype, which is certainly an inferred "mechanism of continuance" in the body. "We know that a structured genotype (morphogenotype) is at work in every living organism, for otherwise there would be no persistence of structural individuality through life,"[9] the phenotype by contrast not even implying its own continuance.

But the genotype is an abstraction, an inferred entity, a construct that cannot be directly measured. Caught between these two possibilities, psychologists have resorted to a number of ways out. On the one hand, one might measure the phenotype, ignoring the fundamental difficulties involved and arriving at what Sheldon had called a "taxonomy of purely static phenotypes," and this, in fact, is how most persons, knowing little of Sheldon's work, understand his somatotypes. On the other hand, one makes whatever measurements are possible and then assigns a reality status not to what is measured but to the measurements themselves. This is a form of methodological operationism, as when the notion of general intelligence arises out of the objective and reliable measurement of it: "Intelligence is what intelligence tests test." Applied to our problem, this approach would seem to wipe away many of the difficulties we face in systematically assessing the living body, but it might at the same time surreptitiously introduce new difficulties. If our description of the body comes to rest on externally imposed conditions of measurement, then from the beginning we have treated the body as though it were a machine.

Sheldon seems to have been aware of the traps in such conventional methods. He concludes that if the static phenotype is "taxonomically worthless" for our purposes and if the dynamic genotype is "but a conceptual abstraction," it becomes necessary to introduce "another concept, the somatotype, which is neither phenotype nor genotype but is the reflection of the continuity which apparently exists between these two aspects of organic life."[10] The somatotype, in this view, is not simply a static category or type to which one or another body may be assigned. It is, rather, "by definition a prediction of the future succession of phenotypes which a living person will present, if nutrition remains a constant factor or varies only within normal limits. We define the somatotype more formally as a trajectory or process through which the living organism will travel under standard conditions of nutrition and in the absence of grossly disturbing pathology . . . (hence) a dynamic abstraction from a series of such (phenotypic) projections"[11] or a summary of "the continuous succession of phenotypes."[12]

Sheldon is quite explicit here in regard to what must be said first of all about the living body, that the observable phenotype, or structure, has no permanence. The living body is not a thing but a process, its shape no more stable than that of a waterfall, its subdivisions not parts but functional components. Thus, for example, endomorphy is the general organization guiding the endodermally derived component; it is not a fixed structure but rather the forming—here meant as both noun and verb—of the body along the lines of one possible trajectory. This explains how it is possible for an infinite number of different bodies all to receive the same somatotype rating.

Sheldon seems to have thought along these lines, although he did not have this vocabulary available to him to express his thinking. He was often forced into statements that were constrained within the existing limitations of the physical science of his day. But more recently a methodology of process has been suggested in a number of quarters, for example in the work of Prigogine,[13] who has emphasized that every part of a system, therefore systems themselves, are in constant change, small though that may be. Process can therefore be either continuous or discontinuous, concerning the part or the whole, slow or fast or changing its rate, for process means more than flow.

Entities to which these statements do not apply are not systems but what I have called in the preceding pages machines. Life is the preeminent set of instances of systems, the living body its most evident consequence. However, the body too may be lived as though it were more machine than system. As Seymour Fisher has described in some detail, many cultural and personal influences combine to lead to bodies lived as depersonalized. "The woman who is repeatedly confronted by clothing style changes that she is supposed to adopt, whether or not they are compatible to her own feelings about her body, comes to perceive her body as not terribly different from a department store mannequin."[14]

Rules and Growth

As the continuously changing expression of an intermixture of its lived components, always in situations rather than in an environment, the body is beyond itself; its actions are not to be fully comprehended by rules that are determined externally or after the fact. What the body is and does—and the two verbs are in this instance inseparable—will flow out of the situational give-and-take, and this in turn presupposes that the body is, as one aspect of its definition, already at home in a situation. Once these propositions are affirmed we are in a position to understand how it is that the most elaborate program of external rules (such as those determining the operation of a computer, for example) will fail to account for even the simplest real-life action carried out by an organism in its body. This is a point that Dreyfus[15] has made in detail in his critique of artificial intelligence research. Because the body acts in an orderly manner in the apparent absence of rules, it always seems to be organized "from the top down," that is, from the most infinitely general to the most concretely particular.

But to state the matter in terms of the general and the particular misses the main point, for differences between these two categories apply to the realm of mechanical rules and causes, not to a bodily world. In the world of living bodies there are nothing but wholes, or entities that are known as such, whether they are objects or events. Some writers describe the world of the newborn infant—at a point in development that is antecedent to cognitive growth—as "a turbulence of noises and odors,"[16] a confusing jumble of singular, disorganized, unexpectedly changing particulars which the infant must somehow put together into a meaningful whole. Such an argument supposes a world of mechanical causes and effects. What I describe here, rather, is the world that is given together with the body, a world that constitutes an ongoing flow of situations rather than a difficult or resistive environment. Only later in development does the growing child create a framework in the form of a system outside itself to which it may then act and react, a framework that becomes the world order the growing child knows.

Once the body is understood in this way we can see how it may serve as a vessel for growth as well as learning. By learning I mean here some form of change that is related to the body's environment, a change that is imposed as an influence from an external source and then directed by external rules. Learning is a change that is testable by means of any formally acceptable procedure. Testing a learner does not depend on the tester knowing more than the testee nor on the tester having ever gone through a similar process of learning. Growth, on the other hand, is always an expression of the body's development, and so it can never be properly assessed except by someone who has already gone through a process of growth in this respect; testing whether growth has occurred requires not an acceptable procedure but a tester who is a "grown" person. Testers and testees thus form an infinite number of mutually interlocking circles, extending outward endlessly in space and backward endlessly in time. Growth is neither instance learning nor rule learning but in effect creates its own ongoing rules. As a result, the consequence of growth is not that the person is taught how to do something in particular but rather is taught how to get some kinds of things done.

MARKS OF THE ECTO STYLE

A capsule summary of the three styles: "What the temptation of adultery is for laymen and the yearning for riches is for secular ecclesiastics, the seduction of knowledge is for monks."—UMBERTO ECO, *The Name of the Rose*

In discussing the body and its process of forming, what needs most to be considered is the ecto style, for this is the one that is least fitted to living the body. Here I point to an important distinguishing characteristic of the ecto style, which I have alluded to earlier but not discussed in depth. It may be summarized in the term *distance*. As was clear in the discussion of styles of memory, in the ecto style the person creates and then uses a gap between what is concretely and immediately present and how one deals with what is present. To take a common example, suppose that I am pushed by a very strong wind. My reaction (for it is usually a reaction, not a response) to such stimulation is likely to be immediate, nonreflective, concretely directed. I do immediately what the wind impels me to do, either giving way or unthinkingly bracing and pushing myself against it. This is a behavioral situation in which there exists no gap between the given and one's reaction to it. Nothing of the ecto style, then, enters the interchange between myself and the stimulation.

As recent work on visual perception indicates, however, this distinction between immediate reaction and a "distanced" apprehension in the form of a response that is self-reflective and organized, may be detected even in common instances of perception, for example, in visual functioning. One may postulate two "independent and dissociable" perceptual modes in vision, the first a focal mode that answers the question of what, the second an ambient mode that answers the question of where.[17] The distinction is not completely congruent with an older and more familiar one between focal and peripheral vision, since it now appears that both modes are processed in the "little brain" we call the retina. An even clearer experimental example of the distinction is reported by Haronian[18] on the basis of responses to the familiar Müller-Lyer illusion (in which lines appear to differ in length depending on the direction of "feathers" at their ends). He finds that persons independently categorized as ectomorphic in constitution take a "keenly analytic" (or distancing) approach to perception of the illusion, thereby markedly reducing its effect.

By the term *distance* I refer to any gap that one sets up between stimulation and response—by delaying it, by assuming a psychological distance from the energizing source, by knowing about the stimulation as much as knowing it directly. When I do this, I am then to some degree in the ecto mode. This holds true for all forms of behavior, from perception to memory. The consequence of creating a gap between the real and the apparent, between what happens to me and what I do about it, or between the world and how it is represented to me, is that stimulation becomes information.

Because of its remarkable elaboration and refinement, in particular in visual perception, ecto functioning in humans has come to dominate human behavior. But as I will show later through consideration of the various perceptual systems, similar perceptual activity, even if not as complex, is to be found in even the simplest forms of animal life. In the present section I want to discuss, not the similarities but the differences between the human and other species; I will indicate how our uniquely human elaboration of the ecto style of distancing enables us to create a world that is unique to our species, even though we utilize essentially the same sensory apparatus as all other animals. My discussion will be based on Erwin Straus's two papers on the upright posture and its consequences for a human world.[19]

One result of developing an upright posture is that the structure and physiognomy of the human face have undergone a dramatic change. In all mammals other than humans the nose and mouth are positioned ahead of the eyes, whereas in humans the mouth has retreated, the nose is smaller and flatter and is vertical rather than horizontal, and the eyes have moved forward to dominate the face. A new term for the face, *visage* in English or French or *Gesicht* in German, both derived from a term for seeing, now becomes applicable. However, this structural change amounts to more than the repositioning of one major sense organ, for it affects as well the functioning of the ears, even though they do not change position.

The change consists in developing a wholly new stance or attitude, one that represents almost a qualitative shift. Animal ears are usually mobile, enabling the creature to point them at specifically located targets, whereas human ears have lost this capacity for being pointed as they changed over to a different function. In this function we are equipped for processing waves of energy into representational information rather than for locating some concretely present stimulus in space. This leads in turn to a possibility that is not open to other animals, to reproduce the sound that we hear.

To all other animals but humans, sounds are like the cry of warning or the shriek of pain. That is, they specify some significant, to-be-attended-to aspect of an immediately present situation. To humans, on the other hand, most sounds serve as indicators *about* an event or state to which both sender and recipient can and often do respond with the same sound. If one chimpanzee should bark in warning to another, the recipient of the sound will be alerted and will then act accordingly. What the recipient will not do is send back the same warning sound, for that would constitute the start of a dialogue between them *about* the event, and this is not the purpose of animal communication. To converse about an event is to refrain from immediately acting in reference to it; it is to interpose a delay between the stimulating event and the person's response to it; everything stops while some talk goes on. Humans, by virtue of their new stance, indicated by the loss of movement of their ears, are able to converse about anything and to do it by means of a language that is universal to the human community. Animal communication is never universal in this sense but only common to those members of the group who share a biological program. Because human languages have this characteristic of universality, they constitute their own worlds. Thus the individual who knows the language but not well enough may be misunderstood, a possibility not open to nonhuman animals of the same species. No chimpanzee can ever misunderstand another; but by the same token, no chimpanzee can ever understand another. This is because programmed sounds, such as those made by most animals and by humans under special conditions—for example, the baby's cry of hunger—can never be "wrong" but equally, are never "right." They simply belong to certain situations, in just the way that the clenched fist belongs to the situation of conflict and the open face to the situation of friendliness.

Distance is the distinctive mark of the upright posture, whether the psychological distance that one can then assume toward what is perceived or the temporal distance that then ensues between stimulus and response. The newfound biological stance expressed in the upright posture of humans is the basis for our unprecedented development of ecto functions. With the exception of certain sounds that we share with other animals, our speech is all dialogue, the formal and grammatical use of language for purposes of referring *to* matters that we and others are concerned with. While other animals are capable of being engaged in matters of concern to them, they have no way of referring *to* these matters.

We are able to engage in dialogue, to refer to, to think about, and to interpose delay because of our developed capacity for *representation*. By this term I refer to our ability to create a world—an unreal world of image, of fantasy, of thought or idea—in which we can place and hold, and then if we wish manipulate, whatever engages us. As an analogy, think of the new breed of electronic typewriters, most of which contain a buffer mechanism to enable one to display a line or more of what has been typed before having it impressed on the page. In this analogy, the original typing corresponds to sensory stimulation, the buffer mechanism to the human capacity for representation, and the impress of typed words on the page to the response to stimulation. By the use of such a buffer, what is typed, or impressed as stimulation, can be changed and even erased independently of the nature of its content, and very much the same can be accomplished by the "buffering" mechanism of representation. It becomes the heart of our ecto functioning.

On Object and Effigy

Erwin Straus has made an important distinction, in this connection, between a picture as object and a picture as *effigy*. Effigies are not produced in nature but only as a consequence of the object—in this case a picture—being viewed by a human who can assume a distance from it and so is able to perceive it as a representation of another object. Paintings, then, are both objects and effigies; they are what they are, of course, but they can also be what we view them as, in consequence of our ecto functioning. Very young children cannot view them in this way, hence the effigy appears as a possibility only about the time the growing child assumes the upright posture and, at about the same time, begins to talk. The family dog cannot see the picture in this way, which is why the portrait of its master, no matter how realistically it is painted, can never be to the dog anything more than one more object to be sniffed. There are no effigies in the world of the dog.

The notion of effigy, as Straus explicates it, helps us to grasp the full significance and the biological importance of that special world of representation to which only humans have access. Without shifting from one sense modality to another or one perceptual system to another, an effigy manages to be a representation; thus we use our visual apparatus to see the painting as an object, and we can tell how big it is, what colors were used in it, whether the canvas is damaged, and whether it is hung straight. But at the same time, and presumably with the same visual apparatus, we see the object that it is a painting of and simultaneously we grasp that this is not an object itself but the painting of an object. We are therefore never puzzled by the fact that the effigy exists in its own (ecto) realm, unchallenged by the forces and the demands imposed by a concrete, everyday world of physical objects. If we should see a painting of a house in a book, we do not expect thereby that the page will be too heavy to lift, nor when we have lifted and turned the page do we expect to see the backside of the house on the reverse of the page. We recognize, as part of our command of a world of representations and effigies, that what we see is not the world but *of* or *about* the world, in a realm that we control because of our ability to function in the ecto style. And because the space captured for representation of the effigy is not our own space of living but part of its own (ecto) realm, we accept the fact that it is usually marked off by a frame—whether the frame of a painting or the proscenium arch of the stage—a fact that has been true of painting since the craft was invented by Paleolithic hunters some 25,000 years ago.[20]

Like other animals, we as humans are capable of using our visual perceptual systems in the service of both endo and meso activities. We can, for example, behave in a manner that Straus calls "orienting seeing . . . [which] is in the service of corporeal existence, of locomotion, approaching, fleeing, capturing, and incorporating. In orienting seeing we are directed to things as objects within a common field of gravity."[21] But as humans we are also capable of ecto functioning in which we turn off the immediate demands of the situation or of our bodies, turning instead to a mode that Straus calls "beholding . . . [a] distance-preserving gaze [to] count and measure, relate replica to original, representation to what it represents."[22] It is the difference between incarnation, when like most animals we are caught in the immediacy of our own bodies, and excarnation. In the latter, "made possible by upright posture, vision perpendicular to one's own body axis confronts things as they rise up vertically in a fronto-parallel plane."[23]

Direct and Indirect Evidence

The legendary Theseus, of Greek mythology, accomplished the feat of clearing the coast road to Athens of its preying swarm of thieves and murderers. One of the villains he defeated was an innkeeper named Polypemon, known as Procrustes from his habit of "stretching out" his victims. It was his practice to offer travelers a night's safe lodging but to fit all his guests to his one or two existing beds, either by stretching out the short ones or chopping off the legs of the taller ones. The grim fate that these travelers suffered provides us with an apt analogue of a second important characteristic of ecto-style perception and measurement, in addition to distancing.

To spell this out, I begin with a distinction between what I will call direct evidence and indirect evidence. In the field of developmental psychology one major approach is called longitudinal. It consists of gathering data on the spot, so to speak, over a succession of measurement occasions that may stretch out over fifty years. In principle, although not always in practice, longitudinal data, or what I here call direct evidence, is gathered in response to phenomena as they naturally and spontaneously occur. In the other major approach in developmental psychology, cross-sectional, or what I term the gathering of indirect evidence, the time and place and manner of getting data are all predetermined in accordance with a research design and, so to speak, then imposed on the data.

An example of this distinction is found in the work of Piaget, who was one of the very few investigators in psychology whose data may properly be termed longitudinal. First, he worked over a long time span in his studies of the developing intelligence of his own children. But he did not simply stick with his subjects over a period of some years, as in the classic longitudinal studies of developmental psychology, but lived with them. As a consequence, he was able to be present, ready to respond to whatever data arose in naturally ongoing situations. He did not, for example, decide in advance to enter the infant's room and make an observation each fifteen minutes or so many times per day or week. He interacted with the children, playing with them, until something happened that struck him as worthy of recording, and he then made his observations and followed them up with variations. It is a procedure that has also been used by parents whose interest was in charting their children's language development, as in the classic study by Leopold.[24]

I have called this type of observation direct evidence because no schema is introduced between observer and target, but it must be admitted at once that "pure" direct evidence is very hard to come by and probably did not occur even in Piaget's case. He must have had some guiding notion, even some theoretical scheme, that helped to direct what he looked for, what he saw, what he thought about it, and what were the next steps that he took. Direct evidence in this pure sense is an ideal, never achieved and—unless we are willing to forgo all the lessons we have learned from our predecessors—not especially desirable. Yet the distinction between direct and indirect evidence is clear enough, and I think important enough, to be preserved, for what it will teach us about ecto and non-ecto styles.

In a cross-sectional study, by contrast, the investigator typically selects groups of subjects rather than individuals, each group representing the values of significant independent variables—for example, a group of first-graders, a group of second-graders, and so on. Then at certain fixed times decided on by the investigator, predetermined measurements are made on the subjects. The resulting data are then analyzed by statistical procedures that have also been selected in advance. In all, the entire investigation is guided by a plan that imposes layer upon layer of patterning on the original data. The cross-sectional study is thus Procrustean; subjects are fitted to a preexisting schema. More, the cross-sectional design may be likened to another characteristic of Procrustean treatment: once the victim has been fitted to the bed, the bed must then be fitted to the room, and the room to the inn and so on. Similarly, the subject in a cross-sectional design is fitted to a preexisting demand as to age and grade, and groups of subjects are then fitted to each other as part of a research design, and specific aspects of their behavior are in turn manipulated, cut off, or discarded so as to result in the data required, and these groupings of data are then further rearranged as needed, and so on.

The kinds of evidence resulting from these two approaches, direct and indirect, are not equivalent but belong in two quite different realms. Indirect evidence, gathered as in cross-sectional studies by imposing a successive series of predetermined patternings on the data, produces what are called facts. It is evidence that is constructed by the investigator in the light of some already known truth; since it results from a prearranged construction that is not itself changed by the data, it is both timeless and dogmatic. And because it is the result of imposing some intelligible scheme, one can talk about it to others or have it shared, supported, or criticized, and even debate whether or not it is true.

But what I have called direct evidence, demonstrated in as pure a form as we will see in longitudinal studies, is not true in this sense. At best it is simply what is so, or perhaps what seems to be so. It is a function of one individual's grasp of the situation at present, and so in the end it rests on whatever the individual can offer as a statement of trust in the world. It is not timeless but deeply embedded in time, specifically in the present. This was Fritz Perl's great insight, that in the pure case psychotherapy dealt only with such evidence, which he properly called the "here and now." And in the terms of a distinction much older than the topic of the present discussion, we have here the difference between dogma and faith.

It will be evident that direct evidence corresponds most closely to an endo style of thought or perception and indirect evidence to the ecto style. It follows that ecto thinking underlies what we call the scientific method. One consequence of this distinction is that in the ecto style truth is gained by discovery, on the assumption that the truth-seeker has applied the appropriate independent schemas. In the ecto mode truth is not given by a kind of armchair meditation nor out of a faith that it will arrive as a gift from God and certainly not by settling for less, by agreeing that it is all a mystery that we will never know. Truth can be discovered, that is the ecto-style dictum. Jerome Bruner[25] has recently made a distinction that is parallel to the one I suggest here, between two modes of what he calls "knowing," between a "logical-scientific mode of thinking" and a "narrative mode." Both occur naturally, but they do not reduce to each other. The major difference between the modes, according to Bruner, lies in their relation to what is accepted as proof. The logical-scientific mode appeals to "formal verification procedures" and forms of proof based on empirical data, whereas the narrative mode appeals finally to "believability."[26] The narrative mode is therefore independent of considerations of truth and falsity. Although the logical-scientific mode looks in the past for causes and the narrative mode toward the future for intentions, both must be accepted as "versions of the real world."

The distinction I am pursuing here helps us to understand the curious place that is occupied by data obtained in the clinical session. In order to be of use in the clinician's practice, evidence gathered in the session must be molded to some degree, that is, mediated through some construction. Most clinicians would agree that only two such schemes are available to us that are of sufficient scope and possess enough historical documentation as support: psychoanalytic theory and some form of behavioral or learning theory. If the clinician does not fit the presented data to some combination of these two constructions, there will be no alternative but to fall back on allowing, accepting, moved by wonder and fascination, and thereby lessening one's professional value to the client.

Unfortunately for this neat arrangement, the clinical data do not always fall into the patterns that we would like. Clinical work is not supposed to be totally directed according to a prearranged schema, for in any event there will often occur moments that, to the trained eye of the clinician (and occasionally, particularly if they are dramatic or moving, to the untrained eye of the client as well), are memorable and need to be taken into account. Here we have instances of direct evidence, not as yet patterned nor fitted to a plan. The clinician might then make use of such direct evidence, fitting it into a schema in relation to other evidence; the data now become a form of evidence about evidence, in the ecto style. At one extreme there is the example of Gottschalk's research on pauses and hesitations in clients' speech, where clinical data are used as experimental data, as in cross-sectional studies, gathered under prescribed conditions for predetermined purposes.[27] At the other extreme are data that are just as significant for the clinician's purposes, when a sudden insight, change of tone, or emotional outburst unexpectedly determines a whole new direction in the session. And between the two extremes are the most common instances of all, in which a kind of direct evidence does occur, both participants permitting it to happen, but the clinician then makes a special, predetermined use of it on the basis of skills and past experience with such cases.

It is because of these possible variations that one cannot fit clinical data into a known category—and perhaps it is just because of these variations that clinical data are so valuable. Clinicians will differ in the way they make use of the same kinds of data, from the routine set of procedures that identify some forms of psychotherapy to the combination of imagination, intuition, and judgment that results in an approach as much art as science. Across the range of clinicians as well as within the practice of the individual clinician, the data of their sessions will be direct and indirect, both. It has been argued by some writers[28] that whether we admit it or not, this is also true of science in general—but that is a point that must remain unsettled, at least in these pages.

BODIES AND THEIR PERCEPTUAL SYSTEMS

In regard to one's center of gravity, the endo center is low and close to the ground, fitting the person who stays put. Recall the statues of the seated Buddha or the relaxing Sumo wrestler. This is the person who is "centered" or "has a lot of guts." For the meso the center is higher, located in the chest; in the extreme case, the pouter pigeon, its chest all puffed up with nothing beneath to support it; or in its military equivalent, the strutting person, a bemedaled chest held up by a tightly drawn belt. For the ecto the center of

gravity is weak and shifting—although from this the ecto may gain the ad-
vantage of being able to take any position and see many alternatives, thus
avoiding danger.

At the opening of this chapter I noted that the body forms itself continuously as a representative of its species, through time and over the
course of evolution. If we take this proposition seriously, however, we
meet the problem of how the ecto component is expressed in species
other than humans. The meso style, as I described it in earlier chapters,
is certainly expressed in all the action-oriented movement patterns of
animals of different species, especially in the type of animal we call a
predator. The endo style, equally, has its typical mode of expression, a
driven, selective, and gut-dominated pattern of evaluation and absorption that we can find in almost all animals. But there is a serious question as to whether similar claims can be made in regard to the ecto
component in behavior.

The Ecto Style in Nonhumans

Consider in this regard the various species of mammals, where distinctions among the three behavioral styles are most evident. The adult
physiques of mammals develop out of three embryonic germinal layers,
as I discussed in chapter 2. Major organs of the mammalian body are
therefore homologous across most species, from the structures of the
sense organs to the organization of the digestive and respiratory apparatus. The meso and endo styles that use these forms are approximately similar across species. By this reasoning, then, there should also
be found an ecto style in mammals that expresses, just as it does in humans, patterns of distancing, symbolizing, and abstracting behavior. If
we do not find this in other species of mammals than the human, we
would be left with a curious anomaly—that I am claiming a biologically
related set of behaviors that is unique to humans even though their biology is not unique.

The difficulty is that no substantial claim has ever been made that
mammals other than humans and perhaps the monkeys and great apes
are capable of an ecto style of symbolizing and distancing behavior. Indeed, after a decade of research claims and counterclaims regarding

language, it now appears that humans alone exhibit these capabilities. If this should prove to be so, we would then have to conclude that the ecto style, involving the use of symbols, abstractions, and grammatical speech, is unique to humans and perhaps cannot even be taught to the animals that most resemble us. We are then brought to a question that cuts close to the basis of my argument in this book: Do other animals use their sensory apparatus as humans do, as an expression of the ecto style?

To answer this question, we may turn to the account given by phylogenetic evidence, beginning with the "sensory" equipment of single-celled organisms such as the amoeba. I will discuss a number of major perceptual "systems," using that term in Gibson's[29] sense as "active perceptual organs . . . that can search out the information in stimulus energy." This definition of a perceptual system accords with the style that I have termed ecto, in the sense that its mission is to make use of information *about* a source—as distinct from merely directly or passively receiving the stimulus energy without turning it into a form of information.

A first kind of evidence as to whether the perceptual systems of organisms other than humans may properly be termed ecto is found in the fact of specific organ systems for the different perceptual systems. If different kinds of stimulation result not in broad categories of response that are similar across stimulus modes—for example, if they result simply in acceptance *versus* rejection or attraction *versus* repulsion—but rather in specialized organ systems, we have the first evidence as to true perceptual systems. Organ systems that are specialized to the task, structurally as well as functionally, would have developed in this way only if they work on information rather than on broadly similar forms of energy. Organisms at the level of planaria, such as flatworms, which are only slightly developed beyond the complex organization of one-celled animals, already show this distinctive mark of the perceptual system; their cells are differentiated for such functions as touching or responding to chemical stimulation.

The visual system provides the most elaborate basis for ecto-style functions, since it answers the question of intensity (How much?) as well as the question of direction (Where is it?) and even questions concerning the nature of a source (What is it?). Probably for this reason, it is the mode of stimulation and the perceptual system most likely to be elaborated into an ecto style, as we see most clearly in the case of humans. But even in perceptual systems that appear more primitive, such as that associated with chemical stimulation, ecto functions can be found well below the human level. One may distinguish three orders of chemical stimulation and response. There is, first, the "general chemical sense" located on part or all of the animal's body, from protozoan to fish, a sensory capacity so widespread among different species that some have considered it synonymous with being alive. Responses based on this sense usually take the form of simple avoidance and so have none of the characteristics of an ecto style.

Second, there is the response that humans experience as taste, in which receptor organs are brought into direct contact with a stimulating source. Finally, there is the distance receptor known as the sense of smell that is found in practically all creatures that live in the air. Below the human level the taste response is most often the simple dichotomy of acceptance-rejection, but the fact that receptor differentiation, in the form of different organs for each system, appears at the insect level would seem to be evidence that smell, at least, begins to serve an ecto function. In fact, in a number of species of insects such as ants, chemical markers are used to lay a trail for communicating elaborately coded information—for example, information concerning the distance and direction of a food source as well as its kind and even quantity. And even at lower phylogenetic levels the chemical system may serve some ecto functions. In many species the direction and distance to a source of food is detected by the animal by means of its sensitivity to gradients of concentration, and if the source happens to be movement, even more precise information becomes available. Planaria will orient toward and then move in the direction of a food source, on the basis of concentrations of smell that they can differentiate, even moving the head so as to utilize separate spots of sensitivity on the body and in this way comparing intensities of stimulation. Similarly, moths following the scent of a female upwind will tack across the airstream so as to zero in on the selected spot. These are ecto behaviors, making use of information about a source, as distinct from merely a direct response to the presence of the source.

The system of what Gibson terms "mechanical stimulation," which includes both touch and hearing, provides further evidence of ecto-style activities in animals other than humans. The irritability of organisms, as evidenced in their response to mechanical stimulation, is perhaps the earliest mode of sensory receptivity to appear in the animal world; it is omnipresent in such one-celled animals as the amoeba or paramecium. Although the results of mechanical stimulation, however produced, usually consist of generalized responses such as avoidance, two characteristics of this perceptual system serve to identify it with an ecto style. The first is that most animals are capable of distinguishing between touching and being touched. The former is an action common to all motile creatures and when it occurs is marked by quite specific actions that follow; these in turn are quite different from the common response known as irritability, which follows on being touched. Crude though this distinction might be in simple animals, it suggests that we have here not simply a matter of mechanical contact, such as might occur in the case of a machine in motion, but a matter of a perceptual mode in which self is distinguished from other, the self-induced differentiated from the other-induced.

A second important characteristic is the sensitivity of the touch system in most animals. Humans are able to recognize one hair being moved on the body. As one review states, "Even with auditory cues excluded, tapping with a fingernail is often sufficient to determine whether an object is made of wood, metal, or plastic. . . . A lightly etched piece of glass having eminences no higher than .001 mm can be successfully discriminated from an entirely smooth one."[30] This is to say that a contact with only a very minute part or aspect of the world is sufficient to provide, by way of tactile perception, information that extends well beyond the raw data itself.

The earliest forms of organs for the system of mechanical stimulation, serving for hearing and touch, appear at the level of coelenterates, which are primitive multicelled animals such as the coral or the sea anemone. A separate organ for hearing then appears at the later stage of the jointed invertebrates, which includes insects and crustaceans. In either case, the system becomes differentiated to a remarkable degree well before the human level.

Schemas in Other Styles

Finally, I now return to a matter left hanging at the conclusion of chapter 2. There I referred to a "motor attitude" as the home, in the meso style, of what corresponds to the independent schema in the ecto style, and I stated that no schema can be identified as corresponding to the endo style. To help us understand in a more general sense this possibility of the living body that I have called the independent schema, I turn to Merleau-Ponty's discussion of his term *structure* as it is applied to behavior.[31]

Merleau-Ponty refers to an analogous problem: how might we understand the phenomenon known as animal learning without falling into a network of theoretical propositions concerning "determined connections," with its implication of an assemblage of mechanically linked parts? He suggests that learning is to be understood as "a general alteration of behavior which is manifested in a multitude of actions, the content of which is variable and the significance constant."[32] His apt example is that of the burnt child who has learned to stay away from the fire, not because there has been established a new habit of moving the arm in response to the visual stimulus of fire but because there has been established a new set of "reactions of protection."[33] Similarly, the dog that has been trained to sit at the command "Sit!" will, if lying down when the command is given, utilize a set of muscles opposite to the customary ones in order to carry out the order.

The precise elements making up the learned movement will, in Merleau-Ponty's words, vary from one occasion to another, but the "significance" will remain constant. In the case of ecto-style learning we can attribute the constancy to the operation of a developed independent schema. In regard to meso and endo behavior, however, of which animal learning is an obvious example, we must turn elsewhere. A long line of experimental evidence suggests that one can distinguish between the phenomenon of an animal learning something and the phenomenon of the animal learning how to learn. Thus, most test animals that are faced with a problem-solving situation improve their performance as the testing proceeds, as a consequence of their learning how one goes about the process of learning. Merleau-Ponty deals with this issue by suggesting that what the animal gains must be "aptitude for choosing," perhaps even a "method of selection."[34] "There must be a principle in the organism which ensures that the learning experience will have a general relevance."[35] In short, the animal learns what Merleau-Ponty calls a *structure*, a set of behavioral possibilities organized around an appropriate principle of relevance. I suggest that the structure, in this special sense, corresponds in the meso and endo styles to what I have discussed as the independent schema in the ecto style.

PART THREE

Applying the Hypothesis to Issues
of Culture

There is a widespread conviction that one cannot truly know something unless one has experienced it in a personal way. Thus, it is often said that in order to understand a set of teachings one has to practice them, as though they were skills in tennis. And that is the point—for such a notion is strongly influenced by the meso style. The meso truly knows something only in the practice of it. The ecto can know it logically, out of knowing about it, and the endo can simply know that it is so. In each style one knows something out of having experienced it—but the experience differs from one style to another.

There are a number of reasons for including a chapter on art and artists in a book such as this, aside from the obvious reason that it will indicate how far my thesis may be extended.

A first reason is that a discussion of art may furnish some useful insights into the topic of artistic style. This term may be understood in a number of ways: for instance, like other persons, artists tend to behave in one or another style or mix of styles; or unlike most persons, artists' styles are not only expressions of their everyday behavior but also the particular ways they express themselves as artists. A new approach to the question of styles may therefore offer a novel stance from which to explore the general topic of artistic expression. I should note, however, that in so doing, I make no attempt at explaining art or artists—whatever that might mean—but rather make a first try at defining and exploring artistic styles from a novel vantage point.

A second reason for including a chapter on art and artists is that the thesis I explore in this book opens up some interesting possibilities concerning body structures and their place within the context of an

artist's life and work, and this is certainly worth examining. The mean-
ing-creating act for which the artist is uniquely primed is often carried
out by way of somatic expression, as in the statement by Matisse that
he knew when a painting was good because he could feel it "in the
hand"[1] or in the well-known remark by Einstein that he could "feel his
mathematical solutions in his musculature."[2] Perhaps more important
is that the human body, in particular the nude body, is the most widely
used subject in the history of art. Artists not only show somatic concerns, as we all do, and use the body as a vehicle of everyday expression, but they find in the body their best arena of expressive activity.
This in turn reflects back on their individual styles as artists and as
persons; the way they depict the body becomes their own signature.
Who could confuse the body as portrayed by El Greco with that portrayed by Rubens? The question of what these differences mean and
how we may understand them goes directly to the center of any artist's
work and of the meaning of art in general as impulse and as style of
living. In the concluding section of this chapter, I deal with this question at some length in regard to the work of Alberto Giacometti.

There is a third, closely related reason for including a chapter on art
and artists, and that is that artists are, by comparison with the rest of
us, uniquely situated. All of us live our own truth as best we may, but
it is granted only to artists to express that truth, to flaunt it in the face
of history. Our behavior is always a continuing and changing statement of how we live our bodies, but the artist is permitted one step
beyond everyday life experience. That too is worth our time to examine.

In all this I refer to individual artists. However, one may apply the
same thinking to collectivities in which the individual artist is anonymous or even to entire societies in which individuals do not appear to
us. For example, in my discussion (chapter 2) of some differences between Paleolithic and Levantine styles of art, my reference was to
characteristics of an entire culture, almost as though individuals in the
ordinary sense did not exist. We can do this in regard to such preliter-
ate cultures because we assume that their styles of activity, and particularly of art, express cultural rather than simply personal aspirations
and experiences. Although we have no evidence one way or another,
we may also assume that within these relatively monolithic cultures

some of the artists were more gifted than others or managed to place an individual mark on their work.

In some more recent Western cultures, as I discuss below, art was more often than not the product of a school or collectivity of artists. Individual artists became the rule rather than the exception in Western history only at the time of the Renaissance, about the beginning of the eleventh century. In pre-Columbian Mexico, in the dynasties of Egypt, in much of the history of Greece and Rome, in the ancient city-states of the Middle East, and even as late as the Middle Ages in European monasteries, the individual artist was usually anonymous and most artistic productions were identified with a group. Various reasons for this suggest themselves, although of course we have no way to decide among them—that outstanding individuals did in fact exist but were not identified, or that major works were produced by teams of artists and craftsmen working together, or even that everyone in a school or group did very much the same thing and so were indistinguishable if their work was preserved.

In contrast with speech as well as most written work, we are fortunate in that the visual arts of painting and sculpture preserve for us a picture of how things were seen at the time, at least how they were seen by the artist or artists. Such evidence as we have remaining in art is usually in much the same form as when it was originally produced, and so we are in the advantageous position of being able to look at the same object (if not the same subject) as the artist saw. We can examine how it was rendered and so make some intelligent guesses as to how the artist transmuted experience into its representation. And this holds true for artistic productions that go as far back in time as the history of art itself, because from the beginning the forms in which artists worked were much the same as those we know today. If we define art rather broadly to include decoration, we can say that the first works of art were patterns and engravings scratched on pieces of bone. This was followed by sculpture in stone and baked clay and then by bas-reliefs in sizes ranging from less than a meter to full-scale wall coverings. Engravings on cave walls followed and then, completing the Paleolithic oeuvre, paintings on cave walls and on the interior walls of cave shelters. In the twenty-five thousand years since, we have not added much to this list of methods in the graphic arts, and much of what was done then is available for our study today.

IN THE ANCIENT CITY-STATES

Many pieces of evidence suggest that it may be useful to look at the specific body structures that are favored by one or another culture. In a number of preindustrial cultures, notably the Bushmen and the Hottentots of Africa, a certain body structure in women is traditionally favored as being sexually attractive. Its main features are a relatively long torso, squat legs, and a kind of steatopygia or prominence of the buttocks, all features that are typically found in the Venus sculptures of prehistoric cultures. Similarly, when the first Portuguese explorers reached the isolated Canary Islands and made contact with a culture that had preserved some very ancient traditions, they too found an esthetic preference for this Venus type of female body: women who were quite obese, large around the middle, and with small feet and small, babyish faces. Some of the earliest known sculptures of pre-Columbian Mexico also consist of figurines of women who have quite full figures and small, tapered feet together with some emphasis on the buttocks, and, in the case of Olmec sculpture, baby faces as well. These examples are widely dispersed in time and space, hinting at a universal pattern of preference related to body structure.

We turn now to a specific culture that came into existence and flourished before the era of written history, the great city-states of Sumer, Babylon, and Assyria in the fourth millennium B.C. Most of their monumental sculptures are much larger than life-size and are modeled on hunting animals—the lion or the eagle, for example—so that regardless of the pose one can see an emphasis on the muscle groups that lie directly beneath the skin. This amounts to an emphasis on and display of a meso component. On the other hand, in smaller friezes or in small carved figures as well as in wall paintings, there is rather a mix of endo and meso characteristics in the bodies. As a first approximation, I would suggest that if the subject were a person of lower class, such as a warrior who might be expendable on tasks necessary for the kingdom, both male and female figures tend to be very much meso. However, if the picture or carving is of a personage of higher status such as a priest or courtier, one usually finds a mix of meso and endo characteristics. In neither case does one find the characteristics of an ecto body structure.

In addition, these rather heavy and muscular bodies seem to bear striking resemblances to the local residents in modern times, at least according to photographic evidence. These persons, usually of the peasant and working classes, were often hired to help out in a dig, and then posed with the archaeologists for photographs when a find was made. Although such evidence is meager, it begins to suggest that a general body type was prevalent at the time the sculptures were produced and that it may be found even today in this area.

There is, however, one striking exception to the above remarks. At the well-known site of the Khorsabad citadel gate, done in the eighth century B.C., there is a group of monumental figures, presumably stationed there to guard the gate. They are winged creatures, half-human and half-mythical, and are often referred to as "geniuses"—that term being used in its original meaning of a local guardian spirit. These figures are also unique in some important respects. For one, they show quite fine and careful detailing, which is an unusual characteristic for artistic works of this period. For example, at the wrists of the figures there are exceptionally careful and detailed rosettes in stone; in addition, there is much more ornamentation than is normally found. Their general style is, in fact, so exceptional that they have been described as "hard to classify."[3] In the Assyrian tradition, works of art are always flat rather than deep, projecting, or round, but these figures are obvious exceptions to that rule. They consist either of bas-reliefs so deep as to approximate sculpture in the round or else sculptures so shallow as to resemble relief work. In either case they fall into a category of their own.

Further, these figures are unique in the "style" that is suggested or the experience that appears to be projected into them by their maker(s). In Assyrian art the monumental figures, or the beings or personages depicted in the figures, are always shown looking directly at the viewer or else are actively engaged in situations into which the viewer might easily step and take part. The arena that is shown or implied, or the space in which the figures are to act, is either a part of our everyday world of action or a place just like our world, even when what is depicted is an act that is more or less mythical. The figures exist in a concrete, practical, familiar world of motor actions, that is, in a meso world.

But this is just what is not true of the curious winged geniuses at the Khorsabad gate. In the words of one critic, their world "is conceived as a self-contained world, from which no glance or gesture moves outward toward the spectator."[4] Paralleling this distinction is another—that these figures, of all that we know in the corpus of near Eastern art in this culture, are the only ones with fairly pronounced ecto characteristics. In sharp contrast to the dense, muscular bodies found in other monumental sculpture or the relatively squat endo-meso mixture found in the smaller figures on wall friezes, these resemble rather muscular ectos. As I have indicated in earlier pages, the ecto style of behavior is well described as "self-contained" and expressed predominantly within that "interior" realm that in Western culture we call the mind. In the meso realm, by contrast, the style is one of forthright action within the recognizable world of concretely realized social interchange. This is close to the distinction that we find in comparing typical Assyrian sculpture and painting with the unique figures from Khorsabad.

A CENTURY OF PRE-RENAISSANCE ART

An ideal arrangement for enabling comparisons between one era and another might be the repeated representation of the same vision or conception through a number of centuries. Fortunately, this is just what we have in the case of the Christ figure. In one of his many studies of such questions, Sheldon undertook to rate on his somatotypic grid a total of 124 paintings of Christ that had been produced before the year 1900. When he rated in sequence their endo, meso, and ecto components, each on a scale of 1 at the low end to 7 at the maximum, he found that 30 percent were rated at 236 and 35 percent at 235, a mixture of components he describes as evidencing "defiant strength," the general portrait of a bright ectomorph who is not a weakling.[5] However, when he rated another seven paintings of Christ that had been done since 1915, he found that the rating on the meso component now averaged 5, leading him to comment: "If our grand-children go to Sunday School they may be shown pictures not of Christ suffering in (ectomorphic) tight-lipped silence on a cross, but of a Christ performing heroic feats of athletic prowess."[6]

Comparisons of this sort are readily available. For more than a thousand years, well into the Renaissance, the religious art of the Catholic Church constituted the most important art of the Western world. In the very center of this work the figure of Christ was always meant to convey the most deeply felt visions of the artists. We can therefore do no better than try to capture the changes in how Christ and some closely related figures were depicted in the centuries preceding the Renaissance. A preliminary survey of these centuries indicates an important change occurring at what we can call a watershed era, extending from approximately 800 to 900 A.D. Before this time Christ was never represented as an ecto figure. Paintings of him between the fifth and ninth centuries show a meso figure, beardless, and often with oversized feet—found often in young males during a meso growth spurt. By about the year 800 he comes to be depicted as a young and still unformed meso or else as a slightly rounded figure, that is, with mixed meso and endo features. The Christ figure on the Saint-Denis crystal, for example, which was made about 867, is almost paunchy; another picture, made about 783 at the court of Charlemagne for the Godescalc Gospel Lectionary, may be described as a round-faced, almost baby-faced, slightly pudgy adolescent.

As we approach the year 900, however, the figure of Christ starts to become stretched out. It develops a gaunt look, at first only in the face but later in other parts of the body. The face that was formerly young and beardless and a little rounded now is bearded and lean. The feet become smaller, some ribs begin to show, and the arms and lower legs get thinner and relatively longer. It is as though the earlier figure is being stretched out into a different somatic pattern, under the call of a different religious vision.

By the year 1000 this change has become quite obvious and has even started to affect the traditionally determined position that Christ assumes on the cross. Where the art of earlier centuries had shown Christ as loosely and almost effortlessly balanced against the cross, with little except a stylized turn of the head to indicate his suffering, later repre-

Cimabue, *Crucifixion*

sentations show a very complex posture. His body now sags in a zigzag line; the knees, the upper pelvis, and the head are inclined toward the viewer's left, while the feet, the lower pelvis, and the shoulders bend toward the viewer's right. It is now a pose of vivid but contained agony, perhaps nowhere more beautifully realized than in Cimabue's magnificent painting of the crucifixion (figure 7). Other male figures in the sacred art of this period show much the same tendency—tall, stretched out, with long and thin necks, thin and pointed feet, thin hands, slightly sunken chests, and long, lean faces. It appears that the familiar meso figure of Christ, like the figures of those closest to him, has been changed to accommodate a new ecto vision.

Does this hold true as well for works that do not fall into the category of sacred art? It would seem that art with a more secular aim—religious figures that were not meant for display in sacred places such as altars, for one example—went through similar changes but only after some delay. Thus, paintings and other works of the period 850 to 900 show figures that are mainly meso but with some endo characteristics. They are heavy in the neck, sturdy and solid, with strong chins. The Stuttgart Psalter of about 820, as one example, shows Christ looking very much like a modern muscle man. This general pattern seems to persist until at least 950, although some exceptions seem to hint at changes that are about to occur. On the Lothair crystal, done about 865, the figures all seem predominantly meso, but in the scene of "Suzanna before the Elders" she is obviously ecto, as are the Elders, thin, gaunt avengers.

In the view of students of these works, the bodies depicted have, by the late 900s, become "attenuated" and have become infused as well with a certain passionate expressiveness. This is especially evident in the works of Liuthar at the great art center of Trier in Germany. By the year 1050, as can be seen in works out of the Echternach school, even figures other than that of Christ show primarily ecto features. They are now all similar to the tall, thin, "spiritual" type so familiar in our modern tradition, according to which we associate spirituality with ecto features. Whatever endo features may have existed earlier seem now to have dropped away, leaving a figure that is mainly ecto but with some meso aspects. For example, in the Pantheon Bible of the twelfth century Adam is shown as rather square and muscular and Eve as square but a little more attenuated, while the angel is perceptibly taller and thinner. Presumably the closer one is to pure spirit, the more likely one is to be shown with ecto features.

The art centers of Trier in Germany and Cîteaux in France were strongholds of artistic development, training, and production, and at the same time great centers of religious life. Consequently, when new styles appeared in their art, they signaled that a significant change of religious vision, perhaps an explosion of new religious fervor, was also occurring. The general change I have just described, in which a concretely realized figure of Christ and of other religious models was altered to appear almost unworldly, did in fact coincide with a high point of religious fervor at these centers. It marked an attempt to return to a more "pure" and more spiritual faith and practice. The vision emerging from this movement is well exemplified in the painting of a saint that was executed for the Cîteaux Lectionary about the year 1130. This site was perhaps the most important center for art in France from 1100 to 1150, and as well a center of the Cistercian reform movement, which pressed for a new adherence to the sanctity of personal toil. In this painting the saint's figure is shown as quite tall and thin, slope-shouldered, with a long neck and an elongated face. All its lines run vertically, from the small feet and thin fingers to the large eyes, from the drawn and nearly absent stomach to the sunken chest. Somatic characteristics that I have identified with the ecto type, such as elongation and a turning inward from the world, are here dramatically emphasized in ways that would not have been attempted a century or two earlier.

This is not to be taken as an explanation of art or of any of its aspects, for I mean this discussion as no more than another avenue for exploring the history of art. This caution is particularly in order when we are faced with work done either by anonymous artists or by a group whose collective stamp is on the product. Thus, in the stained glass windows of the church of Saint-Yves at La Roche-Maurice in northern Brittany, we see a Christ figure that is just as short, sturdy, and muscular as are the fishermen of Finisterre today—although the windows were done about the year 1500. Here, it appears, the parallel is not between a product and the religious vision that gave rise to it but between a product and the then-current model in real life.

"A MOST CAPRICIOUS BRAIN"

We turn now to considering the work of a particular artist, for what it may tell us about the relations between art and behavioral style. Michelangelo Merisi, whom we will consider in this section, is known today by the name of the village where he was born in 1573, Caravaggio in northern Italy. Very little is known about his early life except that his father was a master builder and that the son was at first intended for the same line of work, until he was apprenticed at the age of ten to a painter in Milan. Caravaggio may or may not have had to flee Milan some four or five years later, but in any case he arrived at Rome in his early teens. There he immediately became a part of the local art scene, worked for a number of painters, lived from hand to mouth, and perhaps did some first paintings on his own to help pay for a hospital bill. His work must have shown some promise, for he was soon taken into the studio of one Giuseppe Cesari, later to become Cavaliere d'Arpino. When he left this place to strike out on his own, he was very soon reduced to being destitute and was only rescued by some fellow painters and then by the man who became his first patron, Cardinal Francesco del Monte. It was at this point, as he obtained other patrons among the clerical nobility, that his career may be said to have begun.

It was Cardinal del Monte who made it possible for Caravaggio to express the promise already becoming apparent in his work. By 1600 the young man was receiving commissions on a regular basis for paintings and altarpieces in the churches of the region. At the same time he was becoming involved in a series of more or less serious brushes with the law. His history reveals a string of fights, libel actions, quarrels, assaults, even duels, the exact seriousness of which is difficult to judge at this distance. Some writers on Caravaggio's life have referred to his "destructive fits and frenzies," while others have argued that he was essentially a shy person who was merely defending his rights during an era in which physical violence was commonplace. In any case he was probably never a retiring person but always actively, physically, even passionately involved in the life of his times. Charged in a libel suit in 1603 with helping to circulate satirical verses about a writer, he had to leave Rome for a time. Then, on his return, he again came to public attention because of a fight with a restaurant waiter as well as a number of more serious brawls. With neither wife nor family nor permanent home, he lived in the company of other young artists like himself, worked fiercely at his commissions, and spent all the money he received in a man-on-the-town life. When the money was exhausted, he would pay his fines and go back to work. His friend, mentor, and strongest supporter, Cardinal del Monte, referred to him as "uno cervello stravagantissimo," a most capricious brain. In his painting as well as in his escapades he seemed to pursue a program of actively and fiercely declaring his independence, for he often managed to displease his clients with the odd or even revolutionary detail, the shocking approach, or the antiformalist style.

A turning point in his life occurred on May 29, 1606, when in the course of a tennis game with his friend Ranuccio Tomassoni, Caravaggio got into a fight over the scoring and killed the friend. Wounded himself, Caravaggio had to flee to Palestrina, where he was able to put up with a friend and resume his painting. On the money from two completed works he then fled to Naples, where he produced his *Death of a Virgin*—and the rumor that he had used the drowned body of a prostitute as a model for the Virgin Mary did little to help his reputation. In the late summer of 1607 he was in Malta, still in flight but again busily at work and now in the good graces of Alof de Wignacourt, Grand Master of the Order of the Knights of St. John. He painted two portraits of de Wignacourt and was himself made a knight of the order, but very soon he was in a serious fight with another cavalier, lost his knighthood, and wound up in jail. He either escaped or was freed from the jail and, with de Wignacourt's hired assassins now on his trail, fled to Syracuse. Here he immediately set himself up to work and soon finished a large painting for which he had been commissioned. From there he was off to Messina to complete two more commissions, and then to Palermo where in 1609 he continued his fierce activity on the run.

In Naples the agents of de Wignacourt caught up with him and almost killed him, but at this moment in his career of work and flight there came word that he would be pardoned for the killing at the tennis match. Leaving Naples, he went by boat up the coast to Porto Ercole and there, unfortunately, was arrested again—this time by mistake when he was confused with someone else. Freed after a few days, he rushed to the shore to try to catch his boat, which he thought was leaving with all his possessions. Exhausted by the recent events, by the excitement and frustration, and by the fruitless chase on the beach, he collapsed with a "fever"—it may have been malaria—and died on July 10, 1610, just three months short of his thirty-seventh birthday.

The pattern of Caravaggio's life seems to fall into two major periods in his adulthood. A first period found him an active member of a brawling fraternity of young artists; the second followed on the killing of his friend and saw him as an equally busy but now fugitive loner, still at odds with society but now haunted by his pursuers as well. One critic has suggested that this division may correspond to a later "speeded tempo" that involved both more violent activities and "the increasingly authentic and moving quality of his paintings."[7] But however we understand the sequence of events in his life, it does seem to represent a consistent style of behavior. In an era of increasingly formal and traditional restrictions, a period that we describe today as the orthodoxy of the counter-Reformation, Caravaggio's absolute and almost brutal individualism marked him as a difficult, at times dangerous man, genius or not. One biographer has aptly stressed this independence as the central quality of the man—an independence of all models, all dogma and edicts, all fashion and custom, schools and patrons and clients, demands by those of wealth or noble birth, current standards, no matter what they were, and even polemics about his independence. His only precepts, the only demands or restrictions he placed on himself, were "to paint well" and "to imitate well natural things," as he was quoted as saying during his trial for libel.[8]

If any one characteristic can be discerned in the chaotic sequence of events in his adult life, it may be that he acted like a "child of Nature," always acting directly and immediately on his feelings of the moment, behaving as a man of passion and impulse rather than of preconceived ideas and form. One biographer notes that he was through and through the very antithesis of an intellectual and indeed "at heart, very likely, he was a superstitious peasant."[9] Freely admitting into his work all that was vulgar, even ugly, and then transmuting it into artistic gold, he gained a great reputation as a painter of moving and evocative religious themes of his day while at the same time establishing the foundations for modern social realism.

It is appropriate at this point to mention a corollary of the thesis of this book, suggested at the opening of this chapter. I have said that if what we do as persons has its own somatic tie, its link to how we function as biological creatures, then it follows that since we are evidently biologically unique, our patterns of experience and behavior will also emerge in unique ways. These ways become, for each of us, an individual style of behavior expressing an individual somatic vision. I now suggest that the individual's somatic vision nowhere appears in purer form than in the work of artists. This is one of the lessons that artists have to teach the rest of us—and of course it furnishes one more reason for exploring the life and work of leading artists. Caravaggio is clearly a case in point.

He was, in sum, a touchy, fiery, impulse-ridden, "natural" man, truly a revolutionary genius. In the terms of this book, he was most definitely not ecto, not in any aspect of his life or behavior, and this, in fact, enables us to stake out his position during these years, for it was very much an ecto-dominated time, at least in religion and art. Anyone of talent who was non-ecto, then, would be on principle a revolutionary. But this only tells us what he was not and perhaps helps to explain what he was in rebellion against. As to what he was, one might at first see him as a meso character, on the basis of his life of activity and frenzied action as well as his immediate resort to physical answers to any difficult situation. But the meso quality is by no means all that clear. In spite of his record of brawling escapades, the activity in which he most deeply invested himself, his painting, shows him to be no painter of action. One critic has described his action pictures as "a sort of charade."[10]

Judging his life as a whole, I think it can be said that it is the endo quality that comes through in his painting and in his life. He was "a pictorial existentialist . . . (who) created afresh a primitive, personal imagery."[11] Indeed, I suggest that he teaches us what we might not otherwise have known, the nature of a life of *endo* action—that it is not simply active and physical but that it is rather earthy, vulgar, mundane, human, primitive, direct. This is just what we see in his paintings, where there is no emphasis on a sky or a heaven, no picture of an Ascension. With its "characteristic dread of distant prospects,"[12] its moral values blindly closed in within an earthly and very human realm, it is a pure endo vision. His self-portrait, shown as a detail in his *Martyrdom of St. Matthew,* is not at all the romanticized legend that grew up around the stories of his escapades, but presents rather an expression that has been well described as "bitter sadness."[13]

This is not to say that the story of his life reveals in any way a comfortable or satisfying endo mode. For whatever reason, he seems to have been driven all his life to burst through the very qualities that constrained and therefore defined his personal style, even to break away from the foundations of his own work as an artist. Thus, he was on the one hand led to a truly revolutionary style of depicting eroticlike states of mystical ecstasy, in paintings that for the first time emphasized the "emotional and physical, the passionate side of such experiences,"[14] yet on the other hand he appeared to be unable to realize fully this endo quality. A close examination of one of his greatest works will demonstrate this curiously self-contradictory characteristic.

The painting is Caravaggio's *Bacchus,* sometimes called *Adolescent Bacchus,* probably painted about 1593 when the painter was only a few years older than the subject of the portrait (figure 8). It shows us

Caravaggio, *Bacchus*

an adolescent boy half-reclining on his couch. On a table in front of him, there rests a low basket overflowing with fruit. With the fingers of his left hand, the boy toys with a goblet filled with dark red wine, and the fingers of his right hand are twined around a bow or loop of blue-black velvet ribbon. The drapes of his robe fall over his left shoulder and chest, leaving exposed the curiously grey-white flesh of his right side and arm. His hair is jet black and very full, as black as his very long eyebrows, and a crown of multicolored, casually sprouting leaves mixed with ripe, bluish grapes sits on his head.

A number of features are so striking as to be noticed immediately. The flat, colorless pallor of his skin contrasts almost brutally with his black hair and the crown resting on it and with the pink flesh of his face and hands. The right arm, bent and supporting most of the body's weight, is faintly muscular but already beginning to hint that it will soon turn to fat. One wonders if another kind of somatic organization is somehow trapped in this image of an adolescent. The background of the painting adds to the unease that is created by the figure. Behind the boy's figure, it is all dark and shadowed, and there is no evident source of light. However, the space within the painting is not dark but rather lit in a way just barely suggesting a diffused gloom. Like the boy's skin and the heavy cloth of his robe, everything seems to be bathed in a light grey tinge.

The composition of the painting is such as to create a tension between two rounded, bowl-shaped areas, the face and head of the boy and the bowl of fruit piled high in front of him. Connecting these two areas is the line of the left arm, foreshortened and ending in plump, reddish fingers curled lightly around the stem of the goblet. Holding the two areas apart is the bright, pale chest, showing what has been described as its "obscene flesh." The fruit in the basket is meticulously portrayed and seems at first to present an image of vibrant life; but close examination reveals that most of the pieces of fruit are either bursting from their skin in a destructive orgy of growth or else are bruised and already starting to rot. The whole arrangement is in the most delicate balance, just straining at the limits of a stable physical grouping. One nudge, it seems, and it will all topple out on the table.

These remarks are intended to convey a sense of the threatening disorganization that pervades this painting. It is hard to say what holds things together—certainly not any tension in the boy's body. If his expression conveys anything at all, it is a quality that we see best in his face, a calm and slightly sleepy mockery. We seem to be witnessing all the potential for an orgy momentarily held in check by a certain weariness of attitude, something that says, "There is no hurry. I have been through all this before." If anything, it is the lighted area of the torso that holds our attention and, so to speak, keeps the scene from dribbling and oozing out at its sides, but again, the grey-white color that is no color denies any life to the body's shape. If we find any indication at all of young vibrant life, it may be in the flushed face and the hands that just begin to show a mature pudginess or else in the fruit, so overcome by the sheer inner force of its organic growth that it rots or bursts before its time. But as we know, growth of this sort is really decay, and so this is what the artist has really expressed here: the green life of rot, the grey growth that we call decay.

It is a masterpiece, so delicately balanced at that tipping point just between the anabolic and the catabolic sides of endo life, between desire and satiation. In its ripe and overripe fullness and in its sense of an organic life that can so easily grow wild, we have all the important aspects of the endo component. In this portrait of an endo vision—accomplished almost as fully in another of his early works, *The Boy with a Basket of Fruit*—the artist has presented himself completely, as both carrier and victim of the indulged passions. In this respect his art tells the same story as his life.

AN ARTIST IN NATURE

In this section and the following I discuss two artists of the present century, Alberto Giacometti and Jean Arp, comparing them with each other and with Caravaggio. I have selected them for study because they furnish clearly evident but sharply distinguished styles of life and art and thought and because they demonstrate, as did Caravaggio, how a dedicated artistic vision may be understood in terms of its somatically grounded style.

We are fortunate in having in Jean Arp[15] a modern artist of the first rank whose style as person and as artist is largely endo, as was Caravaggio's, and who can therefore be compared with the latter and contrasted as well with the ecto-style Giacometti. Born in Strasbourg in 1887, Arp was from his earliest years an artist and a poet and contributed importantly in both fields to the movement known as Dada. Like Giacometti, he came in his later years to a sculpture that expressed completely his own somatic vision, although in Arp's case this expression can be found almost completely realized in some of his earlier work.

In his style as an artist as well as in his thoughts and statements about his work, Arp expressed the endo mode almost exclusively. Apparently no other mode of living, thinking, or creating ever occurred to him; the style runs through and dominates all his work. One of his favorite statements was, "I love nature, not its substitutes"—thereby expressing his lifelong preference for a clear, direct, "natural" connection with his inspiration. This was his major reason for supporting the Dada movement, not its revolutionary stance nor its all-out attack on existing cultural values. Dada, he said, is direct; it is for nature and against "art."

This also explains Arp's early attachment to a form of painting in which collages were constructed out of whatever pattern some scraps of paper made as they fluttered to the floor. Here we have an excellent example of an approach in which literally nothing, not even the hand of the artist, intervenes between a first inspiration and a final product. Some critics have associated such accidental art, with its dependence on laws of chance, with fashionable concepts such as the Freudian unconscious or even with that cosmic process to which Jung gave the name synchronicity. But Arp, true to his own vision, would say only that he let it happen "automatically, without will," and that a law of chance "embraces all laws and is unfathomable like the first cause from which all life arises."[16] It would never have occurred to Arp, as it did almost automatically with Giacometti, to develop a theory about how this came about. Arp was content with a fateful and global reference to something "unfathomable," some foundational first cause arising out of the depths of the human spirit and unrelated to the life of reason. His use of the self-contradictory expression "a law of chance" is possible only within an endo mode, for it is only in this mode that chance is experienced as a law.

Arp's work, in whatever medium, consistently followed a pattern that marked his endo style. Even before the work with collages, he had experimented with crumpled paper, with squares of color randomly attached to a background, and with the medium that he himself brought back into modern art, the woodcut. The latter is an example of his insistence on eliminating distance or intermediary steps between the unformed raw material and a final product.

Many critics have noted the contrast between Arp's inspiration and that of others who lean toward the more precise and formal—for example, the contrast between his work and that of his wife Sophie, the latter with its "geometrical regularity,"[17] or the even more dramatic contrast with the "cerebral acrobatics"[18] of the great Dutch artist Piet Mondrian. All the terms that Arp used in reference to himself, his work, and his vision as an artist followed the endo style, as can be seen particularly in the names he gave his later sculptures: *Fruit of a Stone* (1959) and any number of other titles built around the terms bud, seed, growth, fruit, flower. One of his favorite words was *concretion*, which was his term for "something that has grown . . . (through) the natural process of condensation, thickening, growing together."[19] We could not have asked for a better rendering of the endo style of describing a naturally occurring organic movement, a process that is truly visceral, a crystallization and growth leading to a fusion of the human and the natural. As early as 1917, he said, he had found his "decisive forms," which he then "simplified" so that they would become "symbols of the growth and metamorphosis of bodies."[20]

Arp very aptly described his own work as "sans intention cérébrale," and referred to art in general as "a fruit that grows in man" like the fetus in the womb.[21] His definitions have been well echoed by one critic, Jean Cathelin: "He is lucidly aware of artistic events and of their place in the world, but he cannot build up a system."[22] It is this absence of what we usually call rational or systematic thought that makes Arp's pure endo style so difficult to describe without saying what it is not, and it is this same absence that leads so often to our identifying the endo style with pure feeling without reason—but as we can easily see in Arp's life and work, that is too simplistic an inference. As Cathelin remarks, he is "the very reverse of the intellectual theorist . . . in direct communication with that natural universe which lies hidden beneath the universe of man[23] . . . the forerunner of the formless (and) of hitherto unknown, unperceived forms."[24] He is witness to "the underlying, foetal part of ourselves . . . which is the contrary of the social order but in conformity with . . . the innermost order of created things."[25]

In these remarks one sees the perceptive and sympathetic critic struggling for expressions that will do justice to a somatic vision that is almost unique. An attempt along similar lines was made by another critic, Michel Seuphor, in his distinction between a world that is round and a world that is square—both conceptions being necessary principles for governing our lives. Arp, in these terms, is our great witness to the earth's roundness, and his work is therefore a series of "rounds" for which we should be grateful if we want to care for and conserve the earth. "As for the square part of the world, it is invisible from here. It is known by learned calculation, by operations of squaring the circle."[26] The distinction between the two behavioral styles, endo and ecto, has perhaps never been so neatly put.

Arp's own words are the best expression of the style that marks all his work. Art, he insisted, grows "like a fruit on a plant."[27] Nature is "an immense vital process . . . a cycle evolving between birth and death, constantly changing and growing." Hence all his sculptures serve as illustrations of "organic life."[28] To this Herbert Read comments, "To this organic principle he was faithful all his life."[29] It is just this term "organic" that best expresses his endo vision, with its suggestion of a coming into being by way of a process of natural growth. "I allow myself to be guided by the work at the time of its birth, I have confidence in it. I don't reflect. The forms come, pleasing or strange, hostile, inexplicable, dumb or drowsy. They are born of themselves. . : . It is sunfficient to close one's eyes for the inner rhythm to pass into the hands"[30]—for as I have noted in a number of places, the gut is blind to the world. It does not need laws of perception or a theory about creation.

The best evidence in support of the claims I make in this section is the corpus of Arp's work, or indeed any example of it (figures 9 and 10). The forms literally burst with an inner sense of growth—but in contrast with the art of Caravaggio, here the endo vision is fully accepted by the artist and expressed without conflict.

Jean Arp, *Garland of Buds I*, 1936

Jean Arp, *Amphore de Muse*, 1959

AN ARTIST-PHILOSOPHER

Alberto Giacometti, the final artist to consider in this section, was born in 1901 in the Bregaglia Valley of southeastern Switzerland, near the Italian border, and except for some years in World War II during which he lived in Switzerland, he spent his entire adult life in Paris. A private man who lived within a simple and regular routine, he was at various times identified with one or another school or group—for example, in his early years with the Dada group and the surrealists, and in the decade after World War II with existentialist philosophers and writers—but in reality he always pursued his own very personal vision, irrespective of either inspiration or criticism from others. As we see below, his was truly an inner vision. According to his brother Diego, with whom he was very closely associated all his life, Giacometti was always meditative; although a robust child and popular with his peers, "he was from the very first a scholarly type." The very first drawing to which he really applied himself as a young boy was not a drawing of something real, such as a scene from nature, but his own "interpretive" reproduction of another work, the Dürer etching *Knight, Death, and the Devil.*[31]

This is to say that from the beginning the pattern of Giacometti's life and work was ecto. Artists who might be called "intellectuals" or "thinkers" are relatively rare, and perhaps even more unusual is an artist of the first rank whose particular mode of expressing intellectuality is also ecto. Fortunately, we have in Giacometti's case his own frequent discussions of his work, and in one instance at least an example of this kind of discussion that was produced while he was engaged in painting.

Following what I have said in earlier pages, we may repeat here that the central characteristic of the ecto mode is *distance.* In contrast with the endo mode, in which one is immediately and personally caught up, blindly lacking any distance, or in contrast with the meso mode in which one is concretely and actively engaged, the ecto mode puts one at a distance, such that the world is apprehended or constructed by way of mediating elements. A question that is raised in considering the work of artists is whether such activity can be usefully understood in terms of a characteristic such as distance. My aim here is to show that Giacometti can indeed be understood in such terms, but more important, that if we attempt to do so we come to a richer grasp of the ecto mode and of its central characteristics.

As early in his career as the 1930s, Giacometti was clearly struggling with what we would call theoretical questions. "He decides to make in a rather short time a few studies from nature, just enough to be able to understand the structure of a head or of any figure"[32]—that is, not primarily because of some "inspiration" or even a wish but because these works will, he hopes, solve a theoretical question for him. But he soon found himself faced with a problem he could not solve. First he had to give up complete figures as "too difficult." Then when he tried to do only heads, working from models, he could not, somehow, come to terms with their distance from him. He noticed "fearfully" that his statues began to become smaller, almost as though they were moving away from him. In his words, "The more I looked at the model, . . . the more the screen between his reality and mine grew thicker. One starts by seeing the person who poses, but little by little all the possible sculptures of him intervene. . . . One is no longer sure of his appearance, or of his size, or of anything at all. There were too many sculptures between my model and me."[33]

We may ask, who but the ecto thinker, a thinker above all, would be so deeply implicated in "all the possible sculptures?" It is as though the artist's project were not the working of some clay but the working out of some theory, in its infinite number of possible variants. As though to prove the case, each person who comes to this phenomenon, so puzzling and so provocative, quickly creates, in a further infinitude of theories about the theories, his own version of how this could be. Explanation follows on explanation, in an endless regress: the world of ecto thought. James Lord, Giacometti's biographer, for example, states clearly two explanations and hints at a number of others. In the first case, he proposes, the artist's work parallels his sexual life. Just as Giacometti throughout his adult life could have satisfactory relations only with prostitutes, whom he envisioned as "goddesses" by placing them "at an inviolable distance in the realm of the imaginary," so the figurines, "archetypes of such transcendence," consist of "real relations with an illusion."[34] Yet in another passage Lord argues that Giacometti was always seeking some way "to radiate the whole expressive power of a human presence . . . without any loss of perceptual immediacy." How to "provide for (such) largeness" while preserving their very essence? The artist's answer was in "thinness."[35]

It matters not at all that a perceptive and sympathetic biographer of the artist should propose one or many explanations, nor does it matter whether any of them are "correct" (even assuming that such a term has any meaning in this context). For my purposes here, what is important is that explanations seem to be called for and that they come easily to anyone who is able to become devoted to Giacometti's art. I suggest that this is in large part because this artist, perhaps more than any other in this century, presents us with an artistic vision that is inescapably a theoretical problem, and that for this reason it cries for analysis, explanation, theory. Giacometti himself, caught in a seemingly bizarre manifestation of his own style, tried to find simple ways out. For a while he worked from memory only, as though such a mediating operation would either fix the statues at a distance or provide him a measure of control. But they disappeared, either becoming smaller or, if he tried to fix their image by drawing them, by contracting into long, thin, wispy lines.

At this early point in his career, long before he had become famous or had settled into the artistic style with which his name is associated, the central issues were already clear to him and, perhaps, already insoluble. Although he was to become a master of all the media of his field, whether painting, sculpture, drawing, or the graphic arts of lithography and etching, he found no technique in which there seemed to be an answer to his questions. By the time he left for Switzerland at the outset of World War II, he had reduced the size of his work to pieces of sculpture tiny enough to fit into matchboxes, and these he carried with him as the remnants of his quest. Returning to Paris after the war, he again attempted larger figures, trying to approximate the sizes that painters and sculptors seem to adapt to naturally. Again, however, as he made the figures with his hands they seemed to disappear; an uncontrollable "distancing" would invariably take over.

This was a strange situation, one for which we as observers or critics really have no terms. One of Giacometti's most perceptive critics, Jacques Dupin, commented that here is a "real person" and over here is Giacometti working at a "depiction"—for in no sense was the artist attempting an expressionist rendering. He was "seeking only the pure equivalence of the work to his vision of his subject," seemingly very much the same endeavor as occupies other artists. He is apparently copying the model, he is attempting to produce a likeness. In what way, then, does his effort differ from that of other artists who also strive for a kind of realism? Dupin refers here to "a superior realism, at once broader and more precise." It is, in Giacometti's case, a realism that "no longer has as objects man or the world as they are, but as Giacometti's eye sees them."[36]

But now we may ask: Surely this should not pose an insurmountable problem, for what this says of Giacometti's realism is simply true of all artists, perhaps of all creatures that perceive. They are, in the nature of the case, removed by one step; they do not see the thing itself, only their individual version of the thing. Theirs is a perceived world, one that intervenes between the world as-is and the world as-grasped. In what way, then, does Giacometti differ, and why should he be so tortured simply by virtue of being a perceiver? The answer, as every writer on his art has noted, is that Giacometti does not simply interpose one act of perceiving between world and self but a second act of *knowing*. His perceiving is, inescapably, in the constant service of a theory about how things really are out there. In Dupin's analysis, what Giacometti might, under other circumstances, grasp as just a person, as a human, as a subject for study or a model for sculpting, "has given way to the *other*, to be encountered, near and inaccessible being."[37]

Giacometti's theory of things, which from the beginning of his career provided the foundation for his art, might if expressed in other contexts be familiar to us. "We walk and we grope for each other in the darkness; we never know if we are close or far; and if at last my hand by chance goes so far as to touch the other one, I never know what I touched, a nose, a shoulder, or a knee. By the detail that I have reached, I never attain the whole."[38] This is the voice of that modern existentialist despair that surfaced during the decade of World War II. It is hardly an accident that Giacometti was considered the premier existentialist painter of postwar Paris and was a close friend of both Sartre and Genet. Theirs was never a vision based on a spontaneous, empathic, or "natural" grasp of the other person but rather a vision beginning and ending within the lone individual's singular and solitary space. In this philosophy no foundational community of spirit exists, only unique specimens who wander, and vainly reach out, within the void that contains and separates us all.

The curious and touching friendship between Giacometti and the writer Samuel Beckett tells us a great deal about the ecto style that they so closely shared. They knew one another for quite a long time before they began to spend time together, as though it was not easy for either to make a definite approach. And when they had become close friends and could therefore be expected to do things together, perhaps even to share their inner lives, it was as though each was bristling with barbs to hold the other off. If they met, it would be more or less by chance, at night, almost as though their meetings had to be kept secret, and they would walk side by side for long distances, for hours, often without conversation. "It was a very private, almost secretive, and secret friendship."[39] We have here a fine instance, one not too often uncovered, of two supremely ecto styles (and bodies) in the only kind of "contact" that they can permit themselves to enjoy. It was a meeting, an encounter, a sharing that was typical of Giacometti's style, of whom Lord remarks, "The physical self often stands in the way of the intellectual and spiritual self"[40]—a statement that is true, if at all, only for the ecto.

I want to emphasize that it is not Giacometti's avowal of an existentialist philosophy that determines his special character as an artist. That is not the point I am arguing here. Rather, I am claiming that Giacometti held and lived this philosophy in the special way that I have been calling the ecto mode and that this was one of the most important influences on his art. Nor did his philosophical position determine his work as an artist. Rather, he held this philosophy as a body of knowledge and a theory, and in turn he interposed this theory between his artistic inspiration and his finished products.

As an artist, he worked as though he were a teacher trying to expound a theory, using his work as a kind of ongoing demonstration of his lectures. This is why everyone who has written about his work has had no difficulty propounding a theory about it—for it is one of the marks of abstract constructions such as theories that an infinite number of other abstract constructions can be developed that in turn, and at greater or less remove, refer to them. Whereas Caravaggio's work, by contrast, was always an explosion of his soul and his passions and any attempt at a theory about it would have been almost superfluous, it has always seemed appropriate for Giacometti as well as his critics to offer theories and explanations, some of them intellectually very impressive. The artist himself was known as a splendid theoretician of his own work and would expound for hours on the impossibility of ever realizing his theoretical dream of the perfect likeness. "Total realism" being impossible according to the tenets of his theory and "partial realism" being false, at least according to his theoretical preconceptions, he was left with only two alternatives: to "turn one's back on reality and substitute the imaginary as a field of experience,"[41] or else to pursue a reality that could in principle never be grasped. He attempted the former for an initial ten years and the latter during the remainder of his career. But whether his analysis was in fact correct, the important fact is that his typical manner of working was to begin with these theoretical issues. His genius as an artist then rested on a theoretical formulation as his foundation. In this respect, almost uniquely among major figures in art, he was acting in the ecto mode.

If one begins with a theoretical construction—in this case that the human condition is one of separated entities within a void—then the closer one comes through art to realizing the truth about a person as subject, the more acutely one understands that the truth is unrealizable and the person unreachable, "the more one feels and communicates the acute feeling of his separation."[42] This is in every respect a description of activity within the ecto mode, not only in its being founded on a theoretical proposition concerning the human condition but in its posing the notion of the impossible. That which can be visualized or imagined or thought about yet never really grasped is, by definition, within the ecto mode, for in either endo or meso modes it is always the grasping that comes first; hence the self-defeating possibility of the realized unrealizable simply never arises. As Giacometti once said to an interviewer, "I can do your head life-size because I know it's life-size, I don't see directly any more, I see you through my knowledge"[43]—which is practically a summary of an ecto position. In the course of continually expounding a theory underlying all his work, Giacometti became a brilliant phenomenological psychologist, someone well worth studying if one's interest is in the psychology of visual perception. He had some important and original things to say about the innocence of seeing, about the difference between sensation and perception, and about modes of visual distance and their relation to the distance in touching. According to Sartre, he came closer to "solving" the problem of essence than any modern thinker.

In one of the most remarkable and valuable documents in modern art, James Lord[44] has described a sequence of meetings with Giacometti in which he sat for a portrait while they talked about the artist's continuing difficulties in realizing his vision. Giacometti's repeated plaint was that he could not possibly accomplish what he was trying to do, and he said this over and over, day after day, as though each time he said it he would realize it anew. "I can't seem to reproduce what I see,"[45] or "That is what's kept me working . . . that desire to find out why I can't simply reproduce what I see."[46] For this complaint Lord offers an appropriate theoretical explanation: "His indefatigable, interminable struggle via the act of painting to express in visual terms a perception of reality that had happened to coincide momentarily with my head. To achieve this was of course impossible, because what is essentially abstract can never be made concrete without altering its essence."[47] The artist himself has his own theory, one that if satisfied would, we suppose, enable him to realize in one stroke his total vision: "What's essential is to work without any preconception whatever . . . to try to see only what exists. You can't do it. But one must try, all the same, try—like Cézanne—to translate one's sensation."[48]

In the course of a full career, Giacometti tried every way possible to realize this ecto vision, to bypass his thought and thus to build an art within the ecto mode. He was, for example, the most dedicated user of distancing techniques in this century. One of the most interesting of these was his attempt at copying in one medium what he had already accomplished in another medium. Most of his lithographs, themselves works of the first rank, have as their subject matter the completed sculptures in his studio—so that they will show, for example, a sculptured head on which he had already worked for months. In the words of one writer, he did these works so as "to portray the deepest possible witness to his own mind"[49] and so as to express "his meditative surprise before his own creations."[50]

There is a risk in this kind of endeavor, one that lies at the very heart of the ecto mode. Since in the ecto mode one's activity is at one step removed from what it concerns, one gains in terms of freedom; we see this in the often remarkable results of imagination and abstract thought. But the concomitant risk is that such activity also has the potential to turn on itself and then to deal just as freely with itself as with any other concern. Pursuing this road may result in endlessly ruminating in obsessive fashion without ever coming to a conclusion, or it may result in an endless regress into nowhere or even, as in Giacometti's inspiration, in "the black ecstasy of an imagination that is its own prison."[51]

This is not to say that Giacometti's concerns were fundamentally different from those of any other artist. The question that all artists raise for us, the question of which they keep reminding us, is this: How shall we realize the living body—our own, first of all, and because we can live only in community, that of others as well? Or, stated in other terms, is it that the artist starts from some inner truth and then pours that truth out into the world, or is it that the artist begins with the most minimal and malleable ghost of an idea, struggling to work toward some truth, more or less ideal, that is presumed to exist out in the world? What is the source, the original and absolute source of the artist's vision? For the artist who lives and works in the ecto style, as did Giacometti, it is the latter that comes closest to describing what goes on: that by means of a progressive distancing of self from the world one hopes to grasp the truth that must exist out in the world in some ideal form. To do so one must learn means of control of the world, and the ultimate instance of such control is to imagine it, to think about it, to be as removed as possible from an immediate bodily contact with it. "Alberto had created and cultivated . . . a relation with reality [that] was not only external and physical but also, and primarily, inward and psychic. He had developed a capacity for abstraction, a disposition to establish between himself and the objects of his perception a psychic as well as a physical distance."[52]

These are issues that were raised in particularly urgent fashion, in the guiding actions of his own work, minute by minute—not because Giacometti sensed them more keenly than other artists did, but because his ecto style led him to raise the issues to a level of serious intellectual discourse, finally to lead him to make them the very foundation of his thought about his own work. Other artists, usually working in other styles, give us a different answer: that the body can never be fully known or realized because it is water or fire, not an object but a process. In the words of a critic who is writing about the poet Blake but might well be referring to most painters or sculptors: "The form of the risen body is like the form of fire in its continuous change of contours, according to changes in impulse and desire."[53]

For Giacometti, however, although the issue remains the same, the reason is different; his style leads him to deal with this question in a radically different way. For him there is no end to the work that one does as an artist; therefore "the more one works on a picture, the more impossible it becomes to finish it."[54] For him it is the task that is endless, whereas for most other artists it is the body that has no final, static representation. This again suggests to us the style of ecto activity, in which there is no beginning or ending to thought—it can be and is spun out endlessly, in all directions—yet in which the object of thought can always be ideally and finally represented. The prototype of ecto activity is theory making, and the mark of theories is that they neither start nor finish. Once started, a theory gives rise to new possibilities, which in turn open out into still other possibilities, infinitely. Theoretical formulations, having no beginnings and no endings, were just what Giacometti was agonizing over, without end.

In attempting to turn his art into an ecto accomplishment, Giacometti may have finally, in a flash of glory, come close to succeeding, as we see if we consider the sculptures of his later years (figures 11 and 12). They consist of impossibly long, lean bodies, whether of humans or of animals, or else of human heads so thinned down as to become almost like pieces of cardboard. It is surely the most remarkable coincidence of style and product, of mode and content, in all of modern art, that this thinker-philosopher whose activity was driven by an ecto component should also have produced works that represent in pure form the ectomorph structure of the human body. In the end, perhaps, he finally achieved the full promise of his somatic vision.

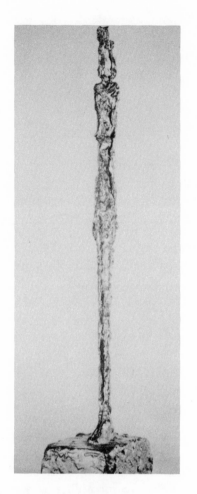

Alberto Giacometti, *Standing Woman (Femme
debout)*, *1947*

Alberto Giacometti, *Head,*
1952–53

In the contrast between Giacometti and Arp, the ecto thinker and the endo disciple of nature, we have in one of its clearest forms a statement about the power of a somatic vision. In Giacometti's final sculptures we have an expression of all that he knew as an artist about the problem of the living body. In Arp's budding, growing, seeding, fulfilling natural forms we have a perfect statement of his endo vision.

Society and the Great Ecto Dream

The endo wants and needs the intimate and personal company of others. The meso will accept others, particularly as competitors, and often makes use of their company. The ecto is basically a loner.

In earlier chapters I have presented a descriptive account of some implications of my hypothesis: that all acts can be carried out in more than one way, and specifically that they may be carried out in some combination of the three behavioral styles that I identified. In my coverage of a number of traditional areas of psychological study, however, my interest has been restricted to styles of individual behavior. In the present chapter, by contrast, I want to apply the thesis to collections of individuals. I will be talking about group and societal styles, about social-historical changes, rather than about individual behavior or development. I began this change in emphasis in chapter 7, in connection with some remarks about schools of artists, and here I will conclude with some additional implications in regard to important cultural and social conditions through history.

I am aware of the dangers in "explaining" human history in terms of some single presumed cause, and I am also aware that what are sometimes identified by observers as radical changes are in reality, and when viewed on a sufficiently large scale, slow and gradual changes. My plan, therefore, is to apply my thesis only tentatively in order to see if it shows some concordance with explanatory attempts by other writers. I will argue that whenever a significant change in human culture can be seen, an important aspect of that change will have been an alteration in the dominant behavioral style and, further, that when

significant distances between cultures or societies can be shown, they
will also demonstrate important differences in collective style.

DETENTION, PUNISHMENT, EXILE

The example of prisons may indicate what can be done with the approach I am suggesting. The prison as we know it is a rather recent
development. Although all societies, no matter what their level of development or complexity, have worked out some means for dealing
with those within their borders whom they consider undesirable, the
idea of a place set aside for incarceration—and, in the past two centuries, for punishment as well—is relatively new. In ancient societies
punishment for crimes consisted of execution or some form of torture;
if a place was used to incarcerate criminals or prisoners of war, this
was for purposes of detention, until some room could be found for
them on the rather busy schedule of the executioner. In Rome, the
most advanced society of ancient times, an additional refinement was
introduced in the form of the galley, which amounted essentially to a
kind of prolonged torture ending in the prisoner's inevitable death.

As officially sanctioned torture slowly died out after the Middle
Ages, the jail became the major form of punishment—yet for some
centuries it was also challenged by various kinds of "transportation"
(that is, sending prisoners to uninhabited areas of their own country)
or banishment (sending them to other countries). France led the way
in the latter, with its notorious penal colonies in French Guiana, of
which the island off the coast known as Devil's Island was perhaps
the worst. Prisons, meanwhile, were often turned into workhouses, or
places of detention in which the inmates might be rehabilitated through
a regimen of hard work. The use of imprisonment specifically as a
mode of punishment is, in the words of one writer, "a child of the
industrial revolution."[1]

Over the past two centuries or so, two countries have led the way
in developing, each in its own fashion, a major form of punishment for
criminals and other undesirables. Russia has specialized in the mode
that we now call exile. This is an elaborate system of prisons that are
located at the end of a road leading out of the prisoner's home—that

is, the prisoner is first removed from his home and then taken a long distance to the prison itself, which is situated in an uninhabitable spot and where conditions may often be worse than would be found in prisons closer to home. Since about the time of World War I the Russian system of such labor or prison camps has been known as the Gulag, defined not by the fact of being an administration of prisons nor by the equally evident fact that the treatment is deliberately brutal but by the prisons' location. There are very few reasons for locating such camps in the far reaches of Siberia, the major one being that imprisonment there is meant to impress on the prisoners a certain kind of experience. It is the experience that we can all appreciate today when we meditate on the connotations of the word *exile*. Prisoners in these place are tossed into a vast, empty wasteland that is impossibly far away from where they feel they belong; in a word, they are made homeless.

By contrast, consider the kind of prison that was pioneered in the United States—which has had, for most if its history as a state, as vast an empty land for exile as the Russians have had. The type of prison invented in America was modeled in its architecture on the Catholic monastery, with its rows of individual cells meant for isolated meditation. The first example of this new prison opened in Philadelphia in 1829 and was soon known as Cherry Hill. It consisted of a large circular building on whose outer circumference was arranged a row of individual cells, each with its tiny, walled exercise yard. Each prisoner passed the entire term of sentence alone in this cell, with no contact with other prisoners or even with the administration. A similar but slightly less extreme arrangement had been built into New York State's Auburn Prison a few years earlier, the difference being that at Auburn the prisoners worked in a group but were forbidden to say even a word to one another.

The regimen is familiar to us today as solitary confinement. When it was first instituted at Cherry Hill, however, largely under the influence of Quaker reformers, it was meant for the prisoners' own good. They were supposed to utilize their time in solitary to meditate on their sins and thereby to become better persons. Hence the term "penitentiary," or place of penitence. But the fact that this style of imprisonment corresponded to Quaker religious practices hardly suffices to explain why it was quickly adopted by the non-Quaker administrations of a number of states. Rather than support a prison system on the known model of the Russians', with prisoners exiled to the empty and dangerous wastelands of the Far West, in the United States the various state governments opted for precisely the opposite—an arrangement in which each prisoner was closed in as far as possible and forbidden even the normal modes of social contact and give-and-take. The American prison has from the beginning been identified by what Robert Sommer has aptly called its "hard architecture,"[2] marked by what he calls "tight spaces" that are aimed at restricting the freedom of action of the inmates.

Sheldon has properly pointed out that for the predominantly meso person hell is *in*action. The prison, then, would seem to be designed so as to provide a hell for the meso, this being the style that defines most criminal activity.[3] The ecto does not particularly mind physical inaction, being more nervous than restless, and in fact, one might surmise that those rare prisoners who manage to make something out of their terms of incarceration—for example, by becoming expert in a small specialty, as did Robert Stroud, the "bird man" of Alcatraz, or by studying for a law degree—are loners, as much ecto as meso in style. The endo, on the other hand, might even choose such a life style, as do those who elect to enter a monastery or a nunnery.

These considerations suggest that the choices in the two countries, Russia and the United States, in regard to what will be considered the worst possible kind of punishment, may be related to the behavioral style that is dominant in the two cultures. Specifically, it may be that Russian culture is dominantly endomorphic and American culture dominantly mesomorphic. Thus, prison administrators responding to the felt needs of their culture might have imagined in Russia that the worst possible punishment would be to toss the prisoner out into an empty wasteland of space, cut loose from his homeland, from what citizens of this country have always called Mother Russia; whereas administrators faced with a similar choice in the United States might have imagined that the worst possible punishment would be to lock up the prisoner, preferably in solitary, where action was very much inhibited and small-scale social interaction impossible. The United States has never had a tradition of exile, although all the conditions for it were available during the first century of its existence. A famous story, "The man without a country," by Edward Everett Hale, was judged a rather shocking work of the imagination for just this reason, that it was not even remotely a historical document.

It is interesting to speculate on the nature of a prison fitting the ecto style. I suggest that the ecto answer to the question, "What is the worst punishment I could mete out to you?" might be: "Bore me. Drain my environment of stimulation and articulation." This may help us to understand the results of studies a few years back on what was called "sensory deprivation," in which subjects were engaged to spend periods of time under conditions of minimal sensory articulation—for example, blindfolded, ears covered, with heavy mittens to minimize tactile stimulation of the hands, and in a closed-in booth without company.[4] Although very little data are available on the behavioral styles of individual subjects, I would hypothesize that those who were predominantly meso became restless and may even have started to hallucinate; the predominantly endo might have become bored or even lonesome; but that those of an ecto style quickly became anxious and would have insisted on discontinuing their participation.

STYLE AND WORLD

If it is appropriate to consider the temporal or historical dimension of stylistic states and changes, a first step might be to discuss the structures of the physical environment that both evoke and express the different styles. I suggest in this connection a most general set of distinctions we can make regarding the instrument, the tool, and the machine.

The Instrument

We may ask concerning, say, a musical instrument: What is the relation that is sustained between the human player and the instrument? What "role" does each play in their interchange? We are familiar with this problem when it is expressed in another realm as the problem of "man-machine interface," although interestingly, we never use such terminology in reference to someone, for example, who is playing a piano.

It is clear that in one sense the instrument serves as an extension of the player, therefore as a "part" of the player. But there is more than this involved. When a musician plays an instrument, there occurs a mutuality of expression that results in something other than the mere quantitative extension of some aspect of the player. The wind instrument does not simply extend or increase the player's lung power. If we listen, we hear some qualitatively new product of the two that could never come from either of the two parties alone. In regard to the music that emerges from the playing, both participants, player and instrument, were silent until they joined.

Additionally, the tone that results from the playing is not simply a result of the player being in the vicinity of the instrument, not even a result of the player breathing normally into the instrument—as students of wind instruments will surely testify. The mutuality involved here is expressed in a behavior that results in something new. To play any instrument you must set up a particular mode of association with it; you must accede to a situation in which each participant, player and instrument, gives in to and uses—literally, "plays upon"—the nature of the other. And all of these statements can, I suggest, be made with equal justification in regard to the human use of oneself, as when the body becomes the instrument in the case of singing.

This special, relational, multiplicative phenomenon that we call playing would appear to be the prototype of a situation created within the endo style. It is an amalgam formed in the fire of two processes that meet and fuse in their mutual expression. Consideration of the instrument and how it is played should help us to understand endo situations that lead to human action. These will occur each time the body "plays" its surround, just as music results each time the player plays upon an instrument. Music may thus be considered a prototypic phenomenon of the endo realm, just as playing music is a prototypic form of the endo event.

The Tool

As we can see on observing a workman using a tool, it is an object that provides an extension or a quantitative increase in some aspect of an act. The hammer, for example, is a kind of fist that hits much harder than the fist; the wrench grips more tightly and therefore exerts more turning power than does the handgrip; and the universal joint covers a greater angular range than do any of our joints. Even the primitive, "found" tools that are used by some animals—such as the sticks that chimpanzees use to extract termites from a mound—fall within this general definition.

There are, however, some tools that do not fall clearly within the category that I have defined; they appear to be more than tools yet less than the machines I will discuss in the next section. An example might be the spear. In one sense it is a tool as I have defined it, for the spear can wound at a greater distance and often with more power than the sharp-pointed stick, the latter in turn being capable of penetrating better than the finger. But the spear must usually be thrown. It exerts its force not at the user's hand but at a distance from the hand. Indeed, this characteristic of the spear's use must have been evident early on to Paleolithic hunters, for they soon devised a spear-throwing attachment in the form of a notched spear-holder to enable them to increase the speed and accuracy of this weapon.

The "pure" tool, however, enables the user to carry out a given muscular act more easily, more powerfully, more quickly than can be accomplished by means of the unaided limb and hand. It does this while always remaining attached to its user, in this way remaining true to its function as an extension of the muscles. Further, the tool itself does not change but in use remains what it is; the knife edge must remain sharp, the spear pointed, the hammer unbroken. This is because the tool is a thing of power, which means that it stays the same even while it effects some adversary change in the world. If the hammer were found to be softer than what it hits, so that it crumbled as it struck the rock, we would very soon stop using it for this purpose. Human culture must have changed in one explosive step when there was discovered a rock, which we call flint, that was harder than any other rock then known, therefore able to be used as a tool. The relation between tool and surround, then, is one of unilaterality, as contrasted with the mutuality marking the endo situation—for the tool is a phenomenon in the meso mode. In place of the ongoing endo situation, we have the meso elaboration or accomplishment, hence the time-boundedness of meso events. And because the user of the tool can always see it in action and see what results from its use, there arises the meso characteristic of concreteness and actuality that marks all actions in this mode.

The Machine

Because of the intrinsic complexity of the ecto realm, a single term such as machine may not be the most satisfactory statement of the prototypic ecto relation with the world. The machine is in a sense a tool, but it differs from the meso tool in one fundamental respect, that it is detachable from the user. As a result it often appears to take on a life of its own, and like the ecto body it becomes worldless and situationless. In Western history the earliest large-scale example of a machine in use was the cannon that could be filled with gunpowder. All earlier weapons had been either tools, such as the axe, or devices that were half tool and half machine and were used on a small scale, such as catapults or spears. Gunpowder, by contrast, enabled the cannon ball to be used at a distance and completely under its own power—from which it followed, as Shakespeare put it, that the user ran the risk of being "hoist by his own petard," that is, blown up by his own machine if it escaped his control. Only a lack of skill will lead to the workman being hurt by his own tool, whereas the power that resides in the machine constantly poses a more serious risk, that it will begin to act on its own.

It is of some significance that although gunpowder had been available from its source in Asia for at least five hundred years, it was not introduced into Western warfare until the fourteenth century, that is, until the first important signs of an ecto style of experience and behavior were awakening Europe.

The machine and the person who uses the machine are separated, each in their own mode of existing. It may even then come about that the contact between them will be in the form of a struggle over control of the event emerging from the person's use of the machine. In our own day we find this struggle expressed in the form of a haunting question in which control is known in the form of identity: Is man a form of machine, or is machine a degraded form of man?

The distinctions that I have described here are these: the endo realm is marked by mutuality within a situation; the meso realm is marked by extension and linkage between parts of an act; and the ecto realm is marked by independence and consequent power struggles over control. These distinctions tell us that you cannot engage in a power struggle with that with which you are mutually engaged or even linked. The machine having its independent existence, its human user will in the course of time maintain less and less contact with it; we will then boast of how advanced are our machines, that they have escaped from their human users. In the end we find ourselves playing at push buttons on a keyboard, utilizing only a symbolic access by way of devices that are in themselves meaningless and are given arbitrary meanings for purposes of convenience. The minimal access we have to machines may then become farther removed if we insert a special, symbolic language referable to the machine, which we build into the machine as a major characteristic of its functioning.

Thus, when I push the buttons on a machine for washing clothes, I activate an elaborate system of relays, motors, gears, and so on, which constitutes its own organization of electrical and mechanical parts. This organization is related in turn not only to me as a user but also to a separate discipline of electrical engineering, and this, while it underpins the operation of the machine, also exists in its own realm and has its own history, development, successes and failures. The only tie that remains between me and the machine is the most minimal of push button contacts; there may be no tie at all between me and the engineering discipline, or between me and the computer if I do not have access to its special language.

In pointing to these contrasts among the ecto machine with its independent character, the meso tool with its concrete and extended character, and the endo instrument with its conjoint and mutually embracing character, I mean to suggest as well some of the ways our collective psyche has developed in the course of modern history. Human history may be understood as the story of our changing interface with the world into which we are cast.

A THEORY OF PAVEMENTS

The history of consciousness, or as I am referring to it here, the socio-historical dimension of behavioral styles, is not a particularly well-worked field within psychology. Aside from attempts by independent scholars such as J. H. van den Berg[5] and the notable contribution by Julian Jaynes,[6] which I treat in a later section of this chapter, psychologists have tended to ignore attempts to view the defining characteristics of persons as embedded in history. I should therefore make clear at the outset that in this chapter I mean to place my descriptions firmly within history and the changes that it accounts for. I will be arguing the thesis that radical and particularly sudden changes in societies and cultures will be found to accompany marked and often sudden changes in the behavioral style that predominates. I do not offer this thesis or its supporting evidence as in any way an "explanation" of historical changes, only as a way of enriching our understanding of history.

To take an obvious example, in his extensive account of the "emergence of man" during the Upper Paleolithic era, John Pfeiffer notes that Neanderthal people were the first to develop burial rituals.[7] On this he remarks that they "invented, or at least formalized, illusion when they invented burial [for] the belief in an afterlife says in effect that death is not what it seems. . . . Reality involves not observed and observable facts, but an abstraction, the idea that death is actually a passage from one world to another."[8] This interesting conjecture may in fact not be true; but whether or not it describes what actually happened, it suggests that from the point of view of the thesis I am pursuing here, this time in history can be understood as showing a rather sudden upsurge in the ecto component of behavior. This might explain not only why an apparent belief in an afterlife occurred at this time but also why the belief appeared in the form of an illusion "invented" as well as an abstraction apprehended. I hope that my attempts to link changes in dominant style with documented historical events or changes will help to enrich our understanding of the latter—as for example might be claimed if I suggest that, if Pfeiffer is right, and if the ecto component came markedly to the fore at this moment in history, it is very probable that this is also the time when humans learned to speak.

The Home

Human history may be traced through the changing physical structures of the human environment. Aside from the practical advantage in having at hand the most durable kinds of evidence, such an examination fits a thesis that has been attractive to many scholars: that humans construct their immediate environments as a reflection of their dominant modes of consciousness, so that from the evidence of the former we may read off inferences about the latter.

We begin with some thoughts about the place of residence we call a home. From the point of view of those living in it, a home is never merely accidental or contingent. Rather, it is created out of the vital relation that its occupant feels toward this area of all areas. Even the most abandoned of persons—for example, prisoners who pass their years alone in a dungeon—usually manage to cross the trembling line dividing the contingent from the residential, coming finally to have a personal knowledge of every bump on every stone. Even centuries later the innocent eye of a tourist may capture the presence of the prisoner, perhaps in a signature scratched painfully in stone.

The home belongs to the occupant as much as the occupant to the home. For this reason having a home is in some ways like having a body, and so we can understand that animals too make their homes. Think of the stickleback, a little fish that fiercely defends its nest at breeding time. Or think of the related phenomenon of territoriality among animals, leading them to fight to the death to defend a space of ground or water against specific other animals. Marking off one's own space in this way seems to be common to most living creatures, although animals other than humans will usually defend it only at specific times or against specific other creatures. George Schaller[9] has observed that mountain gorillas make a new home every night and appear to maintain no tie to a place where they have previously bedded down; we may contrast this with some early human groups, nomadic hunters who returned, year after year, to the same camps over periods of thousands of years.

This is not to say that either animals or the earliest humans appeared to be aware of the distinction we call private *versus* public; we have no basis for assuming that they did. All that we can say about creatures at this level of development is that they may possess some general sense of "belonging" in one location rather than another, and that at certain seasons of the year they denote boundaries to their "belonging" space and indicate that the boundaries mark a division into "mine" and "not mine." Because their places of residence are found spaces, not constructed, no object exists to which they can point and then assign their sense of identity. We are still at the stage of human development when the homesite, like the animal lair, is discovered rather than made. This is why the true home is so important a step in human progress.

Street and Avenue

We are so accustomed to an arrangement in which houses are separated at regular intervals by streets that we may find it hard to imagine the one structure existing without the other. But a street does not inevitably accompany a set of human dwellings. One of the earliest permanent dwelling places for humans, a site now known as Çatal Hüyük in west central Turkey, was first established about 8000 B.C.[10] Recent excavations have shown that it only very gradually became a town in our modern sense. At first it consisted of a maze of interconnected buildings, some of them homes and others shrines, with no spaces between them. One entered an individual living space by clambering over the collective roof and dropping down through the correct hole in a ceiling. Çatal Hüyük had houses but no streets. Similarly, there have been uncovered at Skara Brae, in the Orkney Islands near Scotland, intricate communal warrens consisting of large huts connected by covered paths and covered over with heaps of rubbish—in effect, a complex version of a single-family dwelling but with enough living space for a fair-sized group. A similar arrangement is found at the palace of Knossos on Crete. And even as late as the fourth century B.C., the city of Athens was by no means a city in the modern sense. Its "streets" were in fact randomly placed passageways that were squeezed among a scattered collection of shops, huts, and shrines.

In the sense in which we now use the word, a street consists of a planned area that follows a direction of its own. The modern avenue is an example, to be contrasted with the winding suburban "lane," as it is

called, compliantly following the line dictated by houses whose placement is more important than the direction of the street. Because the
street is meant to provide a passageway for the public movement we
call traffic, it developed first in centers where a strong central government aimed to show its presence and its power. From its beginning, the
street reflected and expressed a mode of consciousness, hence a behavioral style, that differed from that expressed by means of the home.
As I argue below, the street expresses an urban consciousness, specific
to citizens who must cope with governmental power.

The sequence by which a collection of huts became a city differed, of
course, from one location to another, for it was influenced by many
factors—the nature of the economy, the size of the population, the rate
of growth, the climate, the speed and kind of change taking place at
that time, the nature of local political organization, the presence of outstanding leaders, and so on. But certain broad trends can be identified
in places widely separated in space or time. Along the Euphrates River
in what is now Iran, a development began about 8000 B.C. that may
serve as a model.[11] A series of tiny villages began to string out along
a line that may have been a natural waterway. By the year 3500 B.C.
the area had grown to contain at least fifty different sites, one of them
obviously the beginning of a central city, and within another two
hundred years a large administrative center had been built near the
growing city. Here, just as in other locations such as Hierakonpolis, on
the Nile, a central administrative area was constructed with a temple
at its center and a wide avenue was built to lead up to the temple. In
a wide variety of places, at many different times, a pattern repeated:
scattered settlements arose, dependent on farming, with the population
coming together and then migrating elsewhere depending on the vicissitudes of climate and harvest, and finally merging when all the relevant circumstances were favorable to organize a central city. The merging resulted in a kind of city-state, and as its power grew it expressed
that power in a new form of construction, the ceremonial avenue.

In the great showplaces of the Middle East, beginning about 4000 B.C.,
the plan evolved into a gridiron, its layout determined not by buildings
but by streets. Similarly, as late as the Roman empire, rulers often emphasized their secular power by displays of "street furniture," which
consisted of statues and colonnades lining their avenues. Like the main

avenue of the Egyptian city of Alexandria, one hundred feet wide and stretching for four miles, or like the grand avenues that Georges Haussmann cut through a renovated Paris in the 1850s, these streets were demanded by governments either to parade their power or to channel the comings and goings of important citizens on their public business. As ancient Pompeii had its grooved tracks in the streets for the passage of its chariots, so today we have our subways beneath the ground and our freeways above, and the citizens borne along these determinate routes cannot help but feel like mere particles swept along by the impersonal flow of public traffic.

The Sidewalk

The city of London had to be rebuilt after the disastrous fire of 1666. Inspired by the possibilities for a total reconstruction, Christopher Wren, an architect, mathematician, and one of the first city planners, offered a magnificent, though finally unfulfilled, plan for rebuilding the City—that is, the area that was the heart of London. His plan located at the very center not a cathedral, as had been true of cities since time immemorial, but a new kind of shrine, the stock exchange. As if to portend what the modern world was to become, he called for a major city to be built around the needs and behavior of a new kind of citizen, the customer. And so here, for the first time in Western history, space was put aside for the sidewalk, or to give it the name that consumers soon took over from engineers, the pavement. To give him the credit that he is due, we should say that it was Christopher Wren who invented the sidewalk.

As Wren and the other planners of his day envisioned the city of the future, the sidewalk was to be a free area, a kind of neutral ground between building and street, on which the individual consumer might go through a routine of social behavior based on the responsibilities of the window-shopping customer. For the first time this person, in this role, had a place that was neither in the street nor inside the shop nor under some projecting arcade. Whoever was willing to adapt to the new demands now had available three distinct roles, each with its associated physical structure: the home, the street, and the sidewalk.

FROM HALLUCINATION TO SELF

The very broad outline that I have just traced of the development of urban structures that reflect increasingly complex patterns of the behavior of urban citizens, comprises a sociohistorical rather than a psychological account. If I now attempt to add to this account a psychological dimension, I may be running against the tide of thought among psychologists. I will be arguing that important aspects of what we call human nature—one's experience, behavior, styles of intelligence, even personality—may undergo observable changes in the course of history. Fortunately for the purposes of my argument, a challenging recent work by a psychologist, Julian Jaynes, has pursued much the same argument, although resting on different categories and arguing from different evidential sources.[12] Locating the origins of human consciousness in what he calls "the bicameral mind," Jaynes argues that persons in earlier civilizations had "a profoundly different mentality from our own," particularly in regard to their normal mode of consciousness and the sense of personal responsibility associated with it. In place of what we would now consider the natural or normal way of being conscious of one's actions, involving for example the willingness to accept credit or blame, individuals in earlier eras acted by virtue of some part of their nervous system being "ordered about like any slave." This was accomplished through hallucinatory voices that ordered and empowered the person to act, voices that they experienced as coming from their gods "in a carefully established hierarchy."[13]

According to Jaynes's thesis, these persons were, like ourselves, "ruled in the trivial circumstances of everyday life by unconscious habit." However, in regard to circumstances that were "new or out of the ordinary," in which case some volition (as we might call it) would be required, their "voice-visions" took over and determined behavior.[14] The result is called by Jaynes a "bicameral mind," its two "chambers" corresponding approximately to the two hemispheres of the brain, functioning more or less independently but in conjunction taking care of both ordinary or habitual behavior and extraordinary or novel and critical behavior.

The dominant civilizations of the ancient Middle East, in Jaynes's account, were organized according to the arrangement of the individual bicameral mind. During the period beginning about 400 B.C., in a time of vast social disruption and change, the bicameral mind sustained a collective "breakdown" that resulted in the development of the "modern" mind as we know it or experience it—that is, an organization that is marked by the presence to each person of a "self" that is felt to be responsible for one's own behavior. In a detailed comparison of two works of literature, the *Iliad* of about 850 B.C and the *Odyssey* of about 600 B.C., Jaynes traces a series of changes from the full bicameral mind to a state of consciousness rather similar to what we experience today. "Iliadic man did not have subjectivity as we do; he had no awareness of his awareness of the world. . . . Volition, planning, initiative is organized with no consciousness whatever and then 'told' to the individual in his familiar language."[15]

As the culture changed markedly and the old gods began to weaken and die, individuals experienced a high degree of "decision-stress" in any novel situation, "and both the degree and duration of that stress would have had to become progressively more intense before the hallucination of a god would occur."[16] Since stress was usually accompanied by "physiological concomitants" such as alterations in the normal pattern of breathing or heart rate, individuals associated the physiological events with impulses to act, with the result that "mind" was no longer identified with the hallucinated voices of the gods but now with felt sensations in specific bodily organs. Jaynes marshals impressive evidence for this change from passages in the *Iliad*, where the "mind-words" are either the names of gods or such terms as *thumos* (internal activity of the sympathetic nervous system) or *phrenes* (the lungs or respiratory apparatus) or *kradie* (the heart and its activity). In a final shift, the "mind" is relocated from these bodily parts to an "internal space where metaphored actions may occur." In Jaynes's view the modern mind is just such a set of internal spaces wherein occur actions that are metaphors of real-world events and processes. The very last step in this process of change is the uniting of the various parts of earlier minds into a "unitary consciousness" or "one conscious self capable of introspection."[17]

Historians or classicists may quarrel with the specifics of Jaynes's exposition, but its value lies in his insistence that the metaphors by which we claim to know about our selves are by no means immutable. The evidence that he presents, particularly in his highly original reading of the *Iliad*, surely points in this direction. We may even understand the intermediary stage that he describes, when sympathetic nervous system and lungs and heart were identified with the sources of willed acts, as a period when—the gods being in decline—the intelligences of the body were directly apprehended, even named.

PRIVATE, PUBLIC, AND MEDIATE CONSCIOUSNESS

Pursuing the kind of argument marked out by Jaynes, I will now suggest that we can find, associated with the major physical structures of the urban environment—home, street, and sidewalk—three basic styles of experiencing. I will call these the private, the public, and the mediate, associated in turn with the home, the street, and the sidewalk. As will be immediately apparent, I want to link the styles of experiencing to the endo, meso, and ecto styles of behavior that I have been discussing in earlier pages. However, in order to do so I must introduce a number of cautions.

First, my attempt to discuss these linkages is not meant to imply that I offer some fixed historical sequence. I recognize that human history does not present any single line of events conforming to the continual working out of an overarching principle. I have no intention of claiming here that the history of civilization consists of progress from the endo to the meso to the ecto. I will, however, argue that at various points in history there can be seen a more or less sudden and often very significant change or development in the environment and that associated with it may be observed a change or emergence of a different mode of consciousness and a changed style of dominant behavior. There is no overall pattern to such moments in history, and, indeed, they may not be a sudden emergence at all but simply the appearance in observable form of a series of covert changes that have been working beneath the surface for a long time. My concern here is not to stake out a historiographic argument but to see if the use of the categories I propose will aid our understanding of historical changes.

292 ISSUES OF CULTURE

A second caution to be mentioned is that when I discuss a historical change as associated with the emergence of a different behavioral style, I do not mean this as a claim that all the members of the group in question showed this behavioral style as predominant. Individuals always express themselves in some combination of all three styles, and relatively few persons ever show an extreme of one style. When I talk of a particular style in relation to a society or a segment of a society, I mean only that the group of persons, viewed as a collectivity, seem to show primarily that style as a general characteristic. Perhaps when this occurred many individuals in the society felt a kind of pressure, or responded to a kind of pressure without knowing it as such, to act primarily in one or another style. We know relatively little about how such social influences affect what we know and do and think, and any statement that I make about the transmission of influence must be couched in the most cautious terms.

From Endo to Meso

Given these cautions, I will begin with the rather dogmatic claim that in the earliest protohuman settlements and groupings, the dominant component in human behavior was probably endo. Major exceptions can easily be found, an early and notable one being the Levantine culture that I discussed in chapter 2. But the style of hunting, the reliance on grazing and agriculture, the traditional modes of organization centered in small, almost family-sized villages, all suggest more an endo style than a meso or ecto style. Where this occurred, societies were pastoral, dependent on the slow cycling of the seasons, on the earth being fruitful and the blind forces of nature providing appropriate weather and an absence of overwhelming natural catastrophes. This is, in the large sense, an endo existence.

A major series of changes, significant in the sense that where they occurred they changed forever the nature of society in that area, took place in many parts of the world between 8000 B.C. and 3500 B.C. As I discussed above, these changes led to the formation of city-states, to powerful governments controlling large areas and great numbers of persons, and finally to conquering warrior civilizations. The invention of the street, as an expression of these social powers, was, I suggest, accompanied by a major upsurge in the meso component of behavior. This made possible in turn such meso-style activities as the work of artisans and craftsmen, commercially useful skills, and the organization of social exchange through institutional bureaucracies. A relatively sedentary and traditional pastoral life was transformed into the busy, highly socialized, power-hungry life of the urban citizen. The distinction between city and country exists even today, and it suggests that we are touching here on two distinct modes of consciousness, two styles of behavior that cannot be absorbed into each other.

Again, I emphasize that this great change need not have occurred in the case of every developing metropolis, nor need it have affected all the inhabitants of a city. But the changes were indeed occurring, and for those persons who were able and willing to adapt to them, great possibilities must have seemed to open up, then to be felt as challenge, as risk, as danger, as opportunity, or as powerful pressure. Those persons who were then able to respond in terms of the new possibilities would have experienced a kind of psychic growth, from a consciousness restricted to the dichotomy private-other (or mine-not mine) to a vastly more useful division into private and public. A whole new stance would have made its appearance for them, a way of thinking about everything as well as a way of behaving in regard to everything.

But there would always have been clear-cut distinctions within any citizenry, usually manifested as class distinctions. If we look at some aspects of life in societies that appeared later, we can see that the distinction private-public, though it may have surfaced in powerful form as far back as 4000 B.C., did not have a significant impact on the lives of lower class citizens even as much as fifty centuries later. History does not pursue a neat line for the satisfaction of students of history. During the Middle Ages, when upper-class citizens of the sophisticated city of Florence were living lives that were curiously modern, it was still true of the lower classes that the distinction between private and public had almost no meaning, not in social custom nor in everyday experience. Public bathing took place at the community well; night clothes worn for modesty's sake were unknown; animals and children wandered at will through open doorways, in the same spirit in which everyone's cattle and swine grazed freely in the public squares; and it was rare to see individual dishes set for a meal or walls separating rooms within a dwelling-place.

In the lives of the gentry, on the other hand, carefully shut off from the public street, significant events came to take place behind walls that divided the private dwelling from the brawling and frequently criminal street or highway. The seventeenth-century paintings of Vermeer or Jan Steen show the upper-class house as neatly compartmentalized into small rooms, in marked contrast with the vague representation of room areas as mere background that we find in the earlier art of Raphael or Titian. This contrast, which has always been roughly synonymous with class distinctions, is evident even today—between a crowded and action-oriented life in lower-class areas, where behavior is often the immediate expression of inner forces in outer action and where personal life is lived out in the streets, as opposed to the more reserved forms of expression among middle and upper classes whose private dwellings are removed from the street, separated by the functionless apartment house lobby or suburban lawn.

From Meso to Ecto

The argument presented by Jaynes, which I reviewed above, provides one example of the relatively rapid emergence of an ecto style. Between 800 B.C. and 400 B.C. the Hellenic civilization underwent this change, for reasons that are not clear but with consequences that have resounded into our own century. Associated with a change in the society and an associated emergence of a new behavioral style, we find, at least among a segment of the population, a set of developments that have been of profound importance for the consciousness of later eras. In a period that we nostalgically refer to as a golden age, the self-reflective process of reasoning that in our society is called philosophy arose and flourished in true ecto fashion.

For a more recent instance of a similar emergence of the ecto style within a dominant meso culture, I turn to the argument advanced by Neil Postman in his recent work on what he terms the "disappearance of childhood."[18] In a discussion that echoes historical surveys by Walter Ong[19] and, earlier, MacLuhan,[20] Postman singles out the invention of the printing press as the most important causal event in the subsequent development of the modern psyche. The invention is usually attributed to Johannes Gutenberg and dated about 1437; whether he or Laurens Koster or even Pamfilo Castaldi deserves credit for a workable device for which the times were surely ready, the subsequent century and a half responded almost explosively to its spread. By the middle of the sixteenth century there were printing presses all over the Western world, including even the New World, and within a few more years "the machine-made book already had a typographic form and a look . . . comparable to books of today."[21]

The printed word enforces its own mode of presentation and understanding, in what Postman describes as "unyielding linearity . . . the sequential nature of its sentence-by-sentence presentation, its paragraphing, its alphabeticized indices, its standardized spelling and grammar."[22] Almost from the beginning, five hundred years ago, the printed book had exactly the same format, hence almost the same effect, as the page you are now reading. The presentation was, and is, organized around principles of order, clarity, logical sequence, and repeatability. Just as the language of thought comes to be composed of symbols that are neutral and can be endlessly manipulated, so each sentence, each page, and finally each book comes to be formed of the same neutral principles endlessly applied to new content. In chapter 2 I referred to this phenomenon as an independent schema, and this is just what the printed book has been since it was first produced, an independent schema in the ecto mode. In Postman's description of the hundred or so years following the first printed book, "During the course of the century an entirely new symbolic environment had been created. . . . It required new skills, attitudes, and especially a new kind of consciousness. Individuality, an enriched capacity for conceptual thought, intellectual vigor, a belief in the authority of the printed word, a passion for clarity, sequence, and reason."[23] MacLuhan puts the same thought in slightly different terms: "The alphabet and print technology fostered and encouraged a fragmenting process, a process of specialization and of detachment."[24]

I suggest that it is the ecto mode that these writers are describing—although of course that is my term and not theirs. When we act in some combination of meso and endo modes, we are concretely and immediately caught up in the situation. We do not really look at, much less observe or examine or survey, but simply see. We accept for what it is the nature and ordering of things as we work through it one segment at a time. We do not keep our distance from events or situations. But in the ecto mode this all changes, in ways that must have been exciting to a world-shaking degree when they first opened up as a "natural" possibility for large numbers of people. In the ecto mode we draw back, acting at a distance and through mediate forms and symbols; we observe and survey; and we are open to an infinite number of ways of ordering, manipulating, and finally controlling any phenomenon of which we can conceive.

A MODERN WORLD

The considerations raised by such writers as Postman, Ong, and Mac-Luhan introduce us to the possibility of a wholly new breed of citizen acting in a new kind of world. Just as the origin of city-states was associated with developing the public dimension in human experience, so the period of the late Middle Ages saw the development of a sharp distinction between the public and private dimensions. Members of the upper classes who benefited fully from such developments were now in effect bipartite creatures, their consciousness expressing a dual structure and their behavior able to move between two distinct styles. At just this point, I suggest, there began to emerge the first indications of a third role. Its position was midway between the inner and the outer, between behavior that was relatively private and isolated and behavior that was public and outwardly expressive. To meet the needs of the persons who were able to embody this new role, home and street, and eventually city and world, were to be totally transformed.

To an important degree this new role rested on the earlier development of a highly refined inner life among upper-class persons who had honed their sensibilities to an exquisite degree; it is well caricatured in Casanova's *Memoirs*. The third role emerging during the sixteenth and seventeenth century in Europe was neither public nor private, expressed as neither inner nor outer. Rather, it functioned as a kind of lever by which both private, inner lives and public, outer lives might be manipulated. Because it was neither inner nor outer, it provided the person who could adopt it a vantage point, so to speak, from which one might understand how one's covert experience was related to one's overt behavior. As long as only two possibilities of experience or behavior existed, there was no vantage point from which they could be compared, but with the advent of a third, mediate possibility, individuals began to have access to ways of thinking *about* the other two modes.

New Words, New Colors

To service this emerging, Janus-type role, citizens had to develop new facets of consciousness. They were accompanied, as is always true, by new words for their common experiences. Thus, during the period following the invention of the sidewalk there came into use in English most of the words we now use for what seems to us—who are profoundly tripartite in our consciousness—the self-evident characteristics of our experience. Words such as ennui or even consciousness, in its modern sense, would not have been used by Milton; it was only during his lifetime that most of our words beginning with *self* came into the language.[25] The new terms are all "public" names for "private" events, that is, ways for individuals to communicate their grasp of their own inner processes. The terms provide a symbolized form of neutral ground on which two communicators can stand so as to conduct their exchange, much like customers who meet on the sidewalk, out of their houses yet not on the street, to compare prices at the supermarket.

As the change in language occurred, there came along with it a correlative altering in ways of thought. The full data of a new kind of personal experience was now available to each individual. A coherent scheme could be developed for organizing what was known of the person's inner, or as we now call it, psychic life. In short, psychology was about to be born. This labor, long delayed since its first stirrings in the writings of Aristotle, took place in the unlikely guise of John Dalton's description of his own color blindness. It is a story very well known and surprisingly little understood.

There is no sensible way to account for the circumstance that until the end of the eighteenth century it was not known that some persons were color-blind. The phenomenon goes unnoticed and so unmentioned—although even Aristotle was well aware of individual differences and of their effect on differences in behavior, although the physics and geometry of optics were understood, and although the gross anatomy of the visual system was already familiar. Then in 1777 there appeared a brief account of this condition, which a shoemaker named Harris had apparently discovered in himself—the very first mention of the anomaly in any published writing. One or two other amateur investigators soon made similar reports, and in 1798 John Dalton published a long paper in which he surveyed the known evidence, fully described his own case and that of his brother, and even advanced a theory. It is clear that at this point the times were ready for this discovery to be made, and so a number of persons made it independently. But just what was the nature of the state of readiness?

The New Citizen

The question is not easy for us to answer. In order to do so we must adopt a certain set of ideas, beginning with the notion that we have access to two kinds of worlds. The first is outer and belongs to the universe of things, and the second is inner and belongs to a realm of images and perceptions. Whoever has such access exists not simply as an unreflective experiencer, blind to self as an animal is, but on the other hand not as a set of mechanically triggered movements in the manner of a machine. One must be an experiencing and self-reflective behaver, someone capable of knowing about his or her own behavior and experience. Such a tripartite individual is capable, at long last, of discovering his own color blindness, for he is able to know *that* he is color-blind. It is more than simply knowing that all persons, including oneself, may have an inner world of experience as well as an outer repertoire of behavior. As Harris and Dalton were the first to demonstrate, it involves adopting a mediate stance from which to think and talk about one's own two realms and the possible relations between them. The new citizens who can do this will coin new terms such as perception—which had always meant, as it still does in French, the collection of rents or taxes—to refer to aspects of these new-found relations, and they may then construct a discipline of psychology to help them organize the newly understood phenomena.

In the sphere of social engineering these persons are now able to utilize their new place of residence, the sidewalk. Running along the side of the street and confronting equally the private house and the public roadway, the sidewalk becomes a symbol of a new realm of social affairs. Its place is not always clear, however, any more than is the stance of the new citizen who occupies it. To many the sidewalk is still felt to be at best a semipublic thoroughfare, belonging to the house on which it fronts and on temporary loan to passersby. In small, tradition-bound towns of Europe, for example, housewives will feel it their duty to keep their stretch of sidewalk well scrubbed. In France in particular, where the sidewalk cafe expresses the philosophy of an individualistic homeowner preserving a private enclave against anonymous governmental power, the cafe owner puts his chairs out on the sidewalk, holds a policeman in contempt, and proudly cheats on his income tax. In the United States, by contrast, the tradition of conflict between public and private arenas is much less clear-cut. In spite of our ostentatious display of patio and barbecue pit, we have never taken to the sidewalk cafe, and the area between public and private, like the question of government intrusion into our personal lives, remains quite problematic.

But in spite of these national differences, there has been a general trend in Western societies over the past three centuries toward the pedestrian-consumer evolving into protagonist and representative of a society founded on commerce. The complexity of this role reflects how delicately the modern urban consciousness is now carved up: in carrying out our mission of behaving in public on our private business, we behave even as we experience our behavior and ourselves, all the while knowing about behavior, experience, and the relations between them. As a natural consequence we become increasingly susceptible to the blessings and the ills of self-consciousness. Much of our literary fiction has become an agonized process of self-discovery; many of our novels are in the form of authors writing about themselves writing about themselves; and with our invention of the television age we are able to take the next step and spy on ourselves spying on ourselves.

These are some of the marks of an ecto dominance as it shows itself in modern life. One of the first lessons to be learned from even this sketchy survey of recent history is that each combination of styles presents opportunity for gain as well as the chance of loss and that every style may have both its bright side and its dark side. When the ecto style assumes dominance, it presents up ahead the challenge of complete and uninhibited knowledge, and knowledge about knowledge. At the same time it offers the frightening yet exhilarating pit of an endless regress of self, powered only by ideals and seemingly free of any restrictions derived from real life. These are consequences that result not from the presence of a specific style but from some combination of styles that is imbalanced.

ON IMBALANCE

In the course of an individual life or the history of a society, it may happen that an imbalance occurs, one mode or style becoming overdeveloped to the point that it crowds out the other two or two of the styles developing together so as to produce an organization lacking almost completely in a third. Then we see what I will call the dark side of an individual or social existence, organized in ways that seem "wrong" to others, or maladaptive. In late Victorian England there developed an ideal of masculine health, expressed most forcefully in the writings of the novelist Charles Kingsley. It centered on the notion of "muscular Christianity," a term that Kingsley himself deplored but that became closely, and quite appropriately, connected with his views. In the words of one writer, Kingsley called for "the merits of a simple massive unconscious goodness, and for the great importance and value of animal spirits, physical strength, and a hearty enjoyment of all the pursuits and accomplishments which are connected with them."[26]

This describes a style unbalanced in favor of the meso and endo and with an almost complete denial of the ecto. Indeed, this is how many writers have described the late Victorian culture of England—with its colonial imperialism and its trumpeting of the "white man's burden," with its spurious worship of a feminine ideal while constraining female expression and supporting a thriving subculture of prostitution and pornography, and with its worship of an idealized child while permitting shocking abuses of children in factories; at the same time, however, it advocated a vigor and openness and an adventurous attitude in work as well as in play. That this represented an imbalance of values and styles was clear to many thoughtful persons at the time, and they came to be in large measure responsible for major changes in the culture toward the end of the nineteenth century. "If the Victorian age created that manly ideal, Victorian intellectuals initiated the protest against it. They did so, not because it equated health and manliness, but because it envisioned both of these so narrowly."[27] We may restate this remark in the terms of this book, that it was those who felt the need for the significant expression of an ecto component who helped to correct the imbalance in their culture.

Sartre: The Anti-Semite

To extend our understanding of what I have called imbalance in style, I will review the high points of Sartre's masterful phenomenological analysis of the anti-Semitic character—the character of the person who is blindly and passionately prejudiced toward Jews.[28]

In Sartre's analysis, the anti-Semite has "chosen to live on the plane of passion,"[29] in this way hoping to escape one of the major concomitants of the life of reason, that its results are never more than tentative. There are persons, Sartre remarks, who simply want no change, who want to exist as though they are impenetrable, therefore without histories. "They do not want any acquired opinions; they want them to be innate. . . . [T]hey wish to lead the kind of life wherein reasoning and research play only a subordinate role, wherein one seeks only what he has already found, wherein one becomes only what he already was."[30] For the dedicated anti-Semite, all is faith: "At the outset he has chosen to devaluate words and reasons."[31] Unable to comprehend an abstraction, "he is opposed to the Jew, just as sentiment is to intelligence, the particular to the universal, the past to the present, the concrete to the abstract, the owner of real property to the possessor of negotiable securities."[32]

The arena in which the anti-Semite exists is the place of the mob, the "instantaneous society." In such collectivities, equality arises out of the absence rather than the presence of roles and functions; it is "the product of non-differentiation of functions."[33] In this "society," "the social bond is anger; the collectivity has no other goal than to exercise over certain individuals a diffused repressive sanction. . . .

Thus the person is drowned in the crowd."[34] In its turn the anger of the anti-Semite is kept alive by a kind of horror or disgust at what is experienced as a pervasive stigma. In the eyes of the person driven by prejudice, "the Jew contaminates all that he touches with an I-know-not-what execrable quality. . . . Strictly speaking, the Jew contaminates even the air he breathes."[35]

In attempting to state in the most general terms just what is the "principle" to which the anti-Semite blindly pays homage, Sartre concludes that it is a matter of the whole determining "the meaning and underlying character of the parts that make it up."[36] From the perspective of such a stance there cannot exist a neutral part that combines indifferently with other parts, for example in the way that oxygen combines "with nitrogen and argon to form air and with hydrogen to form water."[37] Rather, every person is conceived as "an indivisible totality," to be understood only according to a "spirit of synthesis" as sharply contrasted with the "purely analytical and critical intelligence of the Jews."[38] And the viewpoint that sustains the stance of the anti-Semite is not one that is generally acknowledged in a community, for it is never the consequence of a reasoned discussion that arrives at some decisive consensus. Rather, the viewpoint is simply there, chaotically formed and half-hidden, "the expression of a primitive society that, though secret and diffused, remains latent in the legal collectivity."[39]

Prejudice As Imbalance

If by imbalance of styles we mean that the person is dominated by an excess of one or another form of expression, then I think we may agree that Sartre has presented such a case. I now want to compare his description with another that is perhaps more familiar in the writings of social psychologists. This is the phenomenon known as prejudice, often contrasted with belief or opinion as a special form of the more general category of attitude.

Of these different but related phenomena, opinion comes closest to behavior in the ecto style: a neutral, even bloodless set of cognitions usually supported by the use of reason and referring to a nonperson target. A belief, by contrast, is more in the meso style, particularly when it constitutes a basis for action. A belief resembles a habit. Even though its content may on occasion carry an explosive potential, its origins are likely to lie in a community of beliefs, and it is held as though it were a custom. A prejudice, however, is through and through a form of passion, and as such belongs in the endo style. Can one imagine, for example, that we say of Hitler that he merely held opinions about Jews?

Although these differences locate the three kinds of attitude within one or another behavioral style, we should bear in mind that the same attitudinal content may be expressed in endo, meso, or ecto style or, indeed, in any combination of the styles. To take an example with which we have all become familiar, a prejudicial attitude toward blacks may take the form of a scholarly if opinionated treatise, perhaps even closely reasoned and dispassionately argued—that is, expressed in the ecto style. Persons holding to such opinions and expressing them in this way are likely to be surprised if accused of being prejudiced. Precisely the same attitude can also be held as a habitual, almost casual set of beliefs, often tossed off by means of derogatory terminology in the course of an ongoing and unreflective conversation. This is often the case with uneducated or unsophisticated persons who express, in this meso style, what may be habitual or common in their subculture. Or, in the third instance, such an attitude may be lived as a truly driven state that expresses a passion, in the endo style. Society's laws are so framed as to control meso action while deploring ecto expression and effectively ignoring underlying endo passions.

If we now turn back to Sartre's beautifully composed essay for what it may contribute to our understanding of the phenomenon of prejudice, we find that what he is describing is an endo form. We note that he places his major emphasis on passion as a determinant of the "plane" on which the anti-Semitic person has chosen to live. The determining character of the endo style, as I have said earlier, is that it is built on passion. The ecto style, on the other hand, emphasizes reason—and reason always carries a quality of tentativeness and works through the continuing play of different and equivalent possibilities, each of them held without deep personal conviction and pursued only as one of a set of logical alternatives. On these grounds alone, I think we are justified in saying that Sartre's distinction between Jew and anti-Semite is similar to the one that I have made in this book between ecto and endo styles. The anti-Semite, acting from the basis of a pure and unbalanced endo style, perceives the Jew as the ideal and proto-typic ecto. If the anti-Semite were to retain even a trace of the ecto style, the imbalance would begin to be corrected and a personal endo style would not be expressed in this blind, "dark" way. Each style has its advantages; but each style pays a price, and the price that we pay for being able to be solidly grounded and to participate with others in the endo style is, when the mix is imbalanced, blind and irrational prejudice of this sort.

Sartre contrasts a preference for the concrete, which he finds in the character of the anti-Semite, with abstract possession that may help define the character of the Jew. In the terms I am using, his contrast is between the concrete immediacy of the endo style and the abstract or symbolic distancing that defines the ecto style. In the same passage Sartre evokes a contrast between the innate opinions and reliance on an established past that we see in the anti-Semite with the choice of acquired opinions that we find in the anti-Semite's enemy. Similarly, a major distinction between endo and ecto styles is that the former is embedded in the past and remembering is experienced as innate whereas the latter is organized around qualities continually acquired and discarded, qualities that are experienced as are all abstractions, neutrally and nonpersonally.

An Endo Collectivity

The argument in Sartre's essay, however, goes beyond a phenomeno-logical analysis of a kind of individual character, and for that reason it is particularly appropriate for the present chapter. His concern is not that some individuals may be so driven by passion as to act unreason-ably toward other persons, but that they act as though they were mem-bers of a special collectivity. Badly equipped though the imbalanced endo may be to serve as a member of a community or to act as part of a social collectivity, such a blindly prejudiced person may indeed act out a social role as one individual in a community of equals. Here may be the model for the thesis I have been pursuing in this chapter: that a collectivity and therefore finally a society may be formed out of the temporary modes of imbalance in a segment of its membership.

Sartre asks what such a strange noncommunity might be like, since its members deny any allegiance to abstract principles guiding social conduct, and themselves appear to lack a means of secreting the glue that for the rest of us holds society together. These are fundamental questions in the social psychology of the endo style.

His first answer is that a collectivity representing the joint outpouring of anti-Semitic energy will take the form of a mob rather than a group. It will be an "instantaneous society" molded out of the excitement of their common though not shared anger. To be in this way "drowned in the crowd"—this is the anti-Semite's dream: to be carried along by a fever that creates one's connections to others in a fellowship of pure, shared passion that is now perfectly justified, to be borne on a wave that sweeps them all forward like a tide of feeling instantly made instrumental. Can this be called action? It is surely not goal-directed behavior in the meso style, nor even team behavior, nor is it the planned pursuit of personal or joint aims in the ecto style. It is closer to a mob in panic than to a group sharing a collective situation.

Yet as I have stressed throughout, there are always at least three ways of doing anything. The fact that we do not think of mob frenzy as belonging in the same category of behavior as proving a theorem or running a race is surely not an argument against now considering it in this light. For mob action is in fact just what a collectivity might engage in if they were all dominated at once by a pure endo style. Nor need their behavior always consist of the display of a "dark side." A large number of persons might run in panic to escape a wall of water after the dam has broken, or they might surge forward to welcome a hero who has just saved the community from a terrible fate. As careful studies of panic situations, such as earthquakes or tornadoes, have shown, the behavior displayed by the collectivity is loosely but urgently and meaningfully linked, not disorganized but rather unorganized.[40]

The statement a few pages back concerning the experience of disgust as central is relevant here. In Sartre's analysis it is just this feeling that powers the anti-Semite's behavior. The deeply prejudiced person seems to sniff out the presence of an enemy, behaving as though invaded by a nameless, penetrating substance against which one will "naturally" respond by recoiling. For the endo, this is an experience that must remain wordless, an experience prior to words and to reasoning, even prior to perceptual knowledge. We might say, indeed, that this is just what the gut would perceive if the gut could perceive: a secret and dreadful invasion by the "other" as enemy.

Finally, there is the general "principle" at which Sartre arrives in his analysis. It concerns an opposition between the whole and its parts, between the global and the particular, between a totality and some aspects of it, between what is namelessly felt and what is named and known, at bottom between synthesis and analysis. These are the distinctions that apply to endo *versus* ecto styles of thinking, between the global and synthetic intelligence of the endo style and the particulate and analytic intelligence of the ecto style. The description that Sartre offers accords very well with some of the distinctions I have made in this book; the anti-Semite, as prototype of the deeply prejudiced person, represents in pure form the dark side of the unbalanced endo style.

It is a matter of generalities. The ecto generality is abstract, an analytically distilled essence of many particulars. The endo generality remains concrete; and when driven by hate, as in the case of prejudice, it can become murderously concrete.

One important point remains. The logic of the prejudiced person assumes from the beginning that it is legitimate to discover some characteristics in an individual and then to apply these characteristics to the individual's group. In reference to Jews as a vaguely sensed totality the anti-Semite gathers evidence from this or that individual, which is all that anyone can ever do in one lifetime, and then proceeds to splash the evidence over the collective face of a group—going in one false step from "This Jew is clever" to "Jews are clever." The particular instance is never seen as such, only as a presently available case of a generality already known. This is the deeply flawed logic that distinguishes the anti-Semite from someone who may dislike one or two Jews as individuals.

To some degree I have fallen into this kind of trap, as when I speak of an anti-Semitic "group," and Sartre's analysis is in some measure based on a similar error. The trap awaits anyone who ventures to speak of collectivities in terms derived from the analysis of individual personalities or tries to discuss the dominant culture of an entire group. It may reappear in the pages that follow.

IMBALANCE: THE DREAM OF CONTROL

Pierre Simon de Laplace, one of the scientists who founded modern astronomy, published a work entitled *Analytical Theory of Probability* at the beginning of the nineteenth century. In this work he posed the exciting possibility of human control of the entire universe, a control that, as he thought, might well be brought about by an all-comprehending, analytic intelligence. His words were stunningly prophetic and are therefore worth our consideration almost two centuries later: "Given for one instant an intelligence which could comprehend all the forces by which nature is animated and the respective positions of the beings which comprise it, if moreover this intelligence were vast enough to submit these data to analysis, it would embrace in the same formula both the movements of the largest bodies in the universe and those of the lightest atom: to it nothing would be uncertain, and the future, like the past, would be present to its eyes."

Think about this for a moment. Millennia before Laplace dreamed his dream of absolute control, the Greek philosophers had already recognized the flaw in the dream. Of course (they agreed), with a strong enough lever one could move the world—but where would one rest the lever? Similarly, of course, one could in theory understand all space and all time, but one would be forever limited by the necessity of standing somewhere, at some point in space and time; therefore one's outlook would be bounded and one's understanding to some degree constrained.

This is to say that Laplace's dream will work only if one is nowhere in the world of space and time. It is an ecto dream; that is its great glory and necessarily its central flaw. The universal control that it postulates is simply not possible if one's behavioral style is mixed to any degree with the meso or the endo. As a dream it represents the very limit of ecto possibilities, but to put the dream into practice, to develop and organize it, to communicate it and then act on this full control requires giving up the endo mode and placing the meso component entirely in the service of an ecto style. It is at this moment of imbalance that the dream turns over slowly to reveal its hidden, dark side.

I am saying nothing here that is not already painfully familiar to anyone who has read contemporary criticism of modern, technological society. In the work by Postman that I cited earlier, to take only one example, the author discusses the development of modern forms of communication. It is a sequence that began with the invention of the telegraph in the nineteenth century. Postman notes that electrical communication is essentially impersonal; it is "news from nowhere,"[41] that is to say, ecto rather than meso. It was hardly coincidental that one of the first messages sent by Samuel F. B. Morse, the inventor of the telegraph, was "Attention Universe." As Marshall MacLuhan also sensed, the heart of the process of electrical transmission of information is that it sets up its own spaceless, almost timeless, therefore worldless realm of symbols into which any knowing can be transmuted. The electrical network that results is an extension and analogue of the human central nervous system, hence in the ecto style.

The development of Western culture has been powered by the ecto impulse, in a movement that has been proceeding for at least four hundred years. The aim of this movement has been well summarized by Richard Rorty in the terms of Western philosophy: it is the dream of "finding some permanent neutral framework of all possible inquiry,"[42] a dream in which Laplace would surely have felt at home. The personal self resulting from this pursuit, fully educated in the ecto style, will have no history, for the foundations of our personal histories are laid down, for good or ill, within the endo style. Nor will the ecto-dominated citizen of today be willing to say, "So be it. This is my fate." In our day no one will accept the idea of being fated, for that is associated with being determined. We prefer to speak of being master of our individual fates; and the charged and significant term "destiny," having reversed its meaning, now points to the future rather than the past.

We have been born into an age that is dominated by the ecto dream: what is ideal and abstract will flower into thought and knowledge in the manner of the mystic or the ideologue and will then instruct us in how to act; the work of the world need no longer be in the world but merely of the world or about the world; what counts is information about things and the processing of that information rather than the things themselves, their doing, and their eventual loss. It is a world in which, in the words of one writer, the advice of Francis Bacon has been taken too narrowly: " 'Knowledge is power,' Francis Bacon said, launching the Western bias on a technological course. Not reality, not wisdom, not reconciliation, not compassion, not brotherhood or peace or justice. Power."[43]

The way one goes about solving problems in the ecto style, an approach first clearly spelled out by Galileo, consists of beginning with an ideal or abstract statement and then assessing deductively how one's empirical data deviate from this ideal. One's description is then not of events in the real world but of constructs within some ideal space; the actual data, the report on what is literally going on, is referred to as "raw" and considered a form of "error." Understandably, this approach has come under criticism in recent years. In Polanyi's words, "an unbridled lucidity can destroy our understanding of complex matters."[44] Rorty concludes that "an 'account of the nature of knowledge' can be, at most, a description of human behavior,"[45] which is to say that one cannot account for the nature of knowledge in a "pure" sense, out of an "unbridled lucidity," but only as part of a full report on how people can and do act.

Yet there can be no denying the power of the ecto approach. It has brought us most of the understanding we have gained over the past four centuries, even if it has not brought a metaphysics within which to comfortably locate our knowledge. I suggest that the gain and the loss we now find within the ecto dream may be stated as a paradox: that the great achievements of contemporary science take us farther away from nature at the same time they give us a more intimate understanding of nature, that is, one that brings us closer. In an analogous movement in our scientific understanding of the universe, the more distantly our probes penetrate, in time and space, out to the farthest possible limits of the universe, the more deeply do we penetrate into the primordial units of matter. Thus, the more abstract our description of the physical world, the more particular is our report of that abstraction. As Laplace clearly sensed, it is in the nature of this style of knowing that distance leads to understanding; and as I have said in these pages, it is because this style is ecto.

The recognition of this paradox may perhaps help us to accept that an ecto approach to ultimate knowledge leaves us with both a gain and a loss. It does not, however, sufficiently reveal the dangers of imbalance, of operating exclusively within one style or at the expense of another style. Any single style when driven to its extreme will show its dark side, as I argued in regard to anti-Semitism; and any two styles that completely rule out the third will pose a collective danger. For example, the Pentagon Papers, well described as "that immense compilation of intellectually elaborate, disembodied strategic calculations,"[46] or what I would term an ecto masterpiece, bore so little relation to the ground-level realities of the Vietnam War that, coupled with a meso-style program of military adventurism and at the expense of enduring endo values, its program culminated in a disaster. A harmony of checks and balances was destroyed and inevitably exacted its price.

No style, if pursued with a single voice, is safe from this trap. In the end it is a matter of harmony, of recognizing that "the knower's situation is . . . shot through with time, history, place, and intention."[47] Consider the consequences of an unbridled meso style, as we are now seeing in the realm of information and entertainment. With the growing influence of television, the printed word in the ecto style is slowly washed away under a tidal wave of meso-style pictorial images. In a far deeper sense than we had suspected, television may be the mortal enemy of the book—as writers and critics have long suspected in opposing the use of illustrations in novels. Flaubert, for one, fought a losing battle against the use of drawings to illustrate his novels, arguing that a description in words preserves a "character of generality" whereas a drawing of a woman is simply that one woman, no more. In one critic's words, "A novel presents something deeper than visual images."[48] The picture, whether in a book or on a television screen, is particular and concrete, in the meso style, while the printed word is always at least potentially abstract and suggestive, that is, ecto. In the special form in which word and image are joined in television, the ecto is overcome by the meso and the endo is necessarily lost. Writing offers two intermingled modes, the prosaic and the poetic, referring to the ecto and the endo, but television offers no more than one, the meso.

Not too long ago one of the great heroes of a nation like ours was D'Artagnan. A warrior who lived heartily within his own sphere of dramatic action, his contact with the world was rarely at a greater distance than an arm's length, the length of his personal sword. An equivalent figure in modern times is Luke Skywalker, the hero of the film *Star Wars*, whose very name gives away his identity. It was chosen to convey the specific image of a great figure striding across vast reaches of space, a D'Artagnan of the skies. Yet Luke Skywalker does not in fact stride and indeed does not even walk. He does, of course, move through great distances, but like the contemporary pilot of a fighter plane he moves as though frozen; in the words of one description, as though "encapsulated and propelled."[49] He fights only at a distance, without physical contact, for his enemy is no more than an image, and he himself serves as a drag on the fighting machine he occupies, as so much freight burdening a machine that can react faster than its pilot. His control of his immediate environment seems to be total, but in fact it comes about by way of almost no action on his part. He need only touch a button to do his job, an arbitrary and disconnected movement that is almost as unworldly as a passing thought. In such an environment his body can be nothing other than "unhinged, free-floating, and alienated."[50]

The great risk that is posed by an imbalance in favor of the ecto and meso styles, either alone or in combination, is that they can exercise control in the world and in particular that the control can get out of hand. This is not true of the endo style, even at its worst, as in the collective passion of a mob. Whatever belongs to the person in the endo style belongs as a disease does: the person is both carrier and victim. This is, in the end, the argument for a balance of styles, that the triumphal yet limitless dreams of the ecto style will be held in check by what has been called the "situated and engaged character of human presence"[51] as it is lived out in the meso and endo styles.

PREFACE

1 Sheldon, W. H. (1942). See also the descriptive paragraphs for the individual somatotypes in Sheldon, W. H. (1970).
2 Humphreys, L. G. (1957).
3 Ibid., p. 218.
4 See, for example, Cortés, J. B., and Gatti, F. M. (1970), and especially Sheldon's sophisticated discussion in Sheldon, W. H. (1971, 1975). A definitive discussion can be found in McLaren, D. S. (in press), a very valuable source that was not available to me before the completion of this book.
5 Ekman, G. (1951a, 1951b).
6 Mervis, C. B., and Rosch, E. (1981). See also Gelman, R., and Gallistel, C. R. (1978).
7 Dundes, A. (1968).

1
ON HISTORY
AND METHOD

1 Fisher, S. (1970), pp. 4–5.
2 Poteat, W. H. (1985). Here see in particular Keleman, S. (1975, 1979).
3 Poteat, W. H. (1985), p. 12.
4 Sheldon, W. H. (1942).
5 Merleau-Ponty M. (1963), p. 162.
6 Kretschmer, E. (1951).
7 Bellow, S. (1976), p. 200.

8 Sheldon, W. H. (1940), p. 8.
9 Hall, C. S., and Lindzey, G. (1978), p. 514.
10 Sheldon, W. H. (1942).
11 Haronian F. (1963), should be mentioned as an exception.
12 Even in the example I have given, of the conjunction of posture and facial expression, some theorists have essayed an ecto-style mode of observation and reasoning, theorizing that both aspects are tied to (and therefore caused by) neuromuscular patterns that are "wired in" from birth. See, for example, Izard, C. E. (1977). His thesis is that an event leads to facial expression and behavior, by way of the "somatic nervous system," which in turn leads to our labeling the experience as an emotion.
13 Marcel, G. (1965).
14 Sartre, J-P. (1956).
15 Marcel, G. (1965), p. 155.
16 Ibid., p. 161.
17 Eco, U. (1983), p. 258.
18 Merleau-Ponty, M. (1963).
19 Ibid., p. 127.
20 Ibid., p. 129.
21 Ibid., p. 130.
22 Merleau-Ponty, M. (1962).
23 Kwant, R. C. (1963), p. 41.
24 Merleau-Ponty, M. (1962), p. 160.
25 Ibid., p. viii.
26 Poteat, W. H. (1985), p. 13.
27 Ibid., p. 17.

28 Ibid., p. 16.
29 Tillich, P. (1951), p. 118.
30 Freud, S. (1961), p. 25.
31 Ibid., p. 26.
32 Fenichel, O. (1945).
33 Adler, A. (1969), p. 38.
34 Ibid., p. 41.
35 Ibid., p. 48.
36 Sartre, J-P. (1956), pp. 562–66.
37 Jung, C. G. (1923).
38 Rorschach, H. (1942).
39 Escalona, S. K., and Heider, G. (1959), p. 9.
40 Klein, G. S. (1954); Gardner, R., et al. (1959).
41 Shapiro, D. (1965).
42 Ibid., p. 1.
43 Ibid., p. 177.
44 Ibid., p. 1.
45 Ibid., p. 4.
46 Reich, W. (1949).
47 Groddeck, G. (1937), p. 40.
48 Ibid., p. 24.
49 Groddeck, G. (1951), p. 73.
50 Köllerström, O. (1974), p. 47.
51 Groddeck, G. (1937), p. 58.
52 Groddeck, G. (1949), p. 58.
53 Groddeck, G. (1951), p. 97.
54 Ibid., p. 83.
55 Groddeck, G. (1949), p. 77.
56 Ibid., p. 77.
57 Quoted in Grossman, C. M., and Grossman, S. (1965), pp. 129–30.
58 Schilder, P. (1950).
59 Ibid., p. 7.
60 Ibid., p. 8.
61 Ibid., p. 8.
62 Ibid., p. 11.
63 Fisher, S. (1970). This work brings up to date an earlier review, Fisher, S., and Cleveland, S. E. (1968). Briefer and more popular presentations may be found in Fisher, S. (1968), and Fisher, S. (1973).
64 Fisher, S. (1970), p. 567.
65 Collins, J. K., et al. (1983).

66 Burton, R. V., and Whiting, J. W. M. (1961).
67 Schilder, P. (1950), part 3.
68 Giorgi, A. P. (1970).
69 Husserl, E. (1965). In what follows one might also bear in mind the useful distinctions made by William James (1950, pp. 221–22) between "knowledge-about" and "knowledge of acquaintance."
70 Gardner, H. (1983).
71 Ibid., p. 13.
72 Ibid., p. 282.
73 Ibid., pp. 60–61.
74 Ibid., p. 8.
75 Ibid., p. 9.
76 Ibid., pp. 63–66.
77 Ibid., p. 69.
78 Ibid., p. 10.
79 Ibid., p. 29.
80 Ibid., p. 30.
81 See Buytendijk, F. J. J. (1974).
82 Straus, E. W. (1963). The title of this book, a play on the German word Sinn, may be translated as "On the meaning of the senses."
83 Straus, E. W. (1963), p. 235.
84 Whitehead, A. N. (1929).
85 Polanyi, M. (1967), p. 4.
86 Ibid., p. 5.
87 Ibid., p. 6.
88 See Kluback, W. (1956); Spranger, E. (1928); Bühler, K. (1929).
89 Polanyi, M. (1967), p. 15n.
90 Ibid., p. 16.
91 Ibid., p. 16.

2

THREE STYLES
OF BEHAVIOR

1 Giedion, S. (1962).
2 The evidence in regard to this question is unclear. Stone points resembling arrowheads have been found at a cave site in southeastern

Spain, associated with the remains of a culture earlier than the Levantine, but they may have been used with either arrows or light spears, and they may have been invented by this group or borrowed from another group. See Pfeiffer, J. E. (1978), p. 192.

3 Sandars, N. K. (1968).

4 Sherif, M., and Hovland, C. I. (1953).

5 Eysenck, H. J. (1967).

6 Ibid., p. 6.

7 Ibid., p. 25.

8 Thorndike, E. L. (1898).

9 Sheldon, W. H. (1970), p. 5.

10 Ibid., p. 3.

11 Shapiro, D. (1965).

12 Sheldon, W. H. (1942), p. 277.

13 Dreyfus, H. L. (1979), pp. 274–75.

14 Ibid., p. 275.

15 Quoted in Dunne, J. G. (1983), p. 29.

16 Cross, A. (1981), p. 6.

17 Watson, J. B. (1966).

18 Ibid., p. 110.

19 Dürckheim, K. (1974).

20 Sheldon, W. H. (1942), p. 248.

21 Sacks, O. (1985).

22 Ibid., p. 20.

23 Ibid., p. 20.

24 Ibid., p. 20.

25 Ibid., p. 21.

26 Heider, F. (1959).

27 Ibid., p. 32.

28 Ibid., p. 23.

29 Ibid., pp. 5–6.

30 Head, H. (1920).

31 Bartlett, F. C. (1932). For its use in regard to cognitive development in childhood, see Church, J. (1966); and for a survey, see Hastie, R. (1980).

32 Lyons, J. (1963).

33 Dreyfus, H. L. (1979), p. 245.

34 Polanyi, M. (1967), p. 25.

35 I recognize, of course, that as one writes a book there must ensue a continuing dialogue between the author's creative efforts and the preformed statement embalmed in an existing schema. I am grateful to Kenneth Shapiro for clarification of this point.

36 Postman, N. (1982).

37 Lyons, J. (1964).

3
THINKING, LEARNING, AND TEACHING

1 Straus, E. W. (1959).

2 Romanyshyn, R. D. (1982).

3 Dreyfus, H. L. (1979).

4 Ibid., pp. 291–94.

5 Aikin, P. A. (1979).

6 McGuigan, F. J., and Schoonover, R. A. (1973); McGuigan, F. J. (1978); Zajonc, R. B., and Markus, H. (1984).

7 Jacobson, E. (1967).

8 Pearce, J. C. (1977).

9 Dürckheim, K. (1974).

10 Ibid., p. 25.

11 Ibid., p. 27.

12 Ibid., p. 28.

13 Merleau-Ponty, M. (1962).

14 Ibid., p. 142.

15 Ibid., p. 139.

16 Ibid., p. 137.

17 Parnell, R. W. (1958), p. 71, table 12.

18 Curran, C. A. (1961); Curran, C. A. (1968), especially chapter 14.

19 Krashen, S. D. (1976).

20 Ebbinghaus, H. (1964). For an experimental approach to learning along the lines of the present work, se Haronian, F., and Saunders, D. R. (1967). However, it should also be noted that some learning programs are best mastered by persons with appropriate be-

havioral styles. For example, as recently reported in the press (*San Francisco Chronicle*, March 22, 1986, p. 51), "an outgoing personality, an ability to persuade and a craving for power"—all traits associated primarily with a meso style—characterize the most successful graduates of Stanford University's MBA program.

21 Ryle, G. (1954).
22 Shattuck, R. (1981).
23 Keller, H. (1923).

4
REMEMBERING LANGUAGE

1 Ebbinghaus, H. (1964).
2 Kuhn, T. S. (1962).
3 Lachman, J. L., et al. (1979).
4 Tulving, E., and Thomson, D. M. (1973).
5 Bransford, J. D., and Franks, J. J. (1971).
6 Smirnov, A. A. (1973).
7 Lyons, J. (1983).
8 McGuire, M. T. (1970).
9 White, S. B., and Pillemer, D. P. (1970).
10 Greenwald, A. G. (1981a), p. 217.
11 Ibid., p. 220.
12 Nuttin, J. R., and Greenwald, A. G. (1968).
13 Greenwald, A. G. (1981b).
14 Sacks, O. (1984).
15 Ibid., p. 18.
16 Ibid., p. 19.
17 Ibid., p. 19.
18 Lyons, J. (1981).
19 See the discussion in MacQuarrie, J. (1960), pp. 48–50.
20 Brown, R. W., and McNeill, B. (1966).
21 Merleau-Ponty, M. (1962).
22 See, for example, Brod, R. S. (1983).

For complete descriptions of various approaches to language teaching, see Schulz, R. A. (1979).
23 Lozanov, G. (1978).
24 It should be noted that these results have not been replicated by other investigators; the question of the success of Lozanov's methods must therefore remain very much open.

5
VARIETIES OF INDIVIDUAL DEVELOPMENT

1 Werner, H., and Kaplan, B. (1963).
2 Boden, M. A. (1979), p. 33.
3 Piaget, J. (1979), p. 484.
4 Piaget, J. (1952), p. 21.
5 Ibid., p. 19.
6 Ibid., p. 37.
7 Ibid., p. 37n.
8 Meltzoff, A. N., and Moore, M. K. (1977). The question of how these findings are to be explained is still a matter of lively discussion, but the phenomenon itself, concerning some form of infant "imitative" behavior, appears to have been established. See Meltzoff, A. N., and Moore, M. K. (1983) for one side, and for the other, McKenzie, B., and Over, R. (1983), and Koepke, J. E., et al. (1983).
9 Gleitman, H. (1981), p. 336.
10 Piaget, J. (1952), p. 338.
11 Piaget, J. (1951), p. 39.
12 For example, Gelman, R. (1978).
13 Shapiro, K. J. (1985).
14 Merleau-Ponty, M. (1964), p. 119.
15 Ilg, F. L. and Ames, L. B. (1955), pp. 42–43; and more recently, Ilg, F. L., et al. (1982).
16 McGuigan, F. J. (1978).
17 Breuer, J., and Freud, S. (1955).

18 Ibid., p. 90. Emphasis in original.
19 Ibid., p. 91.
20 Ibid., p. 174. Emphasis in original.
21 Ibid., p. 95.
22 Ibid., p. 116.
23 Ibid., p. 146.
24 Ibid., p. 157.
25 Ibid., p. 173.
26 Ibid., p. 173.
27 Ibid., pp. 177–78.
28 Ibid., p. 179.
29 Ibid., p. 180.
30 Ibid., p. 181.
31 Freud, S. (1966b), p. 169.
32 Jones, E. (1963), p. 164.
33 Freud, S. (1957a).
34 Freud, S. (1966a).
35 Freud, S. (1958).
36 Freud, S. (1962a).
37 Freud, S. (1960).
38 Strachey, J., in Breuer, J., and
   Freud, S. (1955), pp. xxiv–xxv.
39 Masson, J. M. (1984a).
40 Masson, J. M. (1984b).
41 Freud, S. (1962c).
42 Ibid., pp. 191–92.
43 Ibid., p. 201.
44 Ibid., p. 203. Emphasis in original.
45 Ibid., p. 203.
46 Quoted in Jones, E. (1963), p. 226.
47 Freud, S. (1962b).
48 Freud, S. (1953a), p. 190.
49 Freud, S. (1953b).
50 Ibid., p. 274. Emphasis in original.
51 Freud, S. (1957a).
52 Ibid., pp. 17–18. Emphasis in
   original.
53 Freud, S. (1957b).
54 Freud, S. (1959).
55 Ibid., p. 33.
56 Ibid., p. 33.
57 Ibid., p. 34.
58 Condon, W. S., and Sander, L. W.
   (1974). Similar material is presented in the film *Benjamin*, one of
   the Nova television series.
59 Acredolo, L. P., and Goodwyn,

   S. W. (1985). For a complete historical survey of studies of human
   growth, see Boyd, E. (1985).
60 McNeill, D. (1979).
61 Gruber, J. S. (1973), p. 443.
62 Cited in McLaughlin, B. (1978),
   p. 100.
63 Lyons, J. (1982).
64 *The New Yorker* (1950), p. 21.
65 Updike, J. (1981).
66 Neugarten, B. L. (1964).
67 Rosen, J. L., and Neugarten, B. L.
   (1964), p. 99.
68 Neugarten, B. L., and Gutmann,
   D. L. (1958), p. 89.

6

FORMING THE BODY

1 Quoted in Allport, G. W., and
   Vernon, P. E. (1933), pp. 8–9.
2 This apt remark, as well as many of
   the ideas in this chapter, are owed
   to Straus's paper on the upright
   posture (Straus, E. W., 1952).
3 Bieri, R. (1964).
4 I note again that my reference here
   is not to structures of experiencing
   (as in Sartre) nor to structures of
   behavior (as in Merleau-Ponty) but
   to mechanical structures and functions in the engineer's sense.
5 A related usage may be found in
   Bateson, G. (1972).
6 Sheldon, W. H. (1970), p. 9.
7 Ibid.
8 Ibid, p. 19.
9 Ibid.
10 Ibid.
11 Ibid.
12 Ibid., p. 20.
13 Prigogine, I. (1980). See also the
   discussion in Mahoney, M. J.
   (1982), pp. 100–104.
14 Fisher, S. (1973), pp. 14–15.

15 Dreyfus, H. L. (1979). See also
   Dreyfus, H. L. (1967).
16 Pfeiffer, J. E. (1978), p. 370.
17 Leibowitz, H. W., et al. (1982).
18 Haronian, F. (1963).
19 Straus, E. W. (1952 and 1965).
20 Lyons, J. (1967).
21 Straus, E. W. (1965), p. 682.
22 Ibid.
23 Ibid.
24 Leopold, W. F. (1939–49).
25 Bruner, J. (1986). A similar distinction, between "validating" and
   "procedural" forms of evidence,
   was made some years ago by
   Rychlak (Rychlak, J., 1959, p. 645).
   In this connection, see Belenky,
   M. F., et al. (1986).
26 Paul Ricoeur's term is "follow-
   ability."
27 Gottschalk, L. A., and Gleser, G. C.
   (1969); Gottschalk, L. A. (1979).
28 Maslow, A. H. (1966), p. 2.
29 Gibson, J. J. (1966).
30 Geldard, F. A. (1953), pp. 189–90.
31 Merleau-Ponty, M. (1963), pp.
   96–99.
32 Ibid., p. 96.
33 Ibid., p. 98.
34 Ibid., p. 97.
35 Ibid., p. 99.

7
SOMATIC STYLE AND ART

1 Fisher, S. (1973), p. 127.
2 Quoted in Fisher, S. (1973), p. 131.
3 Frankfort, H. (1955), p. 83.
4 Ibid.
5 Sheldon, W. H. (1970), pp. 85, 89.
6 Sheldon, W. H. (1942), p. 68.
7 Gash, J. (1980), p. 13.
8 de Longu, G. (1964), p. 22.
9 Hinks, R. (1953), p. 32.
10 Ibid., p. 58.
11 Ibid., p. 86.
12 Ibid., p. 65.
13 de Longu, G. (1964), p. 46.
14 Gash, J. (1980), p. 14.
15 He was also known as Hans Arp,
   since his background was perfectly
   mixed of French and German.
16 Quoted in Read, H. (1968), p. 38,
   39.
17 Read, H. (1968), p. 38.
18 The phrase is Jean Cathelin's, in
   Cathelin, J. (1959).
19 Quoted in Read, H. (1968), p. 93.
20 Quoted in ibid., p. 82, 83.
21 Arp, J. (1932).
22 Cathelin, J. (1959), p. 12.
23 Ibid.
24 Ibid., p. 52.
25 Ibid., p. 61.
26 Seuphor, M. (1957).
27 Quoted in Read, H. (1968), p. 42.
28 Giedion-Welcker, C. (1957),
   p. xxvii.
29 Read, H. (1968), p. 42.
30 Quoted in ibid., p. 117.
31 Lust, H. C. (1970), p. 214.
32 Bucarelli, P. (1962), p. 30.
33 Quoted in Lord, J. (1985), p. 165.
34 Ibid., p. 227.
35 Ibid., p. 279.
36 Dupin, J. (1962), p. 22.
37 Ibid. Emphasis in original.
38 Quoted in Bucarelli, P. (1962),
   p. 14.
39 Lord, J. (1985), p. 190.
40 Ibid., p. 79.
41 Dupin, J. (1962), p. 32.
42 Quoted in ibid., p. 12.
43 Sylvester, D. (1980), p. 4.
44 Lord, J. (1980).
45 Ibid., p. 23.
46 Ibid., p. 77.
47 Ibid., p. 72.
48 Ibid., p. 79.
49 Lust, H. C. (1970), p. 77.
50 Ibid., p. 91.
51 Ibid., p. 75.
52 Lord, J. (1985), p. 40.
53 Frosch, T. R. (1974), p. 145.
54 Lord, J. (1980), p. 11.

8
SOCIETY AND THE GREAT ECTO DREAM

1 de Ford, M. A. (1962), p. 6. See also Foucauld, M. (1965).
2 Sommer, R. (1974). See also Johnston, N. (1973).
3 However, see Wilson, J. Q., and Herrnstein, R. (1985), where it is argued that although mesomorphs are over-represented in the male prison population, violently criminal persons are more likely to be physically of the endomorphic type, by contrast with the claim made by Sheldon, W. H. (1949).
4 Schultz, D. P. (1965); Zubek, J. P. (1969).
5 van den Berg, J. H. (1975).
6 Jaynes, J. (1976).
7 Pfeiffer, J. E. (1978).
8 Ibid., p. 157.
9 Schaller, G. (1965).
10 Mellaart, J. (1967).
11 Pfeiffer, J. E. (1978), pp. 175, 250–82.
12 Jaynes, J. (1976).
13 Ibid., pp. 201–2.
14 Ibid., p. 213.
15 Ibid., p. 75.
16 Ibid., p. 258.
17 Ibid., p. 260.
18 Postman, N. (1982).
19 Ong, W. J. (1977, 1982).
20 MacLuhan, H. M. (1962).
21 Postman, N. (1982), p. 30.
22 Ibid., p. 31.
23 Ibid., p. 36.
24 MacLuhan, H. M., and Fiore, Q. (1967), no page.
25 Smith, L. P. (1912), pp. 242–45.
26 Haley, B. (1978), pp. 108–9.
27 Ibid., p. 261.
28 Sartre, J-P. (1948).
29 Ibid., p. 18.
30 Ibid., p. 19.
31 Ibid.
32 Ibid., p. 25.
33 Ibid., p. 30.
34 Ibid.
35 Ibid., p. 34.
36 Ibid.
37 Ibid.
38 Ibid., p. 34–35.
39 Ibid., p. 69.
40 Quarantelli, E. L. (1954). See also Bettelheim, B. (1943).
41 Postman, N. (1982), p. 70.
42 Rorty, R. (1980), p. 211.
43 Novak, M. (1973), p. 275.
44 Polanyi, M. (1967), p. 18.
45 Rorty, R. (1980), p. 182.
46 *The New Yorker* (1981), p. 35.
47 Poteat, W. H. (1985), p. 175.
48 Shattuck, R. (1984), p. 40.
49 Bloomer, K. C., and Moore, C. W. (1977), p. 73.
50 Ibid.
51 Boden, M. (1981), p. 43.

Bibliography

Acredolo, L. P., and Goodwyn, S. W. Symbolic gesturing in language development: A case study. *Human Development* 28 (1985): 40–49.

Adler, A. *The science of living*. New York: Doubleday, 1969.

Aikin, P. A. The participation of neuromuscular activity in perception, emotion, and thinking. *Journal of Biological Experience* 1, no. 2 (1979): 12–32.

Allport, G. W., and Vernon, P. E. *Studies in expressive movement*. New York: Macmillan, 1933.

Arp, J. Notes for a diary. *Transition*, no. 21 (1932).

Bartlett, F. C. *Remembering: A study in experimental and social psychology*. London: Cambridge University Press, 1932.

Bateson, G. *Steps to an ecology of mind: Collected essays in anthropology, psychiatry, evolution, and epistemology*. San Francisco: Chandler, 1972.

Belenky, M. F., Goldberger, N. R., Clinchy, B. M., and Tarule, J. M. *Women's ways of knowing: The development of self, voice, and mind*. New York: Basic Books, 1986.

Bellow, S. *Henderson the rain king*. New York: Avon Books, 1976.

Bettelheim, B. Individual and mass behavior in extreme situations. *Journal of Abnormal and Social Psychology* 38 (1943): 417–52.

Bieri, R. Huminoids on the planets? *American Scientist* 52 (1964): 452–58.

Bloomer, K. C., and Moore, C. W. *Body, memory, and architecture*. New Haven: Yale University Press, 1977.

Boden, M. A. *Jean Piaget*. New York: Viking Press, 1979.

————. *Minds and mechanisms: Philosophical psychology and computational models*. Ithaca, N.Y.: Cornell University Press, 1981.

Boyd, E. *Origins of the study of human growth*. Portland, Oreg.: University of Oregon Health Sciences Center Foundation, 1985.

Bransford, J. D., and Franks, J. J. The abstraction of linguistic ideas. *Cognitive Psychology* 2 (1971): 331–50.

Breuer, J., and Freud, S. *Studies on hysteria*. Standard edition, Vol. 2. London: Hogarth Press, 1955.

Brod, R. S. The state of the profession—1983. *Modern Language Journal* 64, no. 4 (1983): 319–29.

Brown, R. W., and McNeill, B. The "tip-of-the-tongue" phenomenon. *Journal of Verbal Learning and Verbal Behavior* 5 (1966): 325–37.

Bruner, J. Two modes of thought. In J. Bruner, *Actual minds, possible worlds*. Cambridge: Harvard University Press, 1986. Pp. 11–43.

Bucarelli, P. *Giacometti*. Rome: Edizione d'Italia, 1962.

Bühler, K. *Die Kreise der Psychologie.* Jena: Fischer, 1929.

Burton, R. V., and Whiting, J. W. M. The absent father and cross-sex identity. *Merrill-Palmer Quarterly of Behavior and Development* 7 (1961): 85–95.

Buytendijk, F. J. J. *Prolegomena to an anthropological physiology.* Pittsburgh: Duquesne University Press, 1974.

Cathelin, J. *Jean Arp.* New York: Grove Press, 1959.

Church, J. *Language and the discovery of reality.* New York: Vintage Books, 1966.

Collins, J. K., McCabe, M. P., and Jupp, J. J. Body percept change in obese females after weight reduction therapy. *Journal of Clinical Psychology* 39, no. 4 (1983): 507–11.

Condon, W. S., and Sander, L. W. Neonate movement is synchronized with adult speech: Interactional participation and language acquisition. *Science* 183 (January 1974): 99–101.

Cortés, J. B., and Gatti, F. M. Physique and propensity for achievement, sex, politics, religion, crime, esthetics, economics, sociality. *Psychology Today,* October 1970, 42–44.

Cross, A. *Death in a tenured position.* New York: Ballantine Books, 1981.

Curran, C. A. Counseling skills adapted to the learning of foreign languages. *Bulletin of the Menninger Clinic* 25 (1961): 78–93.

———. *Counseling and psychotherapy: The pursuit of values.* New York: Sheed and Ward, 1968.

de Ford, M. A. *Stone walls: Prisons from fetters to furloughs.* New York: Chilton, 1962.

de Longu, G. *Caravaggio.* New York: Harry N. Abrams, 1964.

Dreyfus, H. L. Why computers must have bodies in order to be intelligent. *Review of Metaphysics* 21 (1967): 13–32.

———. *What computers can't do: The limits of artificial intelligence.* Rev. ed. New York: Harper and Row, 1979.

Dürckheim, K. *The Japanese cult of tranquility.* London: Rider, 1974.

Dundes, A. The number three in American culture. In A. Dundes, ed., *Every man his way: Readings in cultural anthropology.* Englewood Cliffs, N.J.: Prentice-Hall, 1968. Pp. 401–24.

Dunne, J. G., "Happy days are here again." Review of W. F. Buckley, Jr., *Overdrive: A personal documentary. New York Review of Books,* October 13, 1983, pp. 20–30.

Dupin, J. *Alberto Giacometti.* Paris: Maeght Éditeur, 1962.

Ebbinghaus, H. *Memory: A contribution to experimental psychology.* New York: Dover, 1964.

Eco, U. *The name of the rose.* New York: Warner Books, 1983.

Ekman, G. On typological and dimensional systems of reference in describing personality. *Acta Psychologica* 8 (1951): 1–24. (a)

———. On the number and definition of dimensions in Kretschmer's and Sheldon's constitutional system. In *Essays in psychology dedicated to David Katz.* Uppsala: Elmquist and Wiknells, 1951. (b)

Escalona, S. K., and Heider, G. *Prediction and outcome.* New York: Basic Books, 1959.

Eysenck, H. J. *The biological basis of personality.* Springfield, Ill.: Charles C Thomas, 1967.

Fenichel, O. *The psychoanalytic theory of neurosis.* New York: Norton, 1945.

Fisher, S. Body image. In *International Encyclopedia of the Social Sciences,* vol. 2. New York: Macmillan, 1968. Pp. 113–16.

———. *Body experience in fantasy and behavior.* New York: Appleton-Century-Crofts, 1970.

———. *Body consciousness: You are what you feel.* Englewood Cliffs, N.J.: Prentice-Hall, 1973.

Fisher, S., and Cleveland, S. E. *Body image and personality.* New York: Dover, 1968.

Foucauld, M. *Madness and civilization.* New York: Mentor, 1965.

Frankfort, H. *The art and architecture of the ancient Orient.* Pelican history of art. Baltimore: Penguin Books, 1955.

Freud, S. Three essays on the theory of sexuality. Standard edition, vol. 7. London: Hogarth Press, 1953. Pp. 135–243. (a)

———. My views on the part played by sexuality in the aetiology of the neuroses. Standard edition, vol. 7. London: Hogarth Press, 1953. Pp. 271–79. (b)

———. On the history of the psycho-analytic movement. Standard edition, vol. 14. London: Hogarth Press, 1957. Pp. 7–66. (a)

———. On narcissism: An introduction. Standard edition, vol. 14. London: Hogarth Press, 1957. Pp. 73–102. (b)

———. *The interpretation of dreams.* Standard edition, vols. 4 and 5. London: Hogarth Press, 1958.

———. *An autobiographical study.* Standard edition, vol. 20. London: Hogarth Press, 1959. Pp. 7–74.

———. *Jokes and their relation to the unconscious.* Standard edition, vol. 8. London: Hogarth Press, 1960.

———. *The ego and the id.* Standard edition, vol. 19. London: Hogarth Press, 1961. Pp. 12–66.

———. The neuro-psychoses of defense. Standard edition, vol. 3. London: Hogarth Press, 1962. Pp. 45–61. Further remarks on the neuro-psychoses of defense. Standard edition, vol. 3, 1962. Pp. 162–85. (a)

———. Sexuality in the aetiology of the neuroses. Standard edition, vol. 3. London: Hogarth Press, 1962. Pp. 263–85. (b)

———. The aetiology of hysteria (A lecture presented to the Psychiatric and Neurological Society on April 21, 1896). Standard edition, vol. 3. London: Hogarth Press, 1962. Pp. 191–221. (c)

———. Project for a scientific psychology. Standard edition, vol. 1. London: Hogarth Press, 1966. Pp. 295–391. (a)

———. Some points for a comparative study of organic and hysterical motor paralyses. Standard edition, vol. 1. London: Hogarth Press, 1966. Pp. 160–72. (b)

Frosch, T. R. *The awakening of Albion: The renovation of the body in the poetry of William Blake.* Ithaca, N.Y.: Cornell University Press, 1974.

Gardner, H. *Frames of mind: The theory of multiple intelligence.* New York: Basic Books, 1983.

Gardner, R., Holzman, P. S., Klein, G. S., Linton, H., and Spence, D. P. Cognitive control: A study of individual consistencies in cognitive behavior. *Psychological Issues* 1, no. 4 (1959).

Gash, J. *Caravaggio.* London: Jupiter Books, 1980.

Geldard, F. A. *The human senses.* New York: Wiley, 1953.

Gelman, R. Cognitive development. *Annual Review of Psychology* 29 (1978): 297–332.

Gelman, R., and Gallistel, C. R. *The child's understanding of number.* Cambridge: Harvard University Press, 1978.

Gibson, J. J. *The senses considered as perceptual systems.* Boston: Houghton Mifflin, 1966.

Giedion, S. *The eternal present: A contribution on constancy and change.* Vol. 1. New York: Pantheon Books, 1962.

Giedion-Welcker, C. *Jean Arp.* New York: Harry N. Abrams, 1957.

Giorgi, A. P. *Psychology as a human science: A phenomenologically based approach.* New York: Harper and Row, 1970.

Gleitman, H. *Psychology.* New York: Norton, 1981.

Gottschalk, L. A., ed. *Content analysis of verbal behavior: Further studies.* Jamaica, N.Y.: Spectrum Publications, 1979.

Gottschalk, L. A., and Gleser, G. C. *The measurement of psychological states through the content analysis of verbal behavior.* Berkeley, Calif.: University of California Press, 1969.

Greenwald, A. G. Self and memory. In G. Bower, ed., *The psychology of learning and motivation,* vol. 15. New York: Academic Press, 1981. (a)

————. Ego task analysis: An integration of research on ego-involvement and self-awareness. In A. Hastorf and A. Isen, eds., *Cognitive social psychology.* New York: Elsevier/North Holland, 1981. (b)

Groddeck, G. *The unknown self.* London: C. W. Daniel, 1937.

————. *Exploring the unconscious.* London: Vision Press, 1949.

————. *The world of man.* London: Vision Press, 1951.

Grossman, C. M., and Grossman, S. *The wild analyst: The life and work of Georg Groddeck.* New York: George Braziller, 1965.

Gruber, J. S. Correlations between the syntactic constructions of the child and of the adult. In C. A. Ferguson and D. Slobin, eds., *Studies of child language.* New York: Holt, Rinehart, and Winston, 1973.

Haley, B. *The healthy body and Victorian culture.* Cambridge, Mass.: Harvard University Press, 1978.

Hall, C. S., and Lindzey, G. *Theories of personality.* 3d ed. New York: Wiley, 1978.

Haronian, F. Anthropometric correlates of the size of the Müller-Lyer illusion. *Journal of Psychological Studies* 14, no. 4 (1963): 162–71.

Haronian, F., and Saunders, D. R. Some intellectual correlates of physique: A review and a study. *Journal of Psychological Studies* 15, no. 2 (1967): 57–105.

Hastie, R. Schematic principles in human memory. In E. T. Higgins, C. P. Herman, and M. P. Zanna, eds., *Social cognition: The Ontario Symposium.* Hillsdale, N.J.: Lawrence Erlbaum, 1980.

Head, H. *Studies in neurology.* London: Oxford University Press, 1920.

Heider, F. Thing and medium. In F. Heider, On perception, event structure, and psychological environment: Selected papers. *Psychological Issues* 1, no. 3 (1959): 1–34.

Hinks, R. *Michelangelo Merisi de Caravaggio. His life—His legend—His works.* New York: Beechhurst Press, 1953.

Humphreys, L. G. Characteristics of type concepts with special reference to Sheldon's typology. *Psychological Bulletin* 54 (1957): 218–28.

Husserl, E. Philosophy as a rigorous science. In E. Husserl, *Phenomenology and the crisis of philosophy.* New York: Harper, 1965. Pp. 71–147.

Ilg, F. L., and Ames, L. B. *Child behavior.* New York: Harper, 1955.

Ilg, F. L., Ames, L. B., and Baker, S. M. *Child behavior.* Rev. ed. New York: Barnes and Noble, 1982.

Izard, C. E. *Human emotions.* New York: Plenum Press, 1977.

Jacobson, E. *Biology of emotions.* Springfield, Ill.: Charles C Thomas, 1967.

James, W. *Principles of psychology.* Vol. 1. New York: Dover, 1950.

Jaynes, J. *The origin of consciousness in the breakdown of the bicameral mind.* Boston: Houghton Mifflin, 1976.

Johnston, N. *The human cage: A brief history of prison architecture.* New York: Walker, 1973.

Jones, E. *The life and work of Sigmund Freud.* Edited by L. Trilling and S. Marcus. New York: Doubleday, 1963.

Jung, C. G. *Psychological types, or the psychology of individuation.* Collected works, vol. 6. London: Routledge and Kegan Paul, 1923.

Keleman, S. *Your body speaks its mind: The bio-energetic way to greater emotional and sexual satisfaction.* New York: Simon and Schuster, 1975.

———. *Somatic reality.* Berkeley, Calif.: Center Press, 1979.

Keller, H. *The story of my life.* New York: Doubleday, Page, 1923.

Klein, G. S. Need and regulation. In M. R. Jones, ed., *Nebraska Symposium on Motivation.* Lincoln: University of Nebraska Press, 1954. Pp. 224–74.

Kluback, W. *Wilhelm Dilthey's philosophy of history.* New York: Columbia University Press, 1956.

Koepke, J. E., Hamm, M., Legerstee, M., and Russell, M. Neonatal imitation: Two failures to replicate. *Infant Behavior and Development* 6 (1983): 97–102.

Köllerström, O. *The actual and the real: A way of thinking about eternity.* London: Turnstone Books, 1974.

Krashen, S. D. Formal and informal linguistic environments in language acquisition and language learning. *TESOL Quarterly* 10 (1976): 157–68.

Kretschmer, E. *Physique and character: An investigation of the nature of constitution and of the theory of temperament.* New York: Humanities Press, 1951.

Kuhn, T. S. *The structure of scientific revolutions.* Chicago: University of Chicago Press, 1962.

Kwant, R. C. *The phenomenological philosophy of Merleau-Ponty.* Pittsburgh: Duquesne University Press, 1963.

Lachman, J. L., Lachman, R., and Thornesberry, O. Metamemory through the adult life span. *Developmental Psychology* 15 (1979): 543–51.

Leibowitz, H. W., Post, R. B., Brandt, T., and Dichgans, J. Implications of recent developments in dynamic spatial orientation for vehicle guidance. In A. H. Wertheim, W. A. Wagenaar, and H. W. Leibowitz, eds., *Tutorials in motion perception.* London: Plenum Press, 1982.

Leopold, W. F. *Speech development of a bilingual child: A linguist's record.* 4 vols. Evanston, Ill.: Northwestern University Press, 1939–49.

Lord, J. *A Giacometti portrait.* New York: Farrar, Straus and Giroux, 1980.

―――. *Giacometti*. New York: Farrar, Straus and Giroux, 1985.

Lozanov, G. *Suggestology and outlines of Suggestopedy*. New York: Gordon and Breach, 1978.

Lust, H. C. Some conversations with Diego Giacometti. In H. C. Lust, *Giacometti: The complete graphics*. New York: Tudor Publishing, 1970. Pp. 213–15.

Lyons, J. *Psychology and the measure of man*. New York: Free Press of Glencoe, 1963.

―――. The recognition of expressive patterns as a function of their mode of production. *Journal of Clinical Psychology* 28 (1964): 85–86.

―――. Paleolithic aesthetics: The psychology of cave art. *Journal of Aesthetics and Art Criticism* 26 (1967): 107–14.

―――. Why human development requires more than one mode of experience. *Journal of the Theory of Social Behavior* 11 (1981): 167–88.

―――. Schreber and Freud: The colonizing of taboo. *American Journal of Psychoanalysis* 42 (1982): 335–47.

―――. Remembering and psychotherapy. In A. P. Giorgi, A. Barton, and C. Maes, eds., *Duquesne studies in phenomenological psychology*, vol. 4. Pittsburgh: Duquesne University Press, 1983. Pp. 47–70.

McGuigan, F. J. *Cognitive psychophysiology*. Englewood Cliffs, N.J.: Prentice-Hall, 1978.

McGuigan, F. J., and Schoonover, R. A., eds., *The psychophysiology of thinking*. New York: Academic Press, 1973.

McGuire, M. T. Repression, resistance, and recall of the past: Some reconsiderations. *The Psychoanalytic Quarterly* 39 (1970): 427–48.

McKenzie, B., and Over, R. Young infants fail to imitate facial and manual gestures. *Infant Behavior and Development* 6 (1983): 85–95.

McLaren, D. S. *Body build in biology and medicine*. London: Academic Press, in press.

McLaughlin, B. *Second-language acquisition in childhood*. Hillsdale, N.J.: Lawrence Erlbaum Associates, 1978.

MacLuhan, H. M. *The Gutenberg galaxy: The making of typographic man*. Toronto: University of Toronto Press, 1962.

MacLuhan, H. M., and Fiore, Q. *The medium is the massage*. New York: Bantam Books, 1967.

McNeill, D. *The conceptual basis of language*. Hillsdale, N.J.: Lawrence Erlbaum Associates, 1979.

MacQuarrie, J. *An existentialist theology. A comparison of Heidegger and Bultmann*. London: SCM Press, 1960.

Mahoney, M. J. Psychotherapy and human change processes. In J. H. Harvey and M. M. Parks, eds., *Psychotherapy research and behavior change*. Master Lecture Series, vol. 1. Washington, D.C.: American Psychological Association, 1982. Pp. 73–122.

Marcel, G. *Being and having: An existentialist diary*. Harper Torchbooks—The Cathedral Library. New York: Harper and Row, 1965.

Maslow, A. H. *The psychology of science: A reconnaissance*. New York: Harper and Row, 1966.

Masson, J. M. *The assault on truth: Freud's suppression of the seduction theory*. New York: Farrar, Straus and Giroux, 1984. (a)

———. Freud and the seduction theory. *Atlantic Monthly*, February 1984, pp. 33–60. (b)

Mellaart, J. *Çatal Hüyük. A Neolithic town in Anatolia*. London: Thames and Hudson, 1967.

Meltzoff, A. N., and Moore, M. K. Imitation of facial and manual gestures by human neonates. *Science* 198 (7 October 1977): 75–78.

———. Newborn infants imitate adult facial gestures. *Child Development* 54 (1983): 702–9.

Merleau-Ponty, M. *Phenomenology of perception*. London: Routledge and Kegan Paul, 1962.

———. *The structure of behavior*. Boston: Beacon Press, 1963.

———. *The primacy of perception*. Evanston, Ill.: Northwestern University Press, 1964.

Mervis, C. B., and Rosch, E. Categorization of natural objects. *Annual Review of Psychology* 32 (1981): 89–115.

Neugarten, B. L. *Personality in middle and late life*. New York: Atherton Press, 1964.

Neugarten, B. L., and Gutmann, D. L. Age-sex roles and personality in middle age: A thematic apperception study. *Psychological Monographs* 72 (1958): whole no. 470.

The New Yorker. September 30, 1950, p. 21.

———. May 18, 1981, p. 35.

Novak, M. *The rise of the unmeltable ethnics*. New York: Macmillan, 1973.

Nuttin, J. R., and Greenwald, A. G. *Reward and punishment in human learning*. New York: Academic Press, 1968.

Ong, W. J. *Interfaces of the word: Studies in the evolution of consciousness and culture*. Ithaca, N.Y.: Cornell University Press, 1977.

———. *Orality and literacy: The technologizing of the word*. London: Methuen, 1982.

Parnell, R. W. *Behaviour and physique: An introduction to practical and applied somatometry*. London: Edward Arnold, 1958.

Pearce, J. C. *Magical child: Rediscovering nature's plan for our children*. New York: Dutton, 1977.

Pfeiffer, J. E. *The emergence of man*. 3d ed. New York: Harper and Row, 1978.

Piaget, J. *Play, dreams, and imitation in childhood*. New York: Norton, 1951.

———. *The origins of intelligence in children*. New York: International Universities Press, 1952.

———. Psychology ten years from now. In J. Lyons and J. J. Barrell, *People: An introduction to psychology*. New York: Harper and Row, 1979. P. 484.

Polanyi, M. *The tacit dimension*. London: Routledge and Kegan Paul, 1967.

Postman, N. *The disappearance of childhood*. New York: Delacorte Press, 1982.

Poteat, W. H. *Polanyian meditations: In search of a post-critical logic*. Durham, N.C.: Duke University Press, 1985.

Prigogine, I. *From being to becoming: Time and complexity in the physical sciences*. San Francisco: W. H. Freeman, 1980.

Quarantelli, E. L. The nature and conditions of panic. *American Journal of Sociology* 60, no. 3 (1954): 267–75.

Read, H. *The art of Jean Arp*. New York: Harry N. Abrams, 1968.

Reich, W. *Character analysis*. New York: Orgone Institute Press, 1949.

Romanyshyn, R. D. *Psychological life: From science to metaphor*. Austin: University of Texas Press, 1982.

Rorschach, H. *Psychodiagnostics: A diagnostic test based on perception*. New York: Grune and Stratton, 1942.

Rorty, R. *Philosophy and the mirror of nature*. Princeton: Princeton University Press, 1980.

Rosen, J. L., and Neugarten, B. L. Ego functions in the middle and later years: A thematic apperception study. In B. L. Neugarten, ed., *Personality in middle and late life*. New York: Atherton Press, 1964.

Rychlak, J. F. Clinical psychology and the nature of evidence. *American Psychologist* 14 (1959): 642–48.

Ryle, G. *Dilemmas*. New York: Cambridge University Press, 1954.

Sacks, O. "The lost mariner." *New York Review of Books*, February 16, 1984, pp. 14–19.

———. The autist artist. *New York Review of Books*, April 25, 1985, pp. 17–21.

Sandars, N. K. *Prehistoric art in Europe*. Pelican history of art. Hammondsworth: Penguin Books, 1968.

Sartre, J-P. *Anti-Semite and Jew*. New York: Schocken, 1948.

———. *Being and nothingness*. New York: Philosophical Library, 1956.

Schaller, G. *The year of the gorilla*. New York: Ballantine Books, 1965.

Schilder, P. *The image and appearance of the human body: Studies in the constructive energy of the psyche*. New York: International Universities Press, 1950.

Schultz, D. P. *Sensory restriction: Effects on behavior*. New York: Academic Press, 1965.

Schulz, R. A. *Options for undergraduate foreign language programs: Four-year and two-year colleges*. New York: Modern Language Association of America, 1979.

Seuphor, M. *Arp*. Paris: Collection Prisine, 1957.

Shapiro, D. *Neurotic styles*. New York: Basic Books, 1965.

Shapiro, K. J. *Bodily reflective modes: A phenomenological method for psychology*. Durham, N.C.: Duke University Press, 1985.

Shattuck, R. *The forbidden experiment: The story of the Wild Boy of Aveyron*. New York: Pocket Books, 1981.

———. Not Swann's way. Review of the film "Swann in love." *New York Review of Books*, August 16, 1984, pp. 40–41.

Sheldon, W. H. *The varieties of human physique: An introduction to constitutional psychology*. New York: Harper, 1940.

———. *The varieties of temperament: A psychology of constitutional differences*. New York: Harper, 1942.

——— (with the collaboration of E. M. Hartl and E. McDermott). *Varieties of delinquent youth: An introduction to constitutional psychiatry*. New York: Harper, 1949.

——— (with the collaboration of C. W. Dupertuis and E. McDermott). *Atlas of men: A guide for somatotyping the adult male at all ages*. Darien, Conn.: Hafner Publishing Co., 1970.

————. The New York study of physical constitution and psychotic pattern. *Journal of the History of the Behavioral Sciences* 7 (1971): 119–26.

————. *Prometheus revisited.* Cambridge, Mass.: Schenkman, 1975.

Sherif, M., and Hovland, C. I. Judgmental phenomena and scales of attitude measurement: Placement of items with individual choice of number of categories. *Journal of Abnormal and Social Psychology* 48 (1953): 135–41.

Smirnov, A. A. *Problems of the psychology of memory.* New York: Plenum Press, 1973.

Smith, L. P. *The English language.* New York: Holt, 1912.

Sommer, R. *Tight spaces: Hard architecture and how to humanize it.* Englewood Cliffs, N.J.: Prentice-Hall, 1974.

Spranger, E. *Types of men: The psychology of ethics and personality.* 5th ed. Halle: Niemeyer, 1928.

Straus, E. W. The upright posture. *Psychiatric Quarterly* 26 (1952): 529–61.

————. Human action—Response or project. *Confinia Psychiatrica* 2, nos. 3–4 (1959): 148–71.

————. *The primary world of senses. A vindication of sensory experience.* New York: Free Press, 1963.

————. Born to see, bound to behold. *Tijdschrift voor Filosofie* 27, no. 4 (1965): 659–88.

Sylvester, D. An interview with Giacometti by David Sylvester, Autumn, 1964. In *Giacometti: Sculptures, paintings, drawings.* London: Arts Council of Britain, 1980.

Thorndike, E. L. *Animal intelligence.* New York: Macmillan, 1898.

Tillich, P. *Systematic theology.* Vol. 1. Chicago: University of Chicago Press, 1951.

Tulving, E., and Thomson, D. M. Encoding specificity and retrieval processes in episodic memory. *Psychological Review* 80 (1973): 352–73.

Updike, J. *Rabbit is rich.* New York: Ballantine Books, 1981.

van den Berg, J. H. *The changing nature of man: Introduction to a historical psychology.* New York: Dell, 1975.

Watson, J. B. The unconscious of the behaviorist. In C. M. Child, ed., *The unconscious: A symposium.* First published 1928. Freeport, N.Y.: Books for Libraries Press, 1966.

Werner, H., and Kaplan, B. *Symbol formation.* New York: Wiley, 1963.

White, S. B., and Pillemer, D. P. Childhood amnesia and the development of a socially accessible memory system. In J. Kihlstrom and F. Evans, eds., *Functional disorders of memory.* Potomac, Md.: Lawrence Erlbaum Associates, 1970.

Whitehead, A. N. *Process and reality: An essay in cosmology.* New York: Macmillan, 1929.

Wilson, J. Q., and Herrnstein, R. *Crime and human nature.* New York: Simon and Schuster, 1985.

Zajonc, R. B., and Markus, H. Affect and cognition: The hard interface. In C. E. Izard, J. Kagan, and R. B. Zajonc, eds., *Emotions, cognition, and behavior.* New York: Cambridge University Press, 1984. Pp. 73–102.

Zubek, J. P., ed. *Sensory deprivation: Fifteen years of research.* New York: Appleton-Century-Crofts, 1969.

Name Index

in relation to "structures" of behavior, 239–40; the term *schema*, 83
Individual differences, xi–xiii

Jung, C. G., work and thought of: relation to hypothesis of book, 28–29; in Rorschach's work, 28

Keller, H.: and the ecto realm, 126–27
Knowing: in Giacometti's work, 266; logical-scientific versus narrative, 233–34
Korsakov's syndrome (case study), 148–50
Kretschmer, E., work of, 8–9

Language: development in early years, 200–201; "little" words in, 154; native accent, 156–57; native language learning, 151–57; teaching a second language, 157–63; tip-of-the-tongue experience, 154
Learning: in animals, 127–31; in the ecto mode, 121–25; in the endo mode, 107–16; interference with meso learning, 121; in the meso mode, 117–21; a native language, 153–57; versus growth, 224
Levantine culture: art, 50–52; hunting style, 55–56
Life-span changes: adolescence, 205–6; adulthood, 206–8; childhood, 202–5; infancy and preschool years, 198–201
Longitudinal studies, 230–32

Machine: compared with living body, 216–21
Memory. *See* Memory system; Remembering
Memory system: private, 139–40; socially addressable, 140
Memory trace, 141–42
Mesomorph(ic), 9–12
Meso style, 64–73; in adolescence, 205–6; in ancient Near Eastern art, 246–47; and awareness, 154–55; in Caravaggio, 254–55; as caricature,

64–67; in early childhood years, 203; and early city-states, 286–88, 292–93; an "engineering" approach, 71; and imprisonment, 277–79; independent schema in, 239–40; its expression in animals, 235; of learning, 116–21; meso public figures: T. Roosevelt, 69, and J. B. Watson, 69–71; in older females, 207; and Piaget's scheme, 170–74; in pre-Renaissance art, 249; in regard to time and space, 164–65; relation to attitude and belief, 302; of remembering, 139–40; and the resistance of the world, 101; as sociality, 72–73; in teaching second languages, 160–61; of thinking, 102–5; and the tool, 281–82; in Victorian culture, 300–301
Motor skills, 160

Neanderthal culture: and burial rituals, 284

"Open" and "closed" tasks, 145

Paleolithic culture, 46, 52–53; hunting style, 52–53; painting, 54–56; sculpture, 47–48
Personality: components, x; relation to somatotype, 12; typology of, 5. *See also* Humphreys, L. G., in Name Index
Phenomenology: and a biological view, 35; as meso, 37, 104–5; relation to approach of book, xvi, 34–37; and self in infancy, 181
Phenotype and genotype: in Sheldon's thought, 221–23
Piaget, J., thought of: body-environment relations, 220; and the longitudinal approach, 231; and reality status, 171; in relation to Freud, 170–71; theory of development, 172–74, 178–80, 182
Polanyi, M., thought of, 40–43; proximal and distal structures, 41–42; tacit knowing, 41–42

ABOUT THE AUTHOR

Joseph Lyons is Professor of Psychology at the University of California, Davis. He is the author of *Psychology and the Measure of Man, A Primer of Experimental Psychology, Experience: An Introduction to a Personal Psychology,* and, with J. J. Barrell, *People: An Introduction to Psychology.*

Library of Congress Cataloging-in-Publication Data
Lyons, Joseph, 1918–
Ecology of the body.
Bibliography: p.
Includes indexes.
   1. Typology (Psychology) 2. Personality.
3. Somatotypes. I. Title. [DNLM: 1. Behavior.
2. Psychological theory. 3. Somatotypes. BF 21
L991e]
BF698.3.L94 1987   155.2'64   87–9080
ISBN 0–8223–0710–3

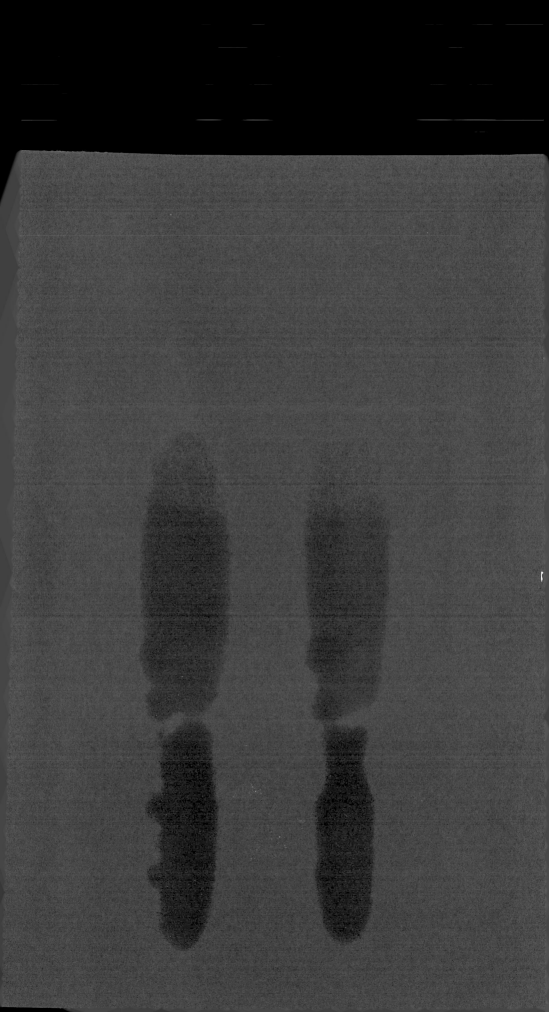